ERIC BENTLEY'S
DRAMATIC REPERTOIRE
VOLUME ONE

BEFORE BRECHT:
FOUR GERMAN PLAYS

Edited and Translated by
Eric Bentley

APPLAUSE
THEATRE BOOK PUBLISHERS
211 West 71 St • New York, NY 10023

BEFORE BRECHT: FOUR GERMAN PLAYS

Library of Congress Cataloging-in-Publication Data
Main entry under title:

Before Brecht.

(Eric Bentley's dramatic repertoire ; v. 1)
Contents: Leonce and Lene / George Büchner—Spring's awakening / Frank Wedekind—La Ronde / Arthur Schnitzler —[etc.]
1. German drama—Translations into English. 2. English drama—Translations from German. I. Bentley, Eric, 1916-   . II. Series.
PT1258.B38   1985   823'.008   85-15623

ISBN 0-87910-249-7
ISBN 0-87910-229-2 (pbk.)

Applause Theatre Book titles are distributed by Harper & Row.

CONTENTS

Leonce and Lena

A Comedy in Three Acts

by GEORG BÜCHNER

English version by Eric Bentley

ALFIERI: E la Fama?
GOZZI: E la Fame?

ILLUSTRATED BY PETER LARKIN

CHARACTERS

KING PETER *of the Kingdom of Popo*

PRINCE LEONCE, his son

PRINCESS LENA *of the Kingdom of Peepee,*
  betrothed to PRINCE LEONCE

VALERIO

THE GOVERNESS

THE PRIVATE TUTOR

THE MASTER OF CEREMONIES

THE PRESIDENT OF THE COUNCIL OF STATE

THE COURT CHAPLAIN

THE PRESIDENT OF THE DISTRICT BOARD

THE SCHOOLMASTER

ROSETTA

SERVANTS, COUNCILLORS, PEASANTS, ETC.

Note on pronunciation of names: The present version being in English, there is no more reason to say Lena in the German way (*Layna*) than to say Peter in the German way (*Payter*). Full Anglicization is recommended: L*ee*na, L*ee*-unce, Val*ee*rio.

ACT ONE

SCENE 1

LEONCE, *half lying on a bench. His* PRIVATE TUTOR.

LEONCE. Well, what do you want from me, sir? You'd like to prepare me for my calling? I'm afraid I have my hands full already, I've more work than I know how to get through. First I have to spit on this stone three hundred and sixty-five times in a row. Did you ever try it? Go ahead. It is peculiarly entertaining. Then again, you see this handful of sand? *He picks up some sand, throws it in the air, catches it on the back of his hand.*

I throw it in the air. Shall we bet? How many grains on the back of my hand—odd or even number?—What? You don't want to bet? Are you a pagan? Do you believe in God? I usually just bet against myself, and I get along pretty well, but if you could find me someone else to bet against once in a while, you'd certainly be doing me a great favor. Then too, I have to figure out how I can contrive to see the top of my head. If a man could but see the top of his own head! That is one of my ideals, it would set my heart at rest. Then too—yes, then infinitely more too. Am I an idler? Do I have nothing to do? Indeed, it is sad . . .

TUTOR. Very sad, your highness.

LEONCE. . . . it is very sad that the clouds have been moving from west to east for three weeks running. It makes me quite melancholy.

TUTOR. And well it might, your highness.

LEONCE. Why don't you contradict me, man? You have urgent business, haven't you? Sorry to have kept you so long.

The TUTOR *withdraws with a low bow.*

When you bow, dear sir, your legs form a beautiful parenthesis. My congratulations! *Alone, he stretches out on the bench.* The bees sit lazily

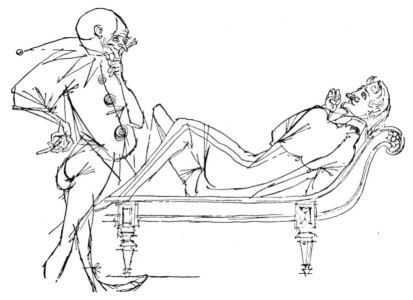

on the flowers, the sunshine lies idly on the ground, a terrible idleness rages!—Idleness is the starting-point of all the vices. What people won't do out of boredom! They study from boredom, they pray from boredom, they fall in love, marry, are fruitful and multiply from boredom, later on they die from boredom, and all this—which is the cream of the jest—without in the least knowing why, though they keep a straight face and think their own thoughts, and what thoughts! These heroes, these geniuses, these blockheads, these saints, these sinners, these heads of families are, one and all, nothing but sophisticated idlers.—Now why must *I* know this? Why me in particular? Why can't

I be important to myself and dress up this poor puppet of a body in a tail coat and put an umbrella in its hand to make sure it's very law-abiding and very useful and very moral. As a jester I'm a fiasco. Then again, why can't I look serious when I make my jokes? This fellow who just left—oh, I envy *him*, I could give him a beating, I envy him so much. If only one could be somebody else for once! Just for a min-ute!——

VALERIO, *a little drunk, enters.*

How that man runs! If only I knew of anything that could still make *me* run!

VALERIO, *coming right in front of the prince, puts one finger to his nose, and stares at him.* Yes!

LEONCE, *also staring.* Correct!

VALERIO. You take my meaning?

LEONCE. Perfectly.

VALERIO. Then let's change the subject. Meanwhile I shall lie on the greensward and let my nose blossom above the blades of grass and get romantic notions when bees and butterflies light on it—

> As if a nose
> Were a rose!

LEONCE. Don't breathe so hard, my dear fellow, or the bees and butterflies will starve: the flowers are their snuffbox, and you're taking great pinches of the snuff.

VALERIO. Oh sir, how much feeling I have for Nature! The grass, for instance. It's so beautiful, I'd like to be an ox to eat it, and then become a man again to eat the ox that ate the grass.

LEONCE. Unhappy man! You, too, seem to labor under ideals!

VALERIO. [*Do I! For eight days now I have run after the ideal of beef without in reality meeting with a single slice. *He sings.*

> Our hostess has a merry maid
> That sits in her garden night and day
> That sits and sits in her garden
> Till twelve o'clock has chimed away
> And the infantry comes ma-arching.

He sits down on the ground. Look at these ants! Is it not marvelous, children dear, the instinct we find in such tiny creatures? Order! Diligence!

* The passage in brackets, ending on page 7, is relegated to an appendix in the Insel edition, as belonging only to a draft.

—There are but three ways, dear sir, of earning money in a humane manner: finding it, winning it in a lottery, and inheriting it, though, of course, you could steal it if you were smart enough to be able to do so without compunction.

LEONCE. You have managed to grow fairly old on these principles without dying of hunger or on the gallows.

VALERIO, *still staring at him.* Oh yes, sir. And my contention is that whoever earns his living in any other way is a rogue.

LEONCE. For work is a subtle form of suicide, and a suicide is a criminal, and a criminal is a rogue. *Ergo*, whoever works is a rogue.

VALERIO. Correct.—And yet ants are a very useful sort of vermin, though not so useful as they would be if they did no harm at all. Nevertheless, worthy vermin, I cannot deny myself the pleasure of kicking some of you on the behind with my heel, wiping your noses, and cutting your nails.

Enter two policemen.

FIRST. Stop! Where is the fellow?

SECOND. There are two.

FIRST. Take a look if anyone's running away.

SECOND. I think no one is.

FIRST. Then we must question them both.—Gentlemen, we are looking for someone, a subject, an individual, a person, a delinquent, a suspect, a fellow. *To* SECOND. Take a look if anyone's started blushing.

SECOND. No one's started blushing.

FIRST. Then we must try something else.—Where is the warrant, the description, the certificate? SECOND *takes a paper out of his pocket and hands it over.* You check these subjects! I'll do the reading. "A man . . ."

SECOND. *A* man? There are two.

FIRST. Blockhead! "A man walks on two feet, has two arms and, to boot, one mouth, one nose, two eyes, two ears. Special characteristics: a highly dangerous individual."

SECOND. That applies to both. Shall I arrest them both?

FIRST. Two? That's dangerous. There are only two of *us*. I'm going to make a report. It's a case of very criminal complication or very complicated criminality. For if I get myself drunk and lie on my bed, that's no one else's business, it's my affair. But if I have to sell the bed to pay for the drinks, then it *is* someone else's business, but *whose*, you rascal?

SECOND. Well, I wouldn't know.

FIRST. I wouldn't know either, but that's the point.

Exeunt both.

VALERIO. And there are people who don't believe in Providence! Think what you can achieve with a single flea! For if this flea hadn't run across me last night, I wouldn't have carried my bed out in the sun this morning. And if I hadn't carried my bed out in the sun this morning, I'd never have got to the Moon Tavern. And if sun and moon hadn't shone on the bed, I could never have pressed the wine out of the mattress and got drunk on it. And if none of all this had happened, I wouldn't be in your company now, worthy ants, letting you pick my bones bare and leave my skeleton to dry in the sun. No, I'd be cutting myself a slice of meat and drying up a bottle of wine—in the hospital, naturally.

LEONCE. "The course of true love never did run smooth."

VALERIO. The wars were running pretty smooth, and the enemy would have run a bullet through me if I hadn't been so handy at running for cover. But anything to save a life. I ran till I had the galloping consumption, at any rate that's what the doctor thought. But of course I *had* to let consumption consume me if I for my part was to consume good soup, good beef, good bread, good wine, and save the life of a patriot and a soldier.] What a pity one can't jump from a church steeple without breaking one's neck! One can't even eat four pounds of cherries complete with the pits and not get belly-ache! Look, sir, I could sit in a corner and all night long to the end of my days sing:

Hey! Just look at that fly on the wall
Fly on the wall
Fly on the wall

—and so on.

LEONCE. Oh shut up with your song! It could make a fool of a man.

VALERIO. Then a man would be something. A fool! A fool! Who will trade me his folly for my reason?—Ha! I'm Alexander the Great! The sun seems a golden crown on my hair, and just look how my uniform glitters! Generalissimo Grasshopper, let the troops advance! Finance Minister Spider, I need money! Lady-in-Waiting Dragonfly, what is my dear wife Beanstalk a-doing of? My good Court Physician Cantharides, I'm in need of an heir to the throne! And on top of these rare fantasies, one gets good soup, good meat, good bread, a good bed and one's hair cut for nothing—in the madhouse, naturally—while with my reason intact I could at best sell my services to a cherry tree for the promotion of ripeness in order to—well?—in order to?

LEONCE. To make the cherry trees turn red with shame at the holes in your trousers. But, noblest one, your craft, your profession, your trade, your rank, your art?

VALERIO, *with dignity.* Sir, what keeps me so busy is idling. I am very good at doing absolutely nothing. I have an infinite capacity for laziness. My hands were never desecrated by a callus, nor has my brow ever given the earth a drop to drink. In work, I am a virgin. And I would take the trouble to explain these merits of mine to you in greater detail, if indeed the trouble were not too much trouble.

LEONCE, *with comic enthusiasm.* Let me clasp you to my bosom! Are you one of those godlike beings who walk the great highway of this life untroubled, with a clear brow, and who, like the blessèd gods themselves, enter Olympus with gleaming feet and blooming bodies? Come! Come!

VALERIO, *singing as he leaves.*

> Hey! Just look at that fly on the wall
> Fly on the wall
> Fly on the wall

Exeunt both, arm in arm.

SCENE 2

A room. KING PETER *is being dressed by two valets.*

KING PETER, *as the dressing proceeds.* Man must think, and I must think for my subjects; for they don't think, they don't think.—Substance is the thing-in-itself, that's me. *He runs about the room nearly naked.* Is that understood? "In-itself" means "in-itself," do you understand? Then come my attributes, qualifications, affections, and accidental properties. Where is my shirt, where are my trousers? Stop! Pah! Free will's flies are undone! Where is morality? Where are my French cuffs? The categories have been shamelessly confused. Two buttons too many have been buttoned. The snuffbox is in my right-hand pocket. My whole system is ruined!—Ha! What does the button in this handkerchief mean? Fellow, what does the button mean, what did I want to remind myself of?

FIRST VALET. When your majesty deigned to tie this button in your handkerchief you wanted——

KING PETER. Well?

FIRST VALET. To remind yourself of something.

KING PETER. A complicated answer!—Indeed! Well, and what do *you* think?

SECOND VALET. Your majesty wanted to remind yourself of something when you deigned to tie this button in your handkerchief.

KING PETER *runs up and down.* What? What? Human beings get me all mixed up. I am in the utmost confusion. I am at my wit's end.

Enter a servant.

SERVANT. The Council of State is met, your majesty.

KING PETER, *joyfully.* That's it, that's it, of course: I wanted to remind myself of my people!—Come, gentlemen. Walk symmetrically! Isn't it very hot? Then take your handkerchiefs and wipe your faces! I'm always so embarrassed when I'm to speak in public!

Exeunt omnes.

Re-enter KING PETER, *this time with the Council of State.*

KING PETER. Beloved friends, faithful retainers, I wanted to announce and make known—announce and make known—for my son either gets married or he doesn't—*with one finger to his nose*—either, or—you do understand me? There's no third way out. Man must think. *Stands musing for a while.* When I speak my thoughts aloud this way, I don't

know who's speaking, myself or someone else. And this frightens me. *After prolonged musing.* I am I.——What do you think of that, Mr. President?

PRESIDENT, *with slow gravity.* Perhaps it is so, your majesty. But perhaps it is also not so.

WHOLE COUNCIL OF STATE IN CHORUS. Yes! Perhaps it is so! But perhaps it is also not so!

KING PETER, *moved*. My wise men!—Well then, what were we talking about? What was I trying to make a speech about? President, why do you have so short a memory on so solemn an occasion? The meeting is adjourned.

He solemnly withdraws, the whole Council of State following him.

SCENE 3

A richly decorated hall. Candles are burning. LEONCE *with several servants.*

LEONCE. Are all the shutters closed? Light the candles! Away with the day, I want night, deep, ambrosial night! Put the lamps under crystal shades among the oleanders so that they peep dreamily out from under the leaves like eyes from under girlish lashes! Bring the roses closer that the wine may sparkle on their petals like dew-drops! Music! Where are the violins? Where is Rosetta?—Away! All of you, away!

Exeunt servants. LEONCE *stretches out on a couch. Prettily dressed,* ROSETTA *enters. Music from the distance.*

ROSETTA, *approaching with flattering mien.* Leonce!

LEONCE. Rosetta!

ROSETTA. Leonce!

LEONCE. Rosetta!

ROSETTA. Your lips are lazy. From kissing?

LEONCE. From yawning.

ROSETTA. Oh!

LEONCE. Oh, Rosetta, I am faced with the terrible task . . .

ROSETTA. Yes, what?

LEONCE. Of doing nothing . . .

ROSETTA. But loving?

LEONCE. A task indeed!

ROSETTA, *offended.* Leonce!

LEONCE. Or an occupation.

ROSETTA. Or pure idleness.

LEONCE. You are right as always. You're a clever girl. I set great store by your perspicacity.

ROSETTA. You love me then out of sheer boredom?

LEONCE. No. I feel boredom because I love you. But I love my boredom as I love you—the two of you are one. *O dolce far niente!* Your eyes are

deep and hidden magic springs, I sit dreaming over them. Your caress-
ing lips lull me to sleep like the rushing of waves. *He embraces her.*
Come, dearest boredom, your kisses are a voluptuous yawning, and
your steps a pretty hiatus.

ROSETTA. You love me, Leonce?

LEONCE. Why not, indeed?

ROSETTA. Forever?

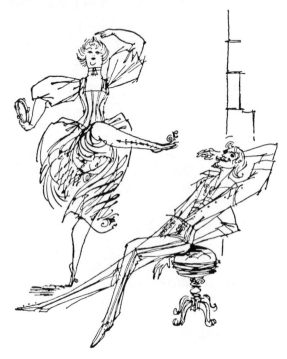

LEONCE. That is a long word: forever. If I love you five thousand years
and seven months, will that do? It's a lot less than forever, but at that
it's quite a time: we could take our time at loving each other.

ROSETTA. Or time could take our love from us.

LEONCE. Or love our time from us. Dance, Rosetta, dance!

> That time may move with the beat
> Of your small attractive feet.

ROSETTA. My feet would rather be out of time. *She dances and sings.*

Tired feet of mine, must you dance
So gaily shod
When you would rather quiet lie
Beneath the sod?

Hot cheeks of mine, must you glow
In the night
When you would rather be
Two roses white?

Poor eyes of mine, must you flash
In torch-lit park
When you would rather sleep away your pain
In the dark?

LEONCE, *dreaming away to himself, meanwhile.* Oh, a dying love is more beautiful than a budding one! I am a Roman: at a fine banquet, during the dessert, golden fishes are sporting in colors of death. See the color die in her cheeks, the light in her eyes go out! How gentle the undulation of her limbs, their rising and falling! *Addio, addio,* my love, I will love your dead body. ROSETTA *approaches him again.* Tears, Rosetta? A delicate Epicureanism—to be able to cry! Stand in the sun so the fine drops will crystallize—they'll make splendid diamonds— you can have yourself a necklace made of them.

ROSETTA. Diamonds, yes. They cut into my eyes. Oh, Leonce! *She tries to embrace him.*

LEONCE. Look out! My head! I have buried my love in it. Look in through the windows of my eyes. You see how dead the poor thing is? You see the two white roses on its cheeks, the two red ones on its breast? Don't push me or it will break an arm, and that would be a shame. I have to carry my head very straight on my shoulders, the way the undertaker woman* carries a child's coffin.

ROSETTA, *playfully.* Fool!

LEONCE. Rosetta! ROSETTA *makes a face at him.* Thank God! *He keeps his eyes shut.*

ROSETTA, *scared.* Leonce, look at me!

LEONCE. Not for anything.

ROSETTA. Just one look!

---

* Strictly, the layer-out, but this term is no longer familiar.

LEONCE. Not a one. What are you after? One little thing like that, and my belovèd love would come back to life again. I am happy to have buried it. I retain the impression.

ROSETTA, *going sadly and slowly away, sings in parting.*

> The poorest orphan child am I
> Afraid, all, all alone
> Grief, my darling
> Will you not come with me home?

LEONCE, *alone.* It's a funny thing about love. You lie half-awake in bed for a full year, then one fine morning you wake, drink a glass of water, put your clothes on, pass your hand lightly over your brow, and bethink yourself—bethink yourself.—Heavens, how many women must one have in order to sing the whole scale of love? One woman can hardly manage a single tone. Why is the vapor around our earth a prism breaking the white ray of love into a rainbow?——*He drinks.* In which bottle is the wine I'm to get drunk on today? Can't I even do that any more? I feel as if I were under an air pump. The air is so sharp and thin, I'm freezing—as if I were to go skating in nankeen trousers.—Gentlemen, gentlemen, do *you* know what Caligula and Nero were like? *I* do.—Come on, Leonce, do me a monologue, I'll be a good listener. My life yawns at me like a great white piece of a paper that I should cover all over with writing, and I don't get a word written, not a letter. My head is an empty dance hall—a few faded roses and crumpled ribbons on the floor—burst violins in the corner –the last dancers have taken their masks off and are looking at each other, their eyes are dead tired. I turn myself inside out twenty-four times a day like a glove. Oh, I know myself, I know what I shall think and dream in a quarter of an hour, in a week, in a year. Lord God, what crime have I committed that You make me do my lesson over so often like a schoolboy?—Bravo, Leonce, bravo! *He claps.* It really does me good to call out to myself like this. Hey, Leonce, Leonce!

VALERIO, *from under a table.* Your highness seems to me well on the way to becoming a *bona fide* fool.

LEONCE. Looked at under the light, that's how it seems to me too.

VALERIO. Wait, we must discuss it more thoroughly in a minute. I've only to eat one more piece of meat that I stole from your kitchen and drink one more glass of wine that I stole from your cellar, and I'll be right with you.

LEONCE. How the fellow smacks his lips, he gives me the most idyllic sensations, I could go back to the beginning and start with the simplest things, eat cheese, drink beer, smoke tobacco. Go ahead, but don't grunt so with that snout, don't make such a racket with those tusks!

VALERIO. Are you afraid for your thighs, most worthy Adonis? Don't worry, I'm neither a broombinder nor a schoolmaster, I don't need twigs for my rods.

LEONCE. You leave nothing unpaid for.

VALERIO. I wish the same could be said of my lord.

LEONCE. You mean I owe you a thrashing? Are you so concerned for your upbringing?

VALERIO. Heavens, we are more easily brought *into* the world than brought *up* in the world. If our first condition is foetal, our second is fatal, isn't that sad? If a man—like an oration—is easy to conceive but hard to deliver . . .

LEONCE. O foul conception when *you* were conceived! Find yourself a better mode of *ex*pression or I'll give you an *im*pression of all the *op*pression that I . . .

VALERIO. What about this? "At the time that my mother was rounding the Cape of Good Hope . . ."

LEONCE. And your father was being shipwrecked on Cape Horn . . .

VALERIO. He *did* have a horn, he was a night watchman. But he didn't put that horn to his lips as often as he put the other one on the heads of noble sons' fathers.

LEONCE. Man, your impudence is heavenly: I feel a certain need to come into closer touch with it. I'm in the grip of a passion—to thrash you.

VALERIO. That is a very striking answer.

LEONCE, *making for him.* Yes, I'll do the striking, and you'll be struck!

VALERIO *is running away when* LEONCE *stumbles and falls.* You are a proof that has yet to be proved, for it falls over its own legs, which certainly are unproven. Those are extremely improbable calves and highly problematic thighs.

Enter the Council of State. LEONCE *remains on the floor.*

PRESIDENT. Forgive us, your highness . . .

LEONCE. As I do myself; I forgive myself for good-naturedly listening to you. Won't you take your places, gentlemen? Just sit on the ground and don't be embarrassed, it's the place where you'll take your place for the last time one day, and it yields nothing to anyone, unless it's the gravedigger.

PRESIDENT, *snapping his fingers in his embarrassment.* Would your highness deign . . .

LEONCE. Don't snap your fingers like that unless you want to make a murderer of me!

PRESIDENT, *snapping more and more violently.* Would you graciously take cognizance . . .

LEONCE. Heavens, stick your hands in your pockets! Or sit on them! He's quite beside himself. Pull yourself together!

VALERIO. One should never interrupt children in the act of pissing, they may get a complex.

LEONCE. Take a hold of yourself, man. Think of your family, think of the country! Let the words come out, it's dangerous to hold them in, you could have a stroke!

PRESIDENT *pulls a paper out of his pocket.* Your highness will permit . . .

LEONCE. Then you can read? Well now . . .

PRESIDENT. That the long-awaited arrival of your highness's betrothed, Her Serene Highness Princess Lena of Peepee, is expected to take place tomorrow—such is the message which His Royal Majesty wishes to convey to your highness.

LEONCE. If my bride awaits me, I'll defer to her wishes and let her wait. I saw her last night—in a dream. She had eyes so big my Rosetta's dancing slippers would have made them a fine pair of eyebrows. And, on her cheeks, instead of dimples, she had a number of ditches to drain off the laughter in. I believe in dreams. Do *you* dream, Mr. President, once in a while? Do you have premonitions?

VALERIO. It goes without saying. Always, the night before a roast burns, a capon drops dead, or His Royal Majesty gets the belly-ache.

LEONCE. By the way, did you have something else on the tip of your tongue? Pray say all you wanted to say.

PRESIDENT. On the day of the nuptials, it is the will of the Highest Will in the land to place the highest expression of that Highest Will in the hands of your highness.

LEONCE. Tell the Highest Will in the land that I shall do everything except what I shall leave undone, which will, however, not be as much, in any case, as if it were twice that amount.—Pardon me, gentlemen, if I don't accompany you myself. A passion for sitting down has just come over me, but my benevolence is so great that I can't measure it with my legs. *He spreads his legs out wide.* Will you take my measure, and remind me later what it was? Valerio, you accompany the gentlemen.

VALERIO. On what instrument? And can they sing? Are they a flock of singing birds in disguise?

LEONCE. Man, you are nothing but a bad pun. You have neither father nor mother, you were begotten by the five vowels.

VALERIO. And you, my prince, are a book with no words in it, nothing but dashes. And now, come, gentlemen! Isn't it sad about this word Come? If you want an *in*come, you have to steal, and the only *out*come of life is death: first you come up to the gallows, then you come down to your grave. Of course, an up-and-coming fellow can always give the oncoming, upcoming generation a becoming come-uppance, and all of us will somehow come through if we keep our wits about us and have nothing more to say, like me for instance right now, or you before you even open your mouth. And so, gentlemen, come!

Exeunt Council of State and VALERIO.

LEONCE, *alone.* How mean of me to act up like that before those poor devils! Though, of course, at times a certain enjoyment lurks in a certain meanness.—Hm! Getting married! It is to drink a well dry. O Shandy, old Shandy,* who will make me a present of your clock?——

VALERIO *returns.*

O dear, Valerio, have you heard?

VALERIO. Well, you're to be king. Which is a funny business. One can go driving for the whole day and make people ruin their hats through having to take them off all the time. Out of the cloth of law-abiding people one can cut law-abiding soldiers, just so everything will stay normal. One can make black tail coats and white cravats into servants of the state. And when one dies, shiny buttons turn blue, and the bell-ropes tear like cotton thread with all the tolling. Isn't that entertaining?

LEONCE. Valerio, Valerio! We must do something different. Advise me.

VALERIO. Science! Knowledge! Let us be scientists and philosophers! A priori? Or a posteriori?

LEONCE. A priori—that can be learnt from my father. And, a posteriori, everything starts like an old fairy tale: once upon a time there was.

VALERIO. Then let us be heroes! *He marches up and down, as with trumpet and drum.* Pom-pom-*pah*-plonk!

LEONCE. But heroism gets revolting tight, it catches a fever and has to be taken to hospital, it can't exist without lieutenants and recruits. Be off with your Alexander and Napoleon romanticism!

VALERIO. Then let us be geniuses!

LEONCE. The nightingale of poetry is at it over our heads all day, but the

---

* Tristram Shandy's father did his duty as a husband whenever he wound up his clock—once a month.

best of the stuff goes to the devil before we've pulled out her feathers and dipped them in ink or paint.

VALERIO. Then let us be useful members of human society!

LEONCE. I'd rather hand in my resignation as a human being.

VALERIO. Then let us go to the devil!

LEONCE. Alas, the devil is only there for the sake of contrast—so we'll grasp the idea that there's something to heaven. *Jumping up.* Ah!

Valerio, Valerio, I have it! Don't you feel a gentle breeze from the south? The undulation of a glowing and dark blue ether? Can't you see the light flashing from the sunny, golden ground, from marble columns, marble bodies, from the salt and sacred sea? Great Pan sleeps, and, in the shade, above the deep and rushing waters, bronze statues dream of the old magician Vergil, of tarentella and tambourine, and of mad, deep nights full of masks, torches, and guitars. A *lazzarone,** Valerio, a *lazzarone!* We're going to Italy!

* "One of the homeless idlers of Naples"—*Webster.*

SCENE 4

A garden. PRINCESS LENA *in her bridal clothes. The* GOVERNESS.

LENA. Yes: now! It's here. I thought of nothing the whole time. It drifted by, and now, of a sudden, this day of days looms up before me. I have the garland in my hair—and the bells, the bells! *She leans back and*

closes her eyes. Look, I wish the green grass were growing over my head with the bees murmuring above. Look, I'm all dressed, and the rosemary's in my hair. Isn't there an old song:

> Beneath a headstone I would rest
> Like a baby at its mother's breast?

GOVERNESS. How pale you are, my child, beneath those flashing stones!

LENA. Lord, Lord, I *could* love. Why not? The journey is very lonely, you reach out, hoping someone will take hold of your hand till the undertaker woman* comes and parts the clasped fingers and folds the hands of both of you, each on his separate breast. But why should a nail be driven through two hands that did not seek each other? What has my poor hand done? *She pulls a ring off her finger.* This ring stings me like an adder.

GOVERNESS. But—they say he's a real Don Carlos!

LENA. But—a man . . .

GOVERNESS. Well?

LENA. That one does not love. *She rises.* Pah! I feel ashamed, you see.— Tomorrow I'm to be robbed of all fragrance, all lustre. Am I then no more than the poor and helpless water in a well that, willy-nilly, must give back from its still depths the image of everything that bends over it? Flowers open and close their cups to the morning sun and the evening wind as they please. Is a king's daughter less than a flower?

GOVERNESS, *weeping.* You're a lamb, a lamb to the slaughter, my angel.

LENA. Too true. And the high priest's knife is poised in the air.—God, God, can it be that we have to redeem *ourselves*—with this grief of ours? Can it be that the world is itself a crucified savior, the sun his crown of thorns, and the stars the nails and spear in his feet and side?

GOVERNESS. My child, my child, I cannot bear to see you so. It cannot continue, it's killing you.—Perhaps there is a way. I believe I have an inkling. We shall see. Come! *She leads the* PRINCESS *off.*

---

* Layer-out, as above.

ACT TWO

How a voice was ringing, ringing
Out within me
In a moment quite extinguishing
My memory.
—ADALBERT VON CHAMISSO

SCENE 1

Open field. A tavern in the background. Enter LEONCE *and* VALERIO, *the latter carrying a bundle.*

VALERIO, *panting.* On my honor, prince, the world *is* a frightfully spacious sort of building.

LEONCE. Not at all, not at all. It's like being in a room full of mirrors, I hardly dare stretch my hands out for fear of hitting them—all the lovely mirrors in fragments on the floor and me staring at the naked walls!

VALERIO. I am lost!

LEONCE. That'll be a loss to no one but the man that finds you.

VALERIO. What I'll do now is place myself in the shadow of my shadow.

LEONCE. You're completely evaporating in the sunshine. You see that lovely cloud? It's equal to at least a fourth part of you. And it's looking down on your coarser constitution rather patronizingly.

VALERIO. To think that if one let that cloud fall on you—drop by drop—it wouldn't harm a hair of your head. A delightful idea, by the way!—We've run through a dozen duchies, half a dozen grand duchies, and a couple of kingdoms, all in the utmost haste, in the course of half a day—and why? Because one is to be king and marry a beautiful princess! And in such a plight, you still live! I don't understand such resignation. I don't see why you haven't taken arsenic, climbed to the top of the church steeple, and put a bullet through your head, just to make a thorough job of it.

LEONCE. Ideals, Valerio, ideals! I have the image and ideal of a female in my head. I must go in quest of it. She is endlessly beautiful and endlessly mindless. Her beauty is as helpless and touching as a newborn infant's. Is the contrast not delightful—eyes both heavenly and dumb, a mouth both divine and moronic, a profile that resembles both a Greek goddess and a sheep's nose, an intellectual death in a body uncontaminated by a single grain of intellect?

VALERIO. Hell, we're at the frontier again! This country is like an onion— nothing but skins. Or Chinese boxes—one inside the other—in the biggest, nothing but boxes, in the smallest, nothing at all. *He throws his bundle to the ground.* Shall this bundle be my tombstone? Look, prince—and now I'm getting philosophical—I give you an image of human life: with aching feet, I drag this bundle through frost and blazing sun because I want to have a clean shirt to wear of an evening, and when evening finally arrives my brow is so deeply furrowed, my cheek so hollow, my eye so dim, I've just enough time left to put that shirt on—and use it as a shroud. Now wouldn't it have been smarter of me to have taken the bundle off the stick and sold it in the first good tavern and got myself drunk and slept in the shade till evening, without the sweat and the corns? And now, prince, I come to the practical application: people today—out of pure modesty—want to put clothes on the inner man too and cover their insides as well as their outsides with coats and trousers. *Both approach the tavern.* Catch a whiff of that, my dear bundle! Oh, the smells of the kitchen, the aromas of the bar! And you, dear old trousers, how you start to thrust your roots into the ground, to put forth leaves, to blossom and bloom! Long, heavy grapes hang down into my mouth, and the must ferments in the winepress! *Exeunt.*

PRINCESS LENA. *The* GOVERNESS.

GOVERNESS. It must be an enchanted day, the sun doesn't set, and it is such an endlessly long time since our flight began.

LENA. Oh no, my dear, the flowers have scarcely wilted that I picked in token of farewell when we left the garden.

GOVERNESS. And where shall we take our rest? Till now we have hit upon nothing. I see no monastery, no hermit, no shepherd.

LENA. I suppose we dreamt it all quite differently behind the garden wall with our books between the myrtles and the oleanders.

GOVERNESS. Oh, the world is revolting! A wandering prince is simply out of the question in such a world!

LENA. The world is wide—endlessly wide and beautiful. I'd like to go on walking forever, day and night. Nothing moves. A glow of red flowers is playing over the meadows, and the distant mountains lie on the earth like resting clouds.

GOVERNESS. Jesus, Mary and Joseph, what will people say? And yet, is it not very tender and feminine? It is a renunciation, it is like the flight of Saint Ottilia.* But we must look for shelter: evening is near.

LENA. Yes, the plants are folding their little leaves together in sleep, and the sunbeams are rocking themselves on blades of grass like tired dragonflies.

SCENE 2

A tavern on a slope by a river. Extensive view. The garden in front of the tavern.
VALERIO, LEONCE.

VALERIO. Well, prince, don't your trousers make a delicious beverage? Don't your boots slip down your throat with the greatest of ease?

* Who fled her father rather than marry any but the Heavenly Bridegroom.

LEONCE. Do you see the old trees, the hedges, the flowers? They all have their history, their secret and charming life-story. Do you see the friendly old faces beneath the grapes at the tavern door? Do you see how they sit holding hands and are afraid because they're so old and the world is still so young? And, oh, Valerio, I am so young, and the world is so old! Sometimes I'm afraid myself, and *about* myself, and could sit in a corner and take pity on myself and weep.

VALERIO *gives him a glass.* Take this bell, this diving bell, and lower yourself into the sea of wine till pearls bubble over your head. *He sniffs it.* What a bouquet! Look! The elves are hovering over its flower-cups, in golden shoes, beating their cymbals!

LEONCE, *jumping up.* Come, Valerio, we must do something, do something! Let us busy ourselves with profound thoughts, and inquire how it is that a chair will stand on three legs and not on two. Come, let us dissect ants and count filaments on flowers! I shall find myself some really princely hobby yet. I'll come across a baby's rattle that only falls out of my hand when I gather wool and pull at the blanket. I still have a certain quota of enthusiasm to use up; but when I've cooked a dish till it's hot enough, I need an endless amount of time to find a spoon to eat it with, and during this time it goes cold.

VALERIO. *Ergo bibamus!* This bottle is no mistress, no theory, it doesn't have labor pains, it doesn't get boring, it's never unfaithful, it is *one* from the first drop to the last. You break the seal, and the dreams that lie slumbering within come sparkling toward you!

LEONCE. Lord, I'd spend half my life giving thanks to God if just one straw were vouchsafed me to ride on like a splendid horse—till the day comes when all I need straw for is to lie dead on.—What a curious evening! Down here everything is still, and up there the clouds change and pass, and the sun keeps coming and going. Look what strange figures are chasing each other up there! Look at the long white shadows with bats' wings and appallingly thin legs! And all so swift and swirling, while down below not a leaf stirs, not a blade of grass. The earth has timorously curled up like a child, while ghosts ride over the cradle.

VALERIO. I don't know what you want, I feel pretty comfortable. The sun looks like an inn sign, and the fiery clouds above it like the inscription: Golden Sun Tavern. The earth and the water below are like a table that wine has been spilt on, and we are on this table like cards that God and the Devil are playing a game with out of boredom— you are a king, and I am a jack, only a queen is missing, a lovely queen

with a big gingerbread heart and a mighty tulip in which her long
nose is sentimentally sunk, and—by God, there she is!

The GOVERNESS *and the* PRINCESS *have come in.*

But it's not a tulip, it's a hunk of tobacco, and it's not a nose, it's a
snout. *To the* GOVERNESS. Why do you hurry so much, worthy lady,
that one sees your late lamented calves right up to your genteel garters?

GOVERNESS, *much enraged, stopping.* Why, honored sir, do you tear your
mouth open so wide that it makes a hole in the view?

VALERIO. So that you, honored madam, won't bump your nose on the

horizon and make it bleed. Such a nose is like the tower of Lebanon that
looketh toward Damascus.

LENA, *to the* GOVERNESS. Is the way so long, my dear?

LEONCE, *dreaming away to himself.* Oh, every way is long. The ticking of
the death-watch beetle within our breasts is slow, every drop of our
blood measures out its time, our life is a creeping fever. To tired feet,
every way is *too* long . . .

LENA, *who listens to him, fearful, musing.* And to tired eyes, every light is
too strong. And to tired lips, every breath is too heavy. *Smiling.* And to
tired ears, every word is one too many. *With the* GOVERNESS, *she goes
into the house.*

LEONCE. Oh, Valerio, I could say what someone said before me:* "Would not this, sir, and a forest of feathers, if the rest of my fortunes turn Turk with me, with two provincial roses on my razed shoes, get me a fellowship in a cry of players, sir?" I spoke the lines quite melancholically, I believe. Thank God I'm beginning to come down with melancholy! The air isn't so cold and bright any more, Heaven glows and sinks down with its arms about me, heavy drops are falling.—Oh, that voice: "Is the way so long?" Many voices are heard in this world, and one can say they talk of other things, but this voice I understood, it rested upon me like the spirit that hovered over the waters before there was light. What fermentation in the depths! Something is growing within me! How that voice pours itself into space—"Is the way so long?" *Exit.*

VALERIO. No. The way to the madhouse isn't as long as all that. It's an easy place to find, and I know the footpaths, trails, and highways that lead there. I see him now taking a broad avenue to it on a winter's day, bitter cold, his hat under his arm, as he walks in the long shadows of the bare trees and fans himself with his handkerchief.—He is a fool! *He follows him.*

SCENE 3

A room. LENA. *The* GOVERNESS.

GOVERNESS. Just don't think about the man.

LENA. He was so old under those yellow locks. Spring on his cheeks, and winter in his heart! That is sad. The tired body can find a pillow anywhere, but when the mind is tired, where shall it rest? An appalling thought comes to me: I believe there are men who are unhappy, incurably so, merely because they exist. *She rises.*

GOVERNESS. Where are you going, my child?

LENA. I want to go down in the garden.

GOVERNESS. But . . .

LENA. "But," dearest mother? I should have been brought up in a pot like a plant, you know that. I need dew and night air, like flowers.— Do you hear the harmonies of the evening? The crickets are singing the day to sleep, and night-violets are lulling it with their scent! I cannot stay indoors. The walls are falling in on me.

---

* *Hamlet*, Act III, Scene 2.

SCENE 4

The garden. Night and moonlight. LENA *is seen sitting on the lawn.*

VALERIO, *at some distance.* It's a fine thing, Nature. But it would be a finer if there were no mosquitoes, if hotel beds were a little cleaner, and

death-watch beetles didn't tick away so in the walls. Inside, men snore. Outside, frogs croak. House crickets chirp inside, field crickets outside.

> There is cause to say alas
> Dear grass.

He lies down on the lawn.
Enter LEONCE.

LEONCE. O night! Balmy as the first night that slowly descended on paradise! *He sees the* PRINCESS *and softly approaches her.*

LENA, *talking away to herself.* The hedge sparrow has twittered in its dream. —The night sinks into a deeper sleep, its cheek is paler, its breath calmer. The moon is like a sleeping child whose golden locks have fallen over his dear little face in his sleep.—Oh, his sleep is death! Look how the dead little angel rests on his dark pillow with stars burning around him like candles! Poor child, it is sad! Dead, and so alone!

LEONCE. Stand up in that white dress of yours and follow the dead body through the night, singing a funeral song.

LENA. Ah! Who speaks?

LEONCE. A dream.

LENA. Dreams are blessèd.

LEONCE. Then dream yourself blessèd, and let me be your blessèd dream.

LENA. Death is the most blessèd of all dreams.

LEONCE. Then let me be your angel of death, let my lips swoop down upon your eyes like his wings. *He kisses her.* O lovely dead body, you rest so charmingly on the black pall of night that Nature hates life and falls in love with death.

LENA. No! Let me go! *She jumps up and rushes away.*

LEONCE. Too much, too much! My whole being is in that moment. Now, die! More were impossible. Creation, breathing freely, is struggling toward me out of Chaos, beautiful, gleaming. The earth is a bowl of dark gold, light foams in the bowl till it overflows, and stars come sparkling over the rim.—This one drop of blessedness makes me a precious vessel. Down, sacred cup! *He tries to throw himself into the river.*

VALERIO *jumps up and takes hold of him.* Stop, Serene Highness!

LEONCE. Let me go!

VALERIO. I'll let you go when you stop letting yourself go and promise to let the water go.

LEONCE. Blockhead!

VALERIO. Lieutenant's romanticism—hasn't your highness got beyond that? Drinking your mistress's health, throwing the glass through the window?

LEONCE. I half-believe you're right.

VALERIO. Take comfort, man. If you aren't to sleep *under* the grass tonight, sleep *on* it. To try and sleep in bed at the tavern would just be another attempted suicide: in that place one lies on straw like a dead man and is bitten by fleas like a live one.

LEONCE. A lot *I* care. *He lies down in the grass.* Man, you have cheated me of the loveliest suicide ever! Never in my life shall I find so exquisite a moment for it again, even the weather is excellent. Now I'm out of the mood already. The fellow has spoiled everything for me with his

yellow waistcoat and sky-blue trousers.—Heaven grant me a disgustingly healthy sleep!

VALERIO. Amen.—Having saved a man's life, I have something to keep me warm tonight—a good conscience!

LEONCE. I hope it works, Valerio.

ACT THREE

SCENE 1

LEONCE, VALERIO.

VALERIO. Getting married? Since when has your highness decided to serve a life sentence?

LEONCE. And do you know, Valerio, that even the least among men is so great that life is much too short to love him? As for a certain kind of people who fancy nothing is so beautiful and holy that they oughtn't to make it still more beautiful and holy, I say: let them have their fun, there is a certain enjoyment in such pleasant arrogance, why shouldn't I let them have it?

VALERIO. Very humane and philobestial. But does she know who you are?

LEONCE. She only knows that she loves me.

VALERIO. And does your highness know who *she* is?

LEONCE. Blockhead! Ask the carnation and the pearly dew their names!

VALERIO. I conclude she is *something*—if the term is not too indelicate and suggestive of police records?—But how can the trick be brought off?— Hmm. Prince, shall I be Minister of State if you and the ineffable Nameless One are this day welded together in holy matrimony in the presence of your father? Your word?

LEONCE. My word.

VALERIO. The poor devil Valerio pays his respects to His Excellency Valerio of Valerianvale, Minister of State.—"What does the fellow want? I do not know him. Get out, you rascal!"

He runs off. LEONCE *follows him.*

SCENE 2

Open space in front of King Peter's castle. PRESIDENT *of the District Board. The* SCHOOLMASTER. PEASANTS *in their Sunday best, holding fir branches.*

DISTRICT PRESIDENT. How are your people holding up, Mr. Schoolmaster?

SCHOOLMASTER. They hold each other up, Mr. District President, and have done this many a day; and so, one may say, for all their little troubles, they hold up well. Of course, in this heat, they couldn't hold themselves up at all, if they didn't have occasional recourse to the bottle. Courage, my men! Stretch your fir branches straight out before you, so everyone will think you're a forest, and your noses are strawberries, and your three-cornered hats are stags' antlers, and your leather pants the moonlight in the trees. And remember: the one that's last has to keep running in front of the one that's first. That way, it will seem that we've raised your number to the second power!

DISTRICT PRESIDENT. And, Schoolmaster: you answer for their sobriety.

SCHOOLMASTER. Of course. I'm so sober, I can barely stand.

DISTRICT PRESIDENT. Now, people, pay attention! In the program it says: "All subjects of the king will of their own free will place themselves along the highway cleanly clothed, well nourished, and with happy faces." Don't you disgrace us!

SCHOOLMASTER. Steady does it, my men! Don't scratch yourselves behind the ears, and don't blow your noses, while the royal couple is driving past. And show you are properly touched, or you'll be improperly touched where you won't like it. And realize what is being done for you: you are being placed where the wind blows straight from the kitchen and for once in your lives you can smell the smell of a roast. Have you remembered your lesson? Huh? *Vi!*

PEASANTS. *Vi!*

SCHOOLMASTER. *Vat!*

PEASANTS. *Vat!*

SCHOOLMASTER. *Vivat!*

PEASANTS. *Vivat!*

SCHOOLMASTER. There, Mr. President, you see: intelligence is on the up-grade! Just think, it's Latin. But we are also presenting this evening a Transparent Ball, in which ingenious use will be made of the holes in our jackets and trousers. And we shall beat cockades onto our heads with our fists.

SCENE 3

Great Hall. Dressed-up ladies and gentlemen, carefully grouped. In the foreground, the MASTER OF CEREMONIES *with a few servants.*

MASTER OF CEREMONIES. It is pathetic. Everything has gone wrong. Every roast has dried up. Congratulations are falling flat. Stand-up collars are all sitting down, and looking like melancholy pigs' ears. The peasant's fingernails and beards have been growing perceptibly. The soldiers' hair is starting to stick up. Among the twelve virgin bridesmaids, there isn't one who wouldn't prefer the horizontal position to the vertical. In those white dresses, they look like worn-out silk rabbits, and the court poet is grunting and snuffling around them like a guinea pig in trouble. The officers are losing their posture, and the ladies-in-waiting stand there like beach shrubbery* at low tide, with the salt crystallizing on their necklaces.

SECOND SERVANT. No one could say they carry too much on their shoulders. And if they aren't openhearted, at least they are open right down to their hearts.

MASTER OF CEREMONIES. Yes, they're like playing cards from the Kingdom

---

* Büchner uses a word ("Gradierbäue") which even in German editions has to be explained in a note.

of Turkey: they show you the Dardanelles and the sea of Marmora. Away, you rascals! To the windows! Here comes his majesty.

Enter KING PETER *and the* COUNCIL OF STATE.

KING PETER. So the princess has disappeared too. Is there still no trace of our beloved son and heir? Have my orders been obeyed? Are the frontiers under observation?

MASTER OF CEREMONIES. Yes, your majesty. The view from this hall allows us to exercise the strictest supervision. *To the* FIRST SERVANT. What did you see?

FIRST SERVANT. A dog looking for his master has been running through the kingdom.

MASTER OF CEREMONIES. How about you?

SECOND SERVANT. There's someone taking a walk on the northern frontier. But it isn't the prince, I'd recognize him.

MASTER OF CEREMONIES. How about you?

THIRD SERVANT. Excuse me—nothing.

MASTER OF CEREMONIES. That is very little. How about you?

FOURTH SERVANT. Also nothing.

MASTER OF CEREMONIES. That is equally little.

KING PETER. But, Council of State, did I not decree that My Royal Majesty would rejoice today and that, today also, the wedding would be celebrated?

PRESIDENT. Yes, your majesty, that was announced. That is protocol.

KING PETER. And, were I not to execute what was decreed, should I not be compromising myself?

PRESIDENT. If it were otherwise possible for your majesty to compromise himself, this would be a case in which he might compromise himself.

KING PETER. Did I not give my royal word?—Yes, I shall at once put my decree into practice: I shall rejoice. *He rubs his hands.* Oh, I am quite extraordinarily merry!

PRESIDENT. And we all share your majesty's feelings insofar as it is possible and proper for subjects to do so.

KING PETER. Oh, I am completely overcome with joy! I'll have red coats made for my chamberlains, I'll make some cadets into lieutenants, I'll permit my subjects to—but, but what about the wedding? Does not the other half of the decree read that the wedding should be celebrated?

PRESIDENT. Yes, your majesty.

KING PETER. Yes, but what if the prince doesn't turn up, and neither does the princess?

PRESIDENT. Yes, if the prince doesn't turn up, and neither does the princess, then—then——

KING PETER. Then? Then?

PRESIDENT. Then, of course, they can't get married.

KING PETER. Stop! Is the conclusion logical? If—then— Correct! But my word, my royal word!

PRESIDENT. Let your majesty take comfort with other majesties! A king's word is a thing—a thing—a thing—that is no thing.

KING PETER, *to the servants*. You still see nothing?

SERVANTS. Nothing, your majesty, not a thing.

KING PETER. And I had decided to rejoice on such a scale! I was going to start precisely on the twelfth stroke of the clock and go on rejoicing for a full twelve hours. I'm going to be quite melancholy.

PRESIDENT. All subjects are earnestly requested to share the feelings of his majesty.

MASTER OF CEREMONIES. Those, however, who have come without their handkerchiefs are strictly forbidden to weep—in the interests of public propriety.

FIRST SERVANT. Stop! I see something! It resembles a protuberance, it looks like a nose, the rest of it hasn't crossed the frontier yet. Now I can see another man. And now two persons of the opposite sex.

MASTER OF CEREMONIES. In which direction?

FIRST SERVANT. They're coming nearer! They're coming to the castle! They're here!

Enter VALERIO, LEONCE, GOVERNESS, PRINCESS, *masked*.

KING PETER. Who are you?

VALERIO. Do I know? *He slowly removes several masks, one after the other.* Is this me? Or this? Or this? Shell the nut! Turn back the leaves! Really, I'm rather afraid I may peel myself completely away!

KING PETER, *nonplussed*. But—but, surely, you must be *something?*

VALERIO. If your majesty commands, yes. But in that case, gentlemen, turn the mirrors to the wall and hide your shiny buttons somewhat and don't look straight at me so I'm forced to see my image in your eyes, or, really, I won't know any more what I actually am.

KING PETER. The man gets me all mixed up! I'm falling into despair, I'm in the utmost confusion!

VALERIO. What I actually had in mind was to announce to an honored and esteemed company like this the arrival of The Two World-Famous

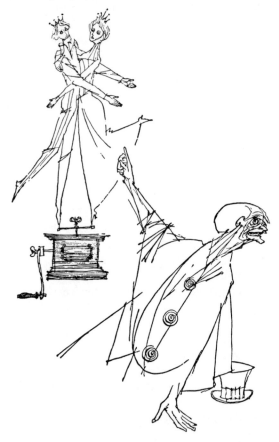

Automata, and to tell you that I am the third of the two, and, at that, perhaps the most remarkable, if, actually, I had any accurate notion, myself, who I was, which shouldn't occasion any astonishment, for not only do I not know what I'm talking about, I don't even know I don't know what I'm talking about, so the probability is that I've just been *caused* to talk, and actually it's some system of tubes and cylinders that's saying all this.

In a barker's voice.

Ladies and gentlemen, you see before you two persons of both the sexes, one little man and one little woman, a gentleman and a lady! It's all mechanism and art, all clock springs and pasteboard! Each of these two persons has a superfine ruby spring in his or her right foot just under the nail of his or her little toe as the case may be. Give it a bit of a push, and the whole mechanism runs a full fifty years. Now, these two persons are so perfectly constructed, you can't tell them from men—from *other* men, I should say—if you didn't know they were just pasteboard. Yes, ladies and gentlemen, you could actually take them for regular members of human society. You can tell they're nobly born: just listen to their Oxford accent. You can tell they're moral: they get up when the clock strikes, have lunch when the clock strikes, and go to bed when the clock strikes; also, they never have indigestion, which proves they have an easy conscience. Oh yes, their moral sense is very highly developed: the lady has no word for underdrawers, and the gentleman would never dream of going upstairs just behind a female or going downstairs just in front of one. They are highly educated: the lady sings all the new operas, and the gentleman wears French cuffs. Take note of this, everyone, they have just come to a very interesting stage, at which stage a new mechanism manifests itself, the mechanism of love. The gentleman has carried the lady's shawl several times. The lady has averted her gaze several times and looked toward heaven. Both have more than once whispered: faith—love—hope. Both look very much as if an understanding had been arrived at. All that's lacking is the one very small word, Amen.

KING PETER, *one finger against his nose.* In effigy, in effigy? President, if you have a man hanged in effigy isn't that just as good as if he received a regulation hanging?

PRESIDENT. Excuse me, your majesty, it is a great deal better, for it gives him no pain, and yet he is hanged.

KING PETER. Now I have it. We'll celebrate the wedding in effigy. *Pointing to* LENA *and* LEONCE. That's the princess, that's the prince.—I shall carry out my decree! I shall rejoice!—Let the bells ring out! Get your congratulations ready! Go to it, Mr. Court Chaplain! *The* COURT CHAPLAIN *steps forward, clears his throat, looks several times toward heaven.*

VALERIO. Begin! Leave thy damnable faces and begin! Now!

COURT CHAPLAIN, *in the utmost confusion.* If we—or—but——

VALERIO. Whereas and in respect of——

COURT CHAPLAIN. For——

VALERIO. It was before the creation of the world——

COURT CHAPLAIN. That——

VALERIO. God was bored——

KING PETER. Make it short, my good man.

COURT CHAPLAIN, *pulling himself together.* If it please Your Highness Prince Leonce of the Kingdom of Popo, and if it please Your Highness Princess Lena of the Kingdom of Peepee, and if it mutually and reciprocally please both of your highnesses mutually and reciprocally to desire to have each other, then, aloud and audibly, say Yes.

LENA *and* LEONCE. Yes!

COURT CHAPLAIN. To which I add Amen.

VALERIO. Well done—terse and to the point. The little man and the little woman are now created, and all the beasts in paradise stand around! LEONCE *takes off his mask.*

ALL. The prince!

KING PETER. The prince! My son! I am lost! I've been deceived! *He makes for the* PRINCESS. Who is this person? I declare the whole thing null and void!

GOVERNESS *removes the* PRINCESS's *mask, in triumph.* The princess!

LEONCE. Lena?

LENA. Leonce?

LEONCE. The flight from paradise? No, Lena, our flight was *to* it.

LENA. I've been deceived.

LEONCE. *I've* been deceived.

LENA. O chance!

LEONCE. O Providence!

VALERIO. I must laugh: it really *was* just chance that your highnesses chanced to meet. Give chance a chance, *I* say. And may you chance to like each other.

GOVERNESS. That I should live to see this sight—at last—a wandering prince! I die in peace.

KING PETER. My children, I am touched, I am quite overcome with emotion. I am the happiest man alive! And herewith I most solemnly place the **government** in your hands, my son. For my part, I shall forthwith begin to think, quite undisturbed. Leave me these wise men, my son, to support me in my endeavors. *He indicates the* COUNCIL OF STATE. Come, gentlemen, we must think, we must think, quite undisturbed! *He starts to withdraw with the* COUNCIL OF STATE. The man got me all mixed up, I must disentangle myself. *Exit.*

LEONCE, *to all present.* Gentlemen, my good wife and I infinitely deplore the fact that you have had to stand so long today at our disposition.

Your situation is so sad, we would not for anything put your constancy to a further test. Get you home now, but don't forget those speeches, sermons, and verses, for tomorrow we're going to start the festivities all over again in peace and comfort. *Au revoir!*

Exeunt all except LEONCE, LENA, VALERIO, *and the* GOVERNESS.

Well, Lena, have you noticed yet that our pockets are full of toys and dolls? What shall we do with them? Shall we make moustaches for the dolls and hang sabres on them? Or shall we dress them in tail coats and have them conduct miniature* politics and diplomacy with us looking on through a microscope? Or do you long to have a barrel organ with very esthetic mice scurrying around on it, white as milk? Or shall we build a theatre? LENA *leans against him and shakes her head.* I know what you'd like: we'll have all the clocks smashed and all the calendars suppressed, then we'll count the hours and the moons only by the flowers, by blossom and fruit. And then we'll surround our little country with burning lenses, so there'll be no more winter, and in summer the heat will shoot us clear up to Ischia and Capri by a process of distillation. And so we'll spend the whole year among roses and violets, oranges and laurel.

VALERIO. And I'll be Minister of State. And a decree will be issued that whoever gets calluses on his hands shall be placed under surveillance; whoever works himself sick shall be punishable under criminal law; whoever boasts that in the sweat of his brow he will eat bread shall be declared insane and dangerous to human society. And then we can lie in the shade and ask God for macaroni, melons, and figs, for musical throats, classic bodies, and a nice, cosy** religion!

* Büchner actually says "infusorial," which explains the microscope. But the word would not be understood in any theatre.

** There are two readings in the German: *commode* and *kommende*. The first has been followed. The second might be rendered: "an up-and-coming religion."

SPRING'S AWAKENING

A Tragedy of Childhood

by

FRANK WEDEKIND

English version by
Eric Bentley

Dedicated
by the author
to
The Man in the Mask

Characters

MRS. BERGMANN

WENDLA BERGMANN
INA MÜLLER } *her daughters*

MR. GABOR

MRS. GABOR

MELCHIOR
their son

RENTIER* STIEFEL

MORITZ STIEFEL
his son

OTTO
GEORG
ROBERT
ERNST
LÄMMERMEIER
HÄNSCHEN RILOW } *schoolboys*

THEA
MARTHA } *schoolgirls*

ILSE
a model

REKTOR SONNENSTICH (Sunstroke)**
AFFENSCHMALZ (Calflove)
KNÜPPELDICK (Cudgelthick)
HUNGERGURT (Starveling)
ZUNGENSCHLAG (Stickytongue)
KNOCHENBRUCH (Bonebreaker)
FLIEGENTOD (Flykiller) } *schoolmasters*

* German title for one who lives on a private income (rents and dividends).

** In cases where the German names are in the tradition of Aguecheek and Belch, English equivalents are supplied in paren-

HABEBALD (Catchemquick)
school porter

PASTOR KAHLBAUCH (Skinnybelly)

FRIEND ZIEGENMELKER (Goatmilker)

UNCLE PROBST (Provost)

DIETHELM ⎤
REINHOLD ⎟
RUPRECHT ⎬ *boys in the Reformatory*
HELMUTH ⎟
GASTON ⎦

DR. PROCRUSTES

LOCKSMITH

DR. VON BRAUSEPULVER (Seidlitz powder)

VINTAGERS

A MAN IN A MASK

THE TIME: 1892

THE PLACE: *Germany*

---

thesis. Wedekind's daughter, Mrs. Kadidja W. Biel, tells me she thinks the English equivalents should actually be used in performance. I, on the other hand, think it is essential not to pretend that the action takes place anywhere but Germany. Besides, many other German names *could* be given such literal translation though no one would propose such a line of action. Should Müller be changed to Miller, Bergmann to Hillman? E.B.

A NOTE on the Language: It is a pity the term "period piece" carries overtones that are wholly unfavorable. For a piece like this is still full of life, while belonging unmistakably to an earlier period. While I have not attempted to reproduce the speech of 1891 with exactitude, neither have I tried to give the effect of the mid-twentieth century.

Even as of 1891, Wedekind's language is peculiar. His background was international, and his German has no single regional root. By consequence, it is always a little abstract and more than a little idiosyncratic.

In addition, his children's talk is the talk, very often, of children pretending to be grown-up. The awkwardness of adolescent gestures is a familiar enough fact: Wedekind explored the awkwardness of adolescent speech. Adolescents of Germany, 1891, differ from adolescents of America, 1960, in carrying a much heavier load of Culture. Some of Wedekind's children know more of literature than of life.

By "Germany" in these notes, I mean the German-speaking part of Europe. The school Wedekind went to and based much of his story on was in Aarau, Switzerland.

E. B.

ACT ONE

SCENE 1

A living room. WENDLA BERGMANN *and her mother.*

WENDLA. Why have you made my dress so long, Mother?

MRS. BERGMANN. You're fourteen today.

WENDLA. If I'd known you were going to make my dress as long as that I'd rather have stayed thirteen.

MRS. BERGMANN. The dress isn't too long, Wendla. What do you expect? I can't help it if my daughter is an inch taller every spring. A big girl like you can't go around in a little-girl dress.

WENDLA. The little-girl dress suits me better than that old sack. —Let me wear it a little longer, Mother! Just for the summer! This penitential robe will keep.—Hold it till my next birthday. I'd only trip on the hem now.

MRS. BERGMANN. I don't know what to say. I'd like to keep you exactly as you are, child. Other girls are gawky and gangling at your age. You're just the opposite.—Who knows what you'll be like when the others are fully developed?

WENDLA. Who knows? Maybe I won't be around.

MRS. BERGMANN. Child, child, where do you get such ideas?

WENDLA. Oh, Mother, please don't be sad!

MRS. BERGMANN, *kissing her.* My little precious!

WENDLA. They just come to me in the evening when I can't go to sleep. And I don't feel sad, either. I know I'll sleep all the better.—Is it sinful to think of such things, Mother?

MRS. BERGMANN. Oh, all right, go and hang the penitential robe in the closet and put your little-girl dress on again if you must.—When I have time I'll put a strip of flouncing on it.

WENDLA, *hanging the dress in the cupboard.* Oh, no! In that case I'd rather be twenty right away!

MRS. BERGMANN. I only hope you won't be cold.—That little dress *was* long enough, but . . .

WENDLA. What, now, with summer coming on?—Oh, Mother, a girl doesn't get diphtheria in the back of her knees, how could you be so fainthearted? You don't feel the cold at my age, specially not in the legs. And would it be any better if I was too hot, Mother?—You can think yourself lucky if one fine morning your little precious doesn't cut her sleeves off or come home in the evening without shoes and stockings. —When I wear my penitential robe I shall be dressed like the queen of the fairies underneath . . . Don't scold, Mother darling. No one will ever see it!

SCENE 2

Out of doors. Sunday evening. MELCHIOR, MORITZ, OTTO, GEORG, ROBERT, ERNST.

MELCHIOR. This is boring. I'm going to stop playing.

OTTO. Then the rest of us will have to stop too!—Have you done the homework, Melchior?

MELCHIOR. You don't have to stop.

MORITZ. Where are you going?

MELCHIOR. For a walk.

GEORG. But it's getting dark!

ROBERT. Finished your homework already?

MELCHIOR. Why shouldn't I take a walk in the dark?

ERNST. Central America!—Louis the Fifteenth!—Sixty lines of Homer!—Seven equations!

MELCHIOR. This damned homework!

GEORG. If only that Latin exercise wasn't for tomorrow!

MORITZ. One can't think of anything without homework getting in the way.

OTTO. I'm going home.

GEORG. I am too. Homework!

ERNST. I am too.

ROBERT. Good night, Melchior.

MELCHIOR. Good night.

All leave but MORITZ *and* MELCHIOR.

What I'd like to know is: why do we exist?

MORITZ. I'd rather be a cab horse than have to go to school! —Why *do* we go?—We go to school to take exams!—And why do they examine us?—So they can flunk us!—They have to flunk seven—the classroom above only holds sixty.—I've felt so strange since Christmas . . . If it wasn't for Father, damned if I wouldn't pack my bag and leave for Hamburg!

MELCHIOR. Let's talk about something else.

They take a walk.

MORITZ. Did you see that black cat with its tail in the air?

MELCHIOR. You believe in omens?

MORITZ. I'm not sure.—She came over from the other side. Doesn't mean a thing, of course.

MELCHIOR. Pull free of the Scylla of religious delusion and you fall victim to the Charybdis of superstition!——Let's sit under this beech tree. A warm breeze is blowing in from the mountains. How I wish I were a young dryad up there in the forest tossed and cradled all night long in the topmost branches!

MORITZ. Unbutton your vest, Melchior.

MELCHIOR. Ah! How it blows one's clothes around!

MORITZ. Darned if it isn't getting so dark you can't see your hand before your face. Where are you actually?——Don't you agree, Melchior, that the sense of shame is simply a product of a person's upbringing?

MELCHIOR. I was thinking about that the day before yesterday. But I must say it seems to me rooted in human nature. Imagine having to undress—completely—in front of your best friend. You wouldn't unless he was doing.—Then again, it's more or less a question of fashion.

MORITZ. If I have children, I'll have them sleep in the same room from the start. If possible in the same bed. Boys *and* girls. I'll make them help each other dress and undress, and in hot weather boys as well as girls will wear nothing but a short white, woolen tunic with a leather strap.—Brought up like this, they'll be, well, less disturbed than we usually are.

MELCHIOR. I'm sure you're right, Moritz.—The only question is, when the girls have babies, what then?

MORITZ. How do you mean, have babies?

MELCHIOR. Well, if you ask me, I believe there's some kind of instinct at work. For example, if you took two kittens, a he and a she, and shut them up together for life, and never let any other cats in—if in short you left them entirely to their instincts—I believe that, sooner or later, the she-cat would become pregnant—even though neither she nor the tom had had any opportunity to learn it by example.

MORITZ. I suppose you're right. With animals it must come all by itself.

MELCHIOR. With humans too! That's *my* theory. May I ask, Moritz, when your boys sleep in the same bed as the girls, and then suddenly feel . . . the first stirrings of their manhood, well, I bet anything—

MORITZ. You may be right.—Even so . . .

MELCHIOR. And at the corresponding age exactly the same thing would happen to your girls! Not that girls are exactly . . . it's hard to judge precisely . . . anyway we can certainly assume . . . and curiosity can be relied on to play its part!

MORITZ. By the way, I have a question.

MELCHIOR. Well?

MORITZ. Will you answer it?

MELCHIOR. Of course!

MORITZ. Really?

MELCHIOR. Cross my heart!—Well, Moritz?

MORITZ. Have you done the exercise yet?

MELCHIOR. Oh, come on! There's no one to see or hear us!

MORITZ. Naturally, my children will have to work all day either in the garden or at the farm or amuse themselves with games that provide physical exercise. Riding, climbing, gymnastics . . . Above all they mustn't sleep on such soft beds as we do. Those beds have made us soft.—I don't believe you dream if you sleep on a hard bed.

MELCHIOR. From now till after grape harvest I'll be sleeping exclusively in my hammock. I've put my bed behind the stove. It folds up.—Once last winter I dreamt I'd been flogging our dog Lolo so long he couldn't move his legs. That's the most horrible thing I ever dreamt.—Why are you looking at me like that?

MORITZ. Have you felt them yet?

MELCHIOR. What?

MORITZ. What did you call them?

MELCHIOR. The stirrings of manhood?

MORITZ. Uh, huh.

MELCHIOR.—Certainly!

MORITZ. Me too. — — — — — — — — — — — — — — — — —

MELCHIOR. I've known for ages.—A year at least!

MORITZ. I felt like I'd been struck by lightning.

MELCHIOR. You'd had a dream?

MORITZ. A short one . . . About legs in sky-blue tights climbing over the lectern. At least I *think* that's what they were trying to do.—I only caught a glimpse of them.

MELCHIOR. Georg Zirschnitz dreamt of his mother.

MORITZ. Did he tell you so?

MELCHIOR. Out on Gallows Lane.

MORITZ. If you only knew what I've been through since that night!

MELCHIOR. The prickings of conscience?

MORITZ. Prickings of conscience? ——— The fear of death!

MELCHIOR. Good God!

MORITZ. I thought there was no hope for me. I was sure I must be suffering from some internal complaint.—In the end I calmed down, but only because I began to write my memoirs. Yes, my dear Melchior, the last three weeks have been my Gethsemane.

MELCHIOR. When it happened to me I was more or less prepared for it. I was a bit ashamed.—But that was all.

MORITZ. And yet you're almost a year younger than me!

MELCHIOR. I wouldn't worry about that, Moritz. In my experience, there's no fixed time for the arrival of these . . . phantoms. You know the big Lämmermeier boy with the straw-colored hair and the hook nose? He's three years older than me. Hänschen Rilow says that he still dreams of nothing but pound cake and apricot jelly.

MORITZ. Now how can Hänschen Rilow know about that?

MELCHIOR. He asked him.

MORITZ. He asked him?—I'd never have dared to *ask* anyone!

MELCHIOR. You asked *me*.

MORITZ. So I did!—It wouldn't surprise me if Hänschen had even made his will!—A strange game they play with us. And we're supposed to be grateful. I can't recall ever feeling any longing for excitements of this kind. Why didn't they let me sleep quietly on till everything had calmed down again? My dear parents could have had a hundred better children than me. Yet here I am, I don't know how I got here, and I'm supposed to answer for not having stayed away.—Haven't you ever wondered, Melchior, how we got into this whirlpool actually?

MELCHIOR. You still don't know, Moritz?

MORITZ. How should I know?—I see that hens lay eggs, and I hear that Mama carried me under her heart. Is that enough? And I can remember even as a child of five feeling embarrassed if anyone turned up the queen of hearts: she wore a décolleté. That feeling has gone. On the other hand, today I can scarcely talk to any girl without thinking something disgusting—though, I swear to you, Melchior, I don't know what.

MELCHIOR. I'll tell you everything.—I got it partly from books, partly from pictures, partly from observing nature. You'll be surprised; it made an atheist of me for the time.—I told Georg Zirschnitz. Georg Zirschnitz wanted to tell Hänschen Rilow but Hänschen learnt it all from his governess when he was still a kid.

MORITZ. I've been through Meyer's *Lexicon* from A to Z. Words! Nothing but words! Not one simple explanation. Oh this sense of shame!—What's the good of an encyclopedia that doesn't answer the most pertinent question in the world?

MELCHIOR. Have you, for instance, ever seen two dogs run across the street?

MORITZ. No!—— Don't tell me any more today, Melchior. I still have Central America and Louis the Fifteenth to take care of. And on top of that the sixty verses of Homer, the seven equations, the Latin exercise. I'd only flunk everything again tomorrow. To get anywhere with studying, I'll have to develop a thick hide.

MELCHIOR. Come back to my room. In three quarters of an hour I'll whip through the Homer, the equations, and *two* exercises. I'll slip in a few harmless mistakes for you, and the job's done. Mama will make us some of her lemonade, and we'll have a nice relaxed talk about reproduction.

MORITZ. I can't.—I can't relax on a subject like reproduction! If you want to do me a favor, give me your explanations in writing. Write down what you know. Make it as brief and clear as you can and stick it among my books during gym. I'll take it home without knowing I've got it. I'll come upon it unexpectedly. I'll have no choice but to glance through it . . . with a weary eye . . . and if it's absolutely necessary, you could add a few illustrations in the margin.

MELCHIOR. You're like a girl.—But just as you say. It's quite an interesting assignment.—— One question, Moritz.

MORITZ. Hm?

MELCHIOR.—Have you ever *seen* a girl?

MORITZ. Yes, I have!

MELCHIOR. All of her?

MORITZ *nods.*

Me too.—Then illustrations won't be needed.

MORITZ. During the Shooting Contest. In Leilich's Anatomical Museum. If they'd ever found out about it, they'd have thrown me out of school.—Beautiful as sunlight! And quite natural!

MELCHIOR. Last summer I was with mother in Frankfort and——Do you have to be going, Moritz?

MORITZ. Homework!—Good night.

MELCHIOR. So long.

SCENE 3

THEA, WENDLA, *and* MARTHA *come up the street arm in arm.*

MARTHA. How the water gets into your shoes!

WENDLA. How the wind whistles about your cheeks!

THEA. How your heart beats!

WENDLA. Let's go out to the bridge. Ilse says the river's sweeping plants and trees along. The boys have a raft on the water. They say Melchi Gabor nearly got drowned last night.

THEA. Oh, he can swim.

MARTHA. I should say so!

WENDLA. If he hadn't been able to, he'd have drowned.

THEA. Your braid's coming undone, Martha, your braid's coming undone!

MARTHA. Pooh, let it! It's a nuisance—all day and all night.
I'm not allowed to wear my hair short like yours or loose
like Wendla's. I can't wear bangs. I have to braid it even
at home. All because of my aunts.

WENDLA. I'll bring a pair of scissors to Bible class tomorrow.
And while we're reciting "Happy is he that walketh" I'll cut
it off.

MARTHA. For heaven's sake, Wendla! Papa would beat me
black and blue, and Mama would lock me in the coalhole
three nights on end.

WENDLA. What does he beat you with, Martha?

MARTHA. I sometimes think they'd feel something was missing
if they didn't have a little mess like me for a daughter.

THEA. But Martha!

MARTHA. Some of you were allowed to thread a blue ribbon
through the yoke of your nightdress, weren't you?

THEA. Mine's pink satin! Mama maintains that pink suits me
—with my coal-black eyes.

MARTHA. Blue looked so lovely on me!—Mama pulled me out

of bed by my braids. I fell on the floor with my hands out like this.—Mama prays with us every evening . . .

WENDLA. If I were you I'd have run away long ago.

MARTHA. . . . "So that's it, that's what you have in mind!" she says. "Well, I just wanted to see it, I just wanted to see it. At least," says she, "you'll have nothing to reproach your mother with later . . ."

THEA. Oh, won't you?

MARTHA. Can you imagine what mother meant by that, Thea?

THEA. I can't.—Can you, Wendla?

WENDLA. I'd have asked her.

MARTHA. I lay on the floor and shrieked and yelled. Enter papa. Rip! Off comes my nightdress! I head for the door. "So that's it," he shouts, "you'd like to go out like that, wouldn't you?"

WENDLA. Oh, now you're telling stories, Martha!

MARTHA. It was freezing. I went back in. I had to spend the whole night on the floor in a sack.

THEA. I could never sleep in a sack as long as I live.

WENDLA. I'd be glad to sleep in your sack for you.

MARTHA. It's only the beatings . . .

THEA. Oh, it's enough to stifle you to death.

MARTHA. Your head sticks out. You tie the sack under your chin.

THEA. And then they beat you?

MARTHA. No. Only when there's something special.

WENDLA. What do they beat you with, Martha?

MARTHA. Oh, I don't know. Anything.—Does *your* mother think it's indecent to eat a piece of bread in bed?

WENDLA. Oh no!

MARTHA. I suppose they have fun, though they never mention it.—If I ever have children I'll let them grow like the weeds in our flower garden. No one bothers about them, and they're so thick, so tall, while the roses—staked out in those beds—bloom more miserably every summer.

THEA. If I have children I'll dress them all in pink. Pink hats, pink dresses, pink shoes. Only the stockings—the stockings shall be as black as night. And when I take them out I'll make them all walk in front of me.—What about you, Wendla?

WENDLA. You both know if you're going to have some?

THEA. Why shouldn't we have some?

MARTHA. Well, Aunt Euphemia hasn't got any.

THEA. Because she's not *married*, silly!

WENDLA. My Aunt Bauer's been married three times and hasn't got a single one.

MARTHA. If you have some, Wendla, which would you rather have, boys or girls?

WENDLA. Boys! Boys!

THEA. Boys for me too!

MARTHA. Me too! I'd rather have twenty boys than three girls.

THEA. Girls are boring.

MARTHA. If I hadn't been a girl up to now I certainly wouldn't want to become one.

WENDLA. I think that's a matter of taste, Martha! I give thanks every day that I'm a girl. Believe me, I wouldn't change places with a king's son.—I want to *have* sons!

THEA. That's a lot of nonsense, Wendla, just nonsense!

WENDLA. But surely, Thea, it must be a thousand times more inspiring to be loved by a man than by a girl!

THEA. You don't mean to tell me Forestry Commissioner Pfälle loves Melitta more than she loves him?

WENDLA. I certainly do, Thea.—Pfälle's proud. Pfälle is proud of being Forestry Commissioner, he doesn't have money.— Melitta is radiantly happy because she gets ten thousand times more than she gives.

MARTHA. Aren't you proud—of yourself, Wendla?

WENDLA. That would be foolish.

MARTHA. How proud *I'd* be in your shoes!

THEA. Just see how she places her feet, how she looks straight ahead, how she carries herself, Martha!—If that isn't pride!

WENDLA. But what for? I'm so happy to be a girl. If I weren't a girl I'd kill myself—so that the next time . . .

MELCHIOR *passes and greets them.*

THEA. He has a marvelous head.

MARTHA. That's how I picture the young Alexander when he was a pupil of Aristotle's.

THEA. Oh Lord, Greek history! All I can remember is how Socrates lay in the barrel when Alexander sold him the ass's shadow.

WENDLA. He's supposed to be third in his class.

THEA. Professor Knochenbruch says if he wanted to he could be first.

MARTHA. He has a lovely forehead, but his friend has a more spiritual look.

THEA. Moritz Stiefel?—*He'll* never be anybody!

MARTHA. I've always got on with him quite well.

THEA. He embarrasses you when you meet him. At the children's party the Rilows gave he offered me some chocolates. Just imagine, Wendla, they were soft and warm! Isn't that . . . ?—He said he'd had them too long in his trouser pocket!

WENDLA. Just think, Melchi Gabor told me that night he didn't believe in anything: God, an afterlife, or anything at all.

SCENE 4

A park in front of the school.—MELCHIOR, OTTO, GEORG, ROBERT, HÄNSCHEN RILOW, LÄMMERMEIER.

MELCHIOR. Can any of you tell me where Moritz Stiefel's hiding?

GEORG. He's headed for trouble. Oh, he's headed for trouble!

OTTO. He goes on and on till he's in the soup!

LÄMMERMEIER. A little bird tells me I wouldn't care to be in that man's shoes!

ROBERT. What a nerve!—What absolute gall!

MELCHIOR. Wha . . . wha . . . what is it you all know?

GEORG. What do we know?—Well, let's see—

LÄMMERMEIER. I'm not talking.

OTTO. Nor me. Good God!

MELCHIOR. If you don't tell me right now . . .

ROBERT. In short: Moritz Stiefel got into the Faculty Room.

MELCHIOR. The Faculty Room?

OTTO. The Faculty Room. Right after the Latin class.

GEORG. He was the last. He stayed behind on purpose.

LÄMMERMEIER. As I turned the corner I saw him open the door.

MELCHIOR. The devil take it . . . !

LÄMMERMEIER. If only the devil doesn't take *him!*

GEORG. The Rektor must've forgotten to take the key away.

ROBERT. Or else Moritz Stiefel has a skeleton key.

OTTO. I wouldn't put it past him.

LÄMMERMEIER. At best, he'll be kept in on Sunday afternoon.

ROBERT. Also a remark on his report card!

OTTO. Provided he isn't kicked out—with the report *he'll* get.

HÄNSCHEN RILOW. There he is.

MELCHIOR. White as a sheet.

Enter MORITZ, *greatly agitated.*

LÄMMERMEIER. Moritz, Moritz, what you have done!

MORITZ.——Nothing——Nothing——

ROBERT. You're feverish!

MORITZ.—With happiness—bliss—jubilation—

OTTO. Did they catch you?

MORITZ. I've got my promotion!—Melchior, I've got my promotion!—Now the world can come to an end!—I've got my promotion!—Who would have thought I'd get my promotion?—I can't take it in even now!—I've read it twenty times.—I can't believe it—great God, it was still there, it was still there! I'VE GOT MY PROMOTION!

Smiling.

I don't know—I feel so strange—the ground's going up and

down . . . Melchior, Melchior, if you knew what I've been
through!

HÄNSCHEN RILOW. Congratulations, Moritz.—Be glad you got
away with it.

MORITZ. You've no idea how much was at stake, Hänschen,
how could you? For the past three weeks I've been slinking
past that door as if it was the jaws of Hell. And then today,
there it was, unlocked. I think if someone had offered me
a million—no, nothing could have stopped me!—So there I
am in the middle of the room, I open the register, turn the
pages, find the place—and the whole time . . . it makes
me shudder—

MELCHIOR. . . . The whole time what?

MORITZ. The whole time the door was standing wide open
behind me. How I got out . . . how I got down the stairs
I don't know.

HÄNSCHEN RILOW.—Has Ernst Röbel got his promotion too?

MORITZ. Oh, surely, Hänschen, surely! Ernst Röbel is up too!

ROBERT. That just shows you must have read the thing wrong.
Not counting the dunce's bench, with you and Röbel we
come to sixty-one, and the classroom upstairs won't hold
more than sixty.

MORITZ. I read it right! Ernst Röbel is just as much going up
as I am. But for both of us it's only provisional. The first
term is supposed to decide which of us must give up his
place to the other.—Poor Röbel!—Heaven knows I no longer
fear for myself. I've been looking too deep into things for
that!

OTTO. I bet you five marks you'll give up the place.

MORITZ. You haven't a penny, and I wouldn't want to rob you.
—God, how I'll grind from now on. Now I can tell you all
—whether you believe it or not—nothing matters any more—
I—I know how true it is: if I didn't get my promotion I was
going to shoot myself!

ROBERT. Show-off!

GEORG. Yellow-belly!

OTTO. I'd like to see you shoot *anything!*

LÄMMERMEIER. I bet you a smack in the eye.

MELCHIOR, *gives him one.*——Come on, Moritz. Let's go to the keeper's cottage.

GEORG. You don't mean you believe that stuff?

MELCHIOR. Mind your business.——Let them gab, Moritz. Let's get out! Into the town!

PROFESSORS HUNGERGURT *and* KNOCHENBRUCH *pass by.*

KNOCHENBRUCH. That my best student should feel himself attracted to my worst is quite incomprehensible to me, dear colleague.

HUNGERGURT. To me also, dear colleague.

SCENE 5

A sunny afternoon. MELCHIOR *and* WENDLA *meet in the forest.*

MELCHIOR. Is it really you, Wendla?—What are you doing all alone up here?—I've been roaming all over the forest for the last three hours without meeting a soul and suddenly *you* pop out of the thickest thicket!

WENDLA. Yes, it's me.

MELCHIOR. If I didn't know you were Wendla Bergmann I'd take you for a dryad fallen from the branches!

WENDLA. No, no, I'm Wendla Bergmann.—What are you doing here?

MELCHIOR. Having my own thoughts.

WENDLA. I'm looking for woodruff. Mama wants to make May wine. At first she wanted to come too, but at the last moment my Aunt Bauer paid us a visit, and she doesn't like to walk uphill.—So I came by myself.

MELCHIOR. Did you find your woodruff?

WENDLA. A basketful. Over there under the bushes it's as thick as clover.—As a matter of fact, I'm looking for a way out, I seem to have got lost. Can you tell me what time it is?

MELCHIOR. Just after half past three.—When are they expecting you?

WENDLA. I thought it was later. I lay a long time in the moss by the stream, just dreaming. The time went so fast. I was afraid evening might be coming on.

MELCHIOR. If they're not expecting you yet, let's lie here a bit longer. Under the oak tree there is my favorite spot. If you lean your head back against the trunk and look up at the sky through the branches you're hypnotized. The ground is still warm from the morning sun.—I've been wanting to ask you something for weeks, Wendla.

WENDLA. But I must be home by five.

MELCHIOR. We'll go together. I'll carry the basket, we'll take the path through the gully, and in ten minutes we'll be on the bridge!—When you lie here with your forehead on your hands you have the strangest thoughts . . .

Both lie down under the oak.

WENDLA. What did you want to ask me, Melchior?

MELCHIOR. I heard that you often visit the poor, Wendla. That you take them food and clothes and money. Do you do it of your own accord, or does your mother send you?

WENDLA. Usually mother sends me. They're poor day laborers with a mob of children. Often the man can't find work, and they go cold and hungry. At home we've got all sorts of things in closets and chests, things we don't use, that are just piling up . . . But what made you think of it?

MELCHIOR. When your mother sends you somewhere like that do you like to go or not?

WENDLA. I love to go, of course!—How can you ask?

MELCHIOR. The children are dirty, the women are ill, their houses are full of vermin, the men hate you because you don't work . . .

WENDLA. That's not true, Melchior. And if it was, all the more reason for me to go.

MELCHIOR. What makes you say that, Wendla?

WENDLA.—It would make me even happier to be able to do something for them.

MELCHIOR. So you visit the poor for your own pleasure?

WENDLA. I visit them because they're poor.

MELCHIOR. But would you go if it didn't give you pleasure?

WENDLA. Can I help it if it gives me pleasure?

MELCHIOR. At that you get yourself into heaven by it.—It's true, then, this thought that's been eating at me for the past month.—Can a man help it if he's closefisted and it *doesn't* give him pleasure to visit dirty, sick children?

WENDLA. It would certainly give you a lot of pleasure!

MELCHIOR. He's supposed to die an eternal death because it doesn't.—I shall write a treatise and send it to Pastor Kahlbauch. He's the cause of it all. How he drools about the joys of self-sacrifice!—If he can't answer me I shall stop going to catechism class, I shall refuse to be confirmed.

WENDLA. Why hurt your parents like that? Go through with your confirmation. It won't cost you your head. If it wasn't for our horrid white dresses and your long pants it could even be something to get excited about.

MELCHIOR. There's no such thing as sacrifice! No such thing as unselfishness!—I see the virtuous rejoicing and the wicked trembling and groaning—I see you, Wendla Bergmann, shaking your curls and laughing, and I can't join in because I feel like an outlaw!——What were you dreaming of just now, Wendla, in the grass by the stream?

WENDLA.——Nonsense—foolishness—

MELCHIOR. With your eyes open?

WENDLA. I dreamt I was a poor, poor beggar child. I was sent into the streets at five in the morning. I had to beg all day, in rain and storm, among rough hardhearted people, and if I came home in the evening, shivering with hunger and cold, and didn't bring as much money as my father expected, I'd get beaten—beaten—

MELCHIOR. I know all about that, Wendla. You have those stupid children's stories to thank for it. Believe me, such brutal people don't exist any more.

WENDLA. They do, Melchior, you're wrong.—Martha Bessel is beaten night after night. Next day you can see the welts. What she must have to suffer! It makes your blood boil to hear her talk about it. I pity her so, I often cry into my pillow in the middle of the night. I've been wondering for months how we could help her. I'd gladly take her place for a week or so.

MELCHIOR. Someone should report her father. They'd take the girl away from him.

WENDLA. I've never been beaten in my life, Melchior. Not once. I can hardly imagine what it's like to be beaten. I've tried beating myself to find out how it feels inside.—It must be a shuddery sensation.

MELCHIOR. I don't believe a child is ever the better for it.

WENDLA. Better for what?

MELCHIOR. For being beaten.

WENDLA.—With this switch for instance?—Phew, it's thin and tough!

MELCHIOR. It would draw blood.

WENDLA. Wouldn't you like to hit me with it once?

MELCHIOR. Hit who?

WENDLA. Hit me.

MELCHIOR. What's got into you, Wendla?

WENDLA. I bet there's nothing to it.

MELCHIOR. Oh, don't worry, I *won't* hit you.

WENDLA. Not if I let you?

MELCHIOR. Never, girl.

WENDLA. Not if I ask you to, Melchior?

MELCHIOR. Are you out of your mind?

WENDLA. I've never been beaten in my life.

MELCHIOR. If you can *ask* for a thing like that . . .

WENDLA. Please! Please!

MELCHIOR. I'll teach you to say please!

He beats her.

WENDLA. Oh dear, I don't feel a thing!

MELCHIOR. I believe you. With all those skirts on.

WENDLA. Then hit me on the legs.

MELCHIOR. Wendla!

He hits her harder.

WENDLA. You're just stroking me!—You're stroking me!

MELCHIOR. Just wait, you little witch, I'll beat the hell out of
you!

*He throws the branch away and pommels her with his fists
till she breaks out in fearful yelling. Not in the least de-
terred, he lets fly at her in a rage, while his tears run down
his cheeks. Suddenly he springs upright, clasps his temples
with both hands, and plunges into the forest sobbing piti-
fully and from the depths of his soul.*

ACT TWO

SCENE 1

Evening in MELCHIOR's *study. The window is open. There is a lighted lamp on the table.—*MELCHIOR *and* MORITZ *on the sofa.*

MORITZ. Now I'm quite cheerful again, only a little excited.—But in the Greek class I slept like the drunken Polyphemus. I'm surprised old Zungenschlag didn't pull my ears.—This morning I was within an inch of being late.—My first thought on waking was of the verbs in *mi*. Christ Almighty, Hell and Damnation—all during breakfast and on the way to school I was conjugating till my head swam.—I must have dropped off just after three. On top of everything, my pen had made a blot on the book. The lamp was smoking when Mathilda woke me. The thrushes were twittering in the lilac bushes below, so glad to be alive, and I started feeling indescribably melancholy again. I put my collar on and drew the brush through my hair.——But you feel so good when you've won a victory over yourself!

MELCHIOR. May I roll you a cigarette?

MORITZ. Thank you, I don't smoke.—If only I can go on like this! I mean to work and work till my eyes pop out of my head.—Ernst Röbel has already failed six times since the vacation, three times in Greek, twice with Knochenbruch, and the last time in Lit. I've only been in that unfortunate situation five times, and from now on it's not going to happen again!—Röbel won't shoot himself. Röbel hasn't got parents who are sacrificing their all for him. He can be a mercenary if he wants to, or a sailor or a cowboy. If *I* don't get through, Papa will have a stroke and Mama will go to the madhouse. That's more than a fellow could bear.—Before the exam I asked God to make me consumptive so that the cup might pass from me. It *has* passed. But even now it kind of glimmers at me from a distance, so I don't dare to raise my eyes, day or night.—Having taken hold of the pole I'll hoist myself up all right. My surety for that is the inescapable fact that I can't fall without breaking my neck.

MELCHIOR. Life's meaner than one could ever have expected. I wouldn't mind hanging myself from a branch.—Where can Mama be with the tea!

MORITZ. Your tea will do me good, Melchior. I'm trembling. I feel so strangely disembodied. Just touch me. I see—I hear —I feel much more clearly—and yet everything's so like a dream—there's such an atmosphere.—The way the park stretches away in the moonlight—so still, so deep, as if into infinity. Dim figures step out from behind bushes, scurry with breathless haste across the clearings, and disappear into the semi-darkness. It seems to me there's a council meeting on under the chestnut tree.—Shall we go down, Melchior?

MELCHIOR. Let's wait till we've had our tea.

MORITZ.—The leaves are whispering so busily.—It's like hearing Grandmother happily telling the story of the queen that had no head.—She was a fabulously beautiful queen, beautiful as the sun, more beautiful than any other girl in the country. Only she'd had the bad luck to be born without a head. She couldn't eat or drink, couldn't see or laugh, she couldn't kiss. She was able to communicate with her attendants only by means of her soft little hand. With her delicate feet she tapped out declarations of war and sentences of death. Then one day she was conquered by a king who happened to have two heads that got in each other's hair all the year round and quarreled so excitedly that neither let the other get a word in edgewise. So the chief court magician took the smaller of the two heads and placed it on the queen. "And lo! It became her passing well." Whereupon the king married the queen, and the two heads no longer got in each other's hair but kissed each other on brow, cheeks, and lips, and lived many years in happiness and joy. . . . What damn nonsense! Since the vacation I can't get the headless queen out of my head. If I see a beautiful girl, I see her without a head, then suddenly I myself seem to be a headless queen. . . . Perhaps I'll get me another head, though.

Enter MRS. GABOR *with the steaming tea, which she places on the table in front of* MORITZ *and* MELCHIOR.

MRS. GABOR. Here you are, boys, I hope you enjoy it.—Hello, Mr. Stiefel, how are you?

MORITZ. Fine, thanks, Mrs. Gabor.—I was just listening to the goings-on down in the park.

MRS. GABOR. You don't look at all well.—Are you feeling ill?

MORITZ. It doesn't mean a thing. I've been to bed rather late the last few times.

MELCHIOR. Just think: he worked all through the night.

MRS. GABOR. But you shouldn't do such things, Mr. Stiefel. You must look after yourself. Consider your health. School is no substitute for health.—Plenty of walks in the fresh air! At your age that's more important than accuracy in Middle High German!

MORITZ. I'll take plenty of walks. You're right. And one can work while walking. Why didn't I think of that myself?— Even so, I'd have the written work to do at home.

MELCHIOR. You can do the written work with me; that will make it easier for us both.—Did you know Max von Trenk has died of brain fever, Mama?—This morning Hänschen Rilow came to Rektor Sonnenstich from Trenk's deathbed. To report that Max had just died in his presence.—"Really?" said Sonnenstich, "don't you still have two hours' detention to do from last week?—Here's the ticket for the school porter. See to it that the matter is finally settled! The whole class will attend the funeral!"—Hänschen was stunned.

MRS. GABOR. What's that book you have there, Melchior?

MELCHIOR. *Faust.*

MRS. GABOR. Have you read it?

MELCHIOR. Not to the end.

MORITZ. We're in the Walpurgisnacht scene.

MRS. GABOR. If I were your age, I'd have waited another year or two.

MELCHIOR. I never found so much in a book before, Mama. It's beautiful. Why shouldn't I read it?

MRS. GABOR.—Because you don't understand it.

MELCHIOR. You can't know that, Mama. I realize I'm in no position to get all the . . . grandeur of it—

MORITZ. We always read together. Amazing how much more you understand.

MRS. GABOR. You're old enough to know what's good for you, Melchior. Do whatever you can answer to yourself for. I shall be the first to welcome the time when you give me no further reason to hold things back.—I only wanted to point out that even the best can be dangerous when one lacks the maturity to interpret it correctly.—But I'd always rather put my trust in *you* than in "disciplinary measures." ——If either of you need anything else, come over and call me, Melchior. I'll be in my bedroom.

Exit.

MORITZ.—Your mother means the business with Gretchen.

MELCHIOR. Why, we only spent half a second on it.

MORITZ. Faust himself can scarcely have dismissed it more cold-bloodedly.

MELCHIOR. After all, artistically speaking, this outrage isn't the high point of the play.—Suppose Faust just promised to marry the girl and then left her; as I see it he wouldn't be a bit less to blame. As far as I'm concerned, Gretchen could die of a broken heart.—To see the frantic way everyone always fastens on to the subject, you'd think the world revolved around penis and vagina.

MORITZ. To be quite frank, Melchior, since I read your essay, I feel that it does.—It fell at my feet in the first days of the vacation. I had Ploetz's *History* in my hand.—I bolted the door and skimmed through the flickering lines as a frightened owl flies through a burning forest.—I think I read most of it with my eyes shut. Your explanations sounded like a series of dim recollections, like a song that one had hummed happily to oneself as a child and then heard on the lips of another as one lay dying. Heartbreaking!—I was the most strongly affected by what you wrote about girls.

I can't get rid of the impression it made. Believe me, Melchior, to have to suffer wrong is sweeter than to do wrong. To have to let oneself undergo so sweet a wrong undeservedly seems to me the essence of all earthly bliss.

MELCHIOR.—I don't want my bliss given to me as charity.

MORITZ. But why not?

MELCHIOR. I don't *want* anything I haven't had to fight for.

MORITZ. Can you still call that enjoyment, Melchior?—Girls enjoy themselves, Melchior, like the gods in *their* bliss. And a girl's nature is self-protective. A girl keeps herself free of everything bitter till the last moment, and then has the pleasure of seeing all heaven break over her. She hasn't stopped fearing hell when suddenly she notices paradise in full bloom. Her feelings are as fresh as water springing from the rock. She takes up a chalice, a goblet of nectar, which no earthly breath has yet blown upon and—even as it flickers and flares—drains it! By comparison, a man's satisfaction seems to me shallow, stagnant.

MELCHIOR. Think of it as you like, only keep it to yourself.— I don't like to think of it . . .

SCENE 2

A living room.

MRS. BERGMANN, *her hat on, a shawl around her shoulders and a basket on her arm, enters through the center door with a beaming face.* Wendla!—Wendla!

WENDLA, *appears in her bodice and petticoat at the side door, right.* What is it, Mother?

MRS. BERGMANN. You're up already, child?—That's a good girl!

WENDLA. Have you been out already?

MRS. BERGMANN. Be quick and get dressed, you must go down to Ina's. You must take her this basket!

WENDLA, *dressing herself completely in the course of what follows.* You were at Ina's?—How is Ina?—Still no better?

MRS. BERGMANN. Just think, Wendla, the stork paid Ina a visit last night. Brought her a little boy.

WENDLA. A boy?—A boy!—Oh, that's wonderful!——*That* explains the never-ending influenza!

MRS. BERGMANN. A splendid boy!

WENDLA. I must see him, Mother!—So I'm an aunt for the third time—aunt to a girl and two boys!

MRS. BERGMANN. And what boys!—That's what comes of living so near the church!—It's only two and a half years ago that she went up the altar steps in her muslin dress.

WENDLA. Were you there when it brought him?

MRS. BERGMANN. It had just flown away.—Wouldn't you like to pin a rose on your dress?

WENDLA. Why didn't you get there a little sooner, Mother?

MRS. BERGMANN. I think he brought something for you too—a brooch or something.

WENDLA. It's a real shame.

MRS. BERGMANN. But I'm telling you he brought you a brooch!

WENDLA. I have enough brooches . . .

MRS. BERGMANN. Then be satisfied, child. What else do you want?

WENDLA. I should so terribly like to know whether he flew through the window or down the chimney.

MRS. BERGMANN. You must ask Ina. Ha, ha, you must ask Ina, dear heart. Ina will give you all details. Ina talked to him a solid half hour.

WENDLA. I shall ask her when I go over.

MRS. BERGMANN. Mind you don't forget, my angel! I should like to know myself whether it came through the window or down the chimney.

WENDLA. Or had I better ask the chimney sweep?—The chimney sweep must know best if it comes down the chimney or not.

MRS. BERGMANN. Not the chimney sweep, child! What does he know of the stork?—He'd tell you all sorts of nonsense he doesn't believe himself. . . . Wh—what are you staring at down in the street?

WENDLA. A man, Mother. And he's three times the size of an ox! With feet like steamboats!

MRS. BERGMANN, *rushing to the window.* Impossible!—Impossible!

WENDLA, *quickly.* He's holding a bedstead under his chin and fiddling "The Watch on the Rhine" on it.——Now he's turning the corner . . .

MRS. BERGMANN. Oh, you're just a big baby still, Wendla. To startle your silly old mother like that!—Come, take your hat. I shall be surprised if you ever learn sense.—I've given up hope.

WENDLA. So have I, Mother darling. It's sad I haven't learned sense.—Here I have a sister married two and a half years. I myself am an aunt three times over. And I haven't the slightest idea how it all comes about. . . . Don't be angry, Mother darling! Who in the world should I ask but you? Please tell me! Tell me, Mother! Don't scold me for asking, I'm ashamed. Just answer. How does it happen?—You can't seriously expect me to believe in the stork—at fourteen.

MRS. BERGMANN. Good gracious child, the things you think of! —I really couldn't!

WENDLA. Why not?—It can't be nasty when everyone is so pleased about it.

MRS. BERGMANN. Oh—oh God preserve me! I'd deserve to be . . . Go and put on your coat, girl, put on your coat.

WENDLA. I'm going . . . What if your daughter goes and asks the chimney sweep?

MRS. BERGMANN. It's enough to drive one crazy!—Come, child, come here. I'll tell you! I'll tell you everything . . . Merciful providence! But not today, Wendla, tomorrow, day after tomorrow, next week. Whenever you like, dear heart . . .

WENDLA. Today. Now. This minute.—Now that I've seen *you* so upset, *I'm* not likely to calm down.

MRS. BERGMANN.—I can't, Wendla.

WENDLA. Why not?—See, I'll kneel at your feet and put my head in your lap. You can put your apron over my head and talk and talk as if you were quite alone. I won't flinch, I won't cry out, I'll take what comes!

MRS. BERGMANN.—Heaven knows it's not my fault, Wendla

. . . Well, I'll tell you how you came into the world.—Are you listening, Wendla?

WENDLA, *under the apron.* I'm listening.

Pause.

MRS. BERGMANN, *beside herself.*—I can't do it.—I couldn't answer for it!—I deserve to be in prison—I deserve to have you taken away from me . . .

WENDLA, *under the apron.* Courage, Mother!

MRS. BERGMANN. Well then, listen . . .

WENDLA, *under the apron, trembling.* Oh dear, oh dear!

MRS. BERGMANN. To have a child—you understand what I'm saying, Wendla?

WENDLA. Quick, Mother, I can't bear it any longer.

MRS. BERGMANN.—To have a child—one must love the man—to whom one is married—love him as only a husband can be loved. One must love him so much, one must love him, Wendla, as you at your age are incapable of loving . . . Now you know.

WENDLA, *getting up.* God in Heaven!

MRS. BERGMANN. Now you know what trials lie before you!

WENDLA.—And that's all?

MRS. BERGMANN. So help me God!——And now take the basket and go over to Ina's. You'll get chocolates and cakes there.—Come, let's have another look at you. Laced boots, silk gloves, sailor blouse, roses in your hair. . . . But that little skirt is definitely too short for you, Wendla.

WENDLA. Have you got the meat for dinner, Mother?

MRS. BERGMANN. May the Lord bless and keep you!—When I have time, I'll put a strip of flouncing on it.

SCENE 3

HÄNSCHEN RILOW, *with a light in his hand, bolts the door behind him and lifts the lid.*

HÄNSCHEN. Hast thou prayed tonight, Desdemona?

He pulls a reproduction of Palma Vecchio's "Venus" out of his shirt.

You don't seem to be at your prayers, fair one—contempla-
tively awaiting whoever might be coming—as in the sweet
moment of dawning bliss when I saw you in Jonathan
Schlesinger's shop window—these supple limbs are just as
beguiling still, the gentle arch of the hips, these firm young
breasts—how intoxicated with happiness the great Master
must have been when the fourteen-year-old original lay before his very eyes on the sofa!

Will you also visit me in dreams sometimes?—I'll receive
you with outstretched arms and kiss you till your breath
gives out. You'll take me over like the rightful mistress entering her deserted castle. The gate and all the doors' are
opened by unseen hands while the fountain joyously begins
to plash in the park below.

"It is the cause!—It is the cause!"—This frightful pounding
in my breast tells you how far from frivolously I murder you.
My throat contracts at the thought of my solitary nights. By
my soul, child, I swear it is not satiety that sways me! Who
would dare boast that he was sated with *you?*

But you suck the marrow from my bones, you crook my
back, you steal the light from my young eyes.—Your inhuman modesty makes excessive claims upon me. Your un-
moving limbs wear me down.—It was you or I; and the victory is mine.

If I were to count them, the dear departed with whom I
have fought the same battle here? "Psyche" by Thumann,
another legacy from that dried up Mademoiselle Angélique,
the rattlesnake in the paradise of my childhood. Correggio's
"Io." Lossow's "Galatea." Then a "Cupid" by Bouguereau.
"Ada" by J. van Beers—I had to abduct Ada from a secret
drawer in father's bureau before I could include her in my
harem. A trembling, twitching "Leda" by Makart that I happened on under my brother's school notebooks. Seven! O
blooming candidate for death, seven have trod this path to
Tartarus before you! Let that be a comfort to you, and do
not seek with those looks of supplication to turn my torments
to excesses!

You are dying, not for your sins, but for mine.—Only to
defend myself from myself do I—with a bleeding heart——

commit this seventh wife-murder. Is there not something tragic in the role of Bluebeard? I believe that all his murdered wives together suffered less than he did strangling any one of them.

But my conscience will rest easier, my body will gain in strength, when you reside no more, you devil, within the red silk cushions of my jewel box. To your place in that voluptuous love-nest I'll admit Bodenhausen's "Lurlei" or Linger's "Forsaken Maiden" or Defregger's "Loni"—they'll help me to recover in short order! Another three months maybe, and your unveiled Jehoshaphat, dear heart, would have begun to eat at my brain like the sun at butter. This separation of bed and board was overdue.

Phew! There's a Heliogabalus in me, I feel it. *Moritura me salutat.*—Girl, girl, why do you press your knees together? —At this late date?—On the threshold of inscrutable eternity? ——One twitch, and I'll release you.—One feminine movement, one sign of lust, of sympathy, my girl, and I'll frame you in gold and hang you over my bed!—Have you no inkling that it's only your chastity that drives me to excesses? —Woe unto ye, inhuman ones!

. . . One never fails to note that she's had an exemplary education.—But then—so have I.

Hast thou prayed tonight, Desdemona?

My heart! I'm having convulsions!—— Nonsense!—St. Agnes also died on account of her abstinence, and she wasn't half as naked as you are!—One more kiss on the blooming body, the budding, child's breast, the sweetly rounded—the cruel knees . . .

It is the cause, it is the cause, my soul.
Let me not name it to you, you chaste stars!
It is the cause!—

The picture falls into the depths. He closes the lid.

SCENE 4

A hayloft.—MELCHIOR *is lying on his back in the new-mown hay.* WENDLA *climbs the ladder.*

WENDLA. So this is where you've crept off to?—Everyone's looking for you. The wagon has gone out again. You must help. A thunderstorm is coming up.

MELCHIOR. Keep away!—Keep away from me!

WENDLA. What's the matter with you?—Why are you hiding your face?

MELCHIOR. Get out of here!—Or I'll throw you down on the threshing floor!

WENDLA. Now I'm certainly not going.

Kneels down beside him.

Why don't you come with us to the meadows, Melchior?— It's dark and stuffy in here. Even if we do get wet to the skin, what do *we* care!

MELCHIOR. The hay smells so wonderful.—The sky must be as black as a pall.—All I can see is the poppy gleaming at your breast—and I can hear your heart beating—

WENDLA.——Don't kiss me, Melchior!—Don't kiss me!

MELCHIOR.—Your heart—I hear it beating—

WENDLA. People love each other—if they kiss — — — — don't, don't——

MELCHIOR. There is no such thing as love! That's a fact.—It's all just selfishness and self-seeking.—I love you as little as you love me.—

WENDLA.——Don't!————Don't, Melchior!——

MELCHIOR.————Wendla!

WENDLA. Oh, Melchior! — — — — — — — don't — — don't — —

SCENE 5

MRS. GABOR, *seated, writing.*

MRS. GABOR.

Dear Mr. Stiefel,

Having for twenty-four hours considered and reconsidered all that you have written to me, I take up my pen with a heavy heart. I am unable, I give you my sacred word on it, to provide you with the cost of a passage to America. I have not so much money at my disposal, and even if I had, it would be the greatest conceivable sin to place in your hand the means of acting on a sudden whim so grave in its consequences. You would do me a bitter injustice, Mr. Stiefel, if you were to attribute this refusal to lack of love. On the other hand, it would be the most brutal violation of my duty as a motherly friend were I to let myself be persuaded by your temporary loss of control into losing my own head and blindly following my own first impulse. Should you wish it, I will gladly write to your parents. I will try to convince them that in the course of the term you have done all you could. You have so used up your strength——I shall point out——that a strict judgment on your failure would be not only unjustifiable but in the highest degree prejudicial to your mental and physical health.

Frankly, Mr. Stiefel, your veiled threats to take your own life, should you be refused the means of escape, have slightly alienated my sympathies. Let a misfortune be never so undeserved, one should not permit oneself to be driven to forbidden measures. The way in which you seek to make me, who have never shown you anything but good will, responsible for a possible dreadful misdeed on your part could all too easily be interpreted by the hostile as attempted blackmail. I must confess that such behavior in you, who otherwise seem so aware of your duty to yourself, is the last thing I would have expected. Meanwhile, I am firmly convinced that you were too much under the influence of the initial fright to be fully aware of what you were doing.

And so I confidently hope that these words of mine will find you already in a more controlled frame of mind. Accept the matter as it stands. In my opinion, it is quite impermissible to judge a young man by his school reports. We have too many examples of very bad students making splendid people, and on the other hand of excellent students acquitting themselves indifferently in life. At all events, I give you my assurance that, as far as it lies in my power, your failure shall change nothing in your relationship with Melchior. It will always be a pleasure to me to see my son associating with a young man who, however the world may judge him, has been able to win my fullest sympathy.

So, chin up, Mr. Stiefel!—Such crises of one kind or another confront each of us and must be overcome. If everyone had recourse to poison or the dagger there would soon be no human beings left in the world. Let me hear from you again soon. With warmest greetings from your still devoted motherly friend,

Fanny G.

SCENE 6

The BERGMANNS' *garden in the morning sunlight.*

WENDLA. Why did you slip out of the room?—To look for violets!—Because Mother can see me smiling.—Why can't you keep your lips together?—I don't know.—I really don't know, I can't find the words . . .

The path is like a plush carpet—not a pebble, not a thorn. —My feet don't touch the ground. . . . Oh, how sweetly I slept last night!

This is where they were.—I feel as solemn as a nun at Communion.—Sweet violets!—All right, Mother dear, I'm ready now for the penitential robe.—Oh God, if only someone would come that I could embrace, that I could tell the whole story to!

SCENE 7

Dusk. The sky is slightly overcast. The path winds through low brush and reeds. From a little distance the murmur of the river can be heard.

MORITZ. It's better this way.—I don't belong. Let the rest of them knock their heads together.—I'll close the door behind me and step out in the open.—Pay for the privilege of being kicked around? I never pushed before. Why should I now? —I've signed no contract with the Almighty. People will make of this what they want to make of it. I've been driven to it.—I don't hold my parents responsible. All the same they must have been prepared for the worst. They were old enough to know what they were doing. I was an infant when I came into the world, or no doubt I'd have been smart enough to become someone else.—Why should I suffer because everyone else was already there?

One would have to be a perfect fool . . . if someone makes me a present of a mad dog I give him his mad dog back again. And if he doesn't want to take his mad dog back, well, I'm human, and . . .

One would have to be a perfect fool.

One is born entirely by chance. And if, after mature consideration————oh, it's enough to make one want to shoot oneself!

—At least the weather's being considerate. It's been looking like rain all day, but it's kept fine after all.—An unusual peace reigns. In all Nature, not a discordant note. Earth and sky—one transparent cobweb. Everything seems to be feeling fine. The whole landscape's as sweet as a lullaby. "Sleep, princeling, sleep," as Fräulein Snandulia sang. Pity she holds her elbows so ungracefully.—— The last time I danced was at the party on St. Cecilia's day. Fräulein Snandulia only dances with "eligible" men. Her silk dress was cut low back and front. Down to her belt behind and, in front, so low you could almost pass out.—She couldn't have been wearing a slip . . .

— —

—That might be something that could still hold me.—More for curiosity's sake.—It must be an extraordinary sensation ——it must feel like being swept away by a torrent——I won't tell anyone I've returned with the job not done. I shall act as if I've taken part . . . There's something to be ashamed of in having been human without getting to know the most human thing of all.—You were in Egypt, dear sir, and did not see the Pyramids?—

I mustn't cry again today. I mustn't think of my funeral. ——Melchior will put a wreath on my coffin. Pastor Kahlbauch will condole with my parents. Rektor Sonnenstich will cite examples from history.—I don't suppose they'll give me a gravestone. I should have liked a snow-white marble urn on a column of black granite—fortunately I won't miss it. Memorials are for the living, not the dead.

I'd need a year to say good-by to everyone in my thoughts.

I mustn't cry again. I'm glad to be able to look back without
bitterness. How many happy evenings I've spent with
Melchior!—under the willows on the riverbank; at the
keeper's cottage; out on the military road where the five
lindens are; on the hillside among the peaceful ruins of the
Runenburg.——When the time comes, I'll think as hard as
I can of whipped cream. It won't hold me up, but it's filling
and the aftertaste is pleasant . . . And I thought human
beings were a lot worse too. Never found one that wouldn't
have wished to do his best. I pitied many—on my own
account.

I proceed to the altar like the young man in ancient Etruria
whose death rattle purchased his brothers' good fortune in
the coming year.—I savor the mysterious terrors of parting,
drop by drop. I sob with grief at this my destiny.——Life
has given me the cold shoulder. From the other side, kind,
grave faces beckon: the headless queen, the headless queen
—sympathy awaiting me with soft arms . . . Your com-
mandments are for minors. I have a complimentary ticket
in my heart. If you put down the cup, off flies the butterfly,
and the mirage stops giving trouble.—But why must you all
play fast and loose with the deception?—The mists dissolve.
Life is a matter of taste.

ILSE, *her clothes torn, a colored kerchief on her head, grabs
him by the shoulder from behind.* What have you lost?

MORITZ. Ilse!

ILSE. What are you looking for here?

MORITZ. Why did you give me such a fright?

ILSE. What are you looking for?—What have you lost?

MORITZ. Why did you frighten me so dreadfully?

ILSE. I've come from the town. I'm going home.

MORITZ. I don't know what I've lost.

ILSE. Then looking for it won't help.

MORITZ. Hell, hell, hell!

ILSE. I haven't been home in four days.

MORITZ.—And quiet as a cat!

ILSE. Because I'm wearing my ballet slippers.—Mother's eyes

will pop when she sees me.—Come with me as far as our house!

MORITZ. Where've you been loafing this time?

ILSE. In the Priapia.

MORITZ. Priapia?

ILSE. At Nohl's, at Fehrendorf's, at Padinsky's, at Lenz's, Rank's, Spühler's—everybody.—Will she be mad? Wow!

MORITZ. Are they painting you?

ILSE. Fehrendorf is painting me as a saint on a pillar. I stand on a Corinthian column. Fehrendorf is a real nut, let me tell you. Last time I trod on one of his tubes of paint. So he wipes his brush in my hair. I give him a whack on the ear. He throws his palette at my head. I upset his easel. He comes after me with his mahlstick, over sofas, tables, chairs, all around the studio. Behind the stove I found a sketch. "Be good, or I tear it up!"—He called a truce and in the end kissed me something terrible—absolutely terrible.

MORITZ. Where do you spend the night when you stay in town?

ILSE. Yesterday we were at Nohl's—day before yesterday at Boyokevich's—Sunday at Oikonomopulos's. At Padinsky's there was champagne. Valabregez had sold his "Sick with the Plague." Adolar drank from the ash tray. Lenz sang "She Murdered Her Child," and Adolar played the guitar to shreds. I was so drunk they had to carry me to bed.—— You still going to school, Moritz?

MORITZ. No, no . . . I'm leaving this term.

ILSE. Quite right, too. Goodness, how time flies when one's earning a living!—Do you remember how we used to play robbers—Wendla Bergmann and you and I and the others? You'd come over in the evening and drink milk fresh from the goat?—What's Wendla doing? I saw her lately watching the floods.—What's Melchi Gabor doing?—Does he still look so solemn?—We used to stand opposite each other in singing lesson.

MORITZ. He philosophizes.

ILSE. Wendla came over not long ago and brought Mother some jam. I was sitting that day for Isidore Landauer. He's using me as Holy Mary, Mother of God, with the infant Jesus. He's an idiot, and disgusting, too. Ugh, like a weather-cock!—D'you have a hang-over?

MORITZ. From last night!—We soused like hippopotami. I came reeling home about five o'clock.

ILSE. One need only look at you.—Any girls there?

MORITZ. Arabella, the beer-nymph of Andalusia!—The land-lord left us alone with her all night . . .

ILSE. One has only to look at you, Moritz!—I never had a hang-over in my life. At the last Carnival I didn't go to bed or take my clothes off for three days and three nights. From the ball to the café, afternoons to the Bellavista, evenings to the cabaret, nights to the ball again. Lena was there, and fat Viola.—The third night Heinrich found me.

MORITZ. Was he looking for you?

ILSE. He stumbled over my arm. I'd passed out in the snow on the street.—Then I moved in with him. Didn't leave for fourteen days—a terrible time! Mornings, I had to put on his Persian bathrobe, and, evenings, I had to walk about the room in a black page outfit—white lace at the neck, knees, and sleeves. Every day he photographed me in a different pose—once on the arm of the sofa as Ariadne, once as Leda, once on all fours as a female Nebuchadnezzar. And all the time he raved about killing, about shooting, suicide, gas fumes. In the early morning he'd bring a pistol into bed, fill it with cartridges, and stick it into my chest. "Wink just once, and I fire!"—Oh, and he would have fired, Moritz, he would have!—Then he'd put the thing in his mouth like a blowpipe. To awaken my self-preservation in-stincts. After which—brrrr—he'd have put a bullet right through my spine.

MORITZ. Is Heinrich still alive?

ILSE. How would I know?—There was a mirror in the ceiling over the bed. Made the little room seem high as a tower and brilliant as an opera house. There you are large as life hanging down from the sky! At night I had ghastly dreams. God, O God, would day ever come?—"Good night, Ilse. When you're asleep, you look lovely for murdering!"

MORITZ. Is this Heinrich still alive?

ILSE. I hope to God not!—One day while he was getting some absinthe I threw my coat around me and crept out onto the street. The Carnival was over. The police pick me up and ask me what I'm doing in men's clothes. They take me to the station. Then Nohl came, and Fehrendorf, Padinsky, Spühler, Oikonomopulos, the whole Priapia! They bailed me out. Transported me in a cab to Adolar's studio. Since then I've been faithful to the gang. Fehrendorf is an ape, Nohl is a pig, Boyokevich an owl, Loison a hyena, Oikonomopulos a camel, yet I love them one and all and wouldn't want to be tied to anyone else if the world was full of archangels and millionaires!

MORITZ.—I must go back, Ilse.

ILSE. Come as far as our house!

MORITZ.—What for?—What for?—

ILSE. To drink warm goat's milk.—I'll curl your hair for you and hang a little bell round your neck.—And we still have a rocking horse you can play with.

MORITZ. I must go back.—I've still got the Sassanids, the Sermon on the Mount, and the parallelepipedon on my conscience.—Good night, Ilse!

ILSE. Sweet dreams! . . . D'you all still go to the wigwam where Melchi Gabor buried my tomahawk?—Brrr! By the time any of you are ready, I'll be on the rubbish heap.
Rushes away.

MORITZ, *alone.* ———A single word would have done it.—
He shouts.

—Ilse!—Ilse!——Thank God she can't hear now.

—I'm not in the mood.—You have to have a clear head and feel good.—A pity to miss such a chance, though, a great pity!

. . . I'll say I had great crystal mirrors over my bed—trained an unruly filly—made her strut across the carpet before me in long, black, silk stockings and black patent-leather shoes and long, black, kid gloves and black velvet round her neck —stifled her with my pillow in a sudden attack of madness . . . when the talk is of lust I shall smile . . . I shall—

SCREAM! I SHALL SCREAM!—TO BE YOU, ILSE!
—PRIAPIA!—UNCONSCIOUSNESS!—IT SAPS MY
STRENGTH!—THIS CHILD OF FORTUNE, CHILD OF
SUNSHINE, DAUGHTER OF JOY UPON MY WAY OF
SORROWS!—OH!—OH!

———————————————————————————
———————————————————————————

In the bushes on the riverbank.
How did I get back here? That grassy bank. The king's-tapers[1] seem to have grown since yesterday. The view through the willows is the same though.—How sluggish the river is—like molten lead.—Don't let me forget . . .
He takes FRAU GABOR's *letter from his pocket and burns it.*
—Look at those sparks! "In and out and roundabout!"—Ghosts!—Shooting stars!—
Before I lit that match, you could still see the grass and a strip of light on the horizon.—It's got dark now. I won't go home again now.

[1] I have used this rarer name for Great Mulleins because it is so precise an equivalent of the German *Königskerzen* and preserves the sexual connotation here and at the end of Act Three, Scene 2. E.B.

ACT THREE

SCENE 1

Faculty Room.—Portraits of Pestalozzi and J. J. Rousseau on the walls. Around a green table over which several gas lamps are burning sit PROFESSORS AFFENSCHMALZ, KNÜP-PELDICK, HUNGERGURT, KNOCHENBRUCH, ZUNGENSCHLAG *and* FLIEGENTOD. At the head of the table on a raised chair, REKTOR SONNENSTICH. HABEBALD, *the porter, cowers by the door.*

SONNENSTICH. . . . Have any of you gentlemen further remarks to make?——Gentlemen—if we have no alternative but to apply to the Ministry of Education for the expulsion of this delinquent student, it is for the most weighty reasons. It is because we must atone for the evil which has already befallen and equally because we must protect this institution against similar calamities in the future. It is because we must chastise this delinquent student for the demoralizing influence he has exercised upon his classmate; and above all it is because we must prevent him from exercising such influence upon his other classmates. It is, and this, gentlemen, may well be the weightiest reason of all, because we have the duty to protect this institution from the ravages of a suicide epidemic such as has broken out already in various other schools, and which till now has set at nought all efforts to teach the boys—by way of giving them an education— the obligations of an educated existence.——Have any of you gentlemen further remarks to make?

KNÜPPELDICK. I can no longer resist the conclusion that the time has come at last to open a window somewhere.

ZUNGENSCHLAG. The a-a-atmosphere which p-prevails here resembles that of underground ca-ca-ca-catacombs, or the archives of the lawcourts in old Wetzlar.

SONNENSTICH. Habebald!

HABEBALD. Yes, Herr Rektor?

SONNENSTICH. Open a window! There is atmosphere enough outside, thank God.—Have any of you gentlemen further remarks to make?

FLIEGENTOD. If my colleagues wish to have a window open I have nothing against it. All I ask is that it should not be the window immediately behind my back.

SONNENSTICH. Habebald!

HABEBALD. Yes, Herr Rektor?

SONNENSTICH. Open the other window!——Have any of you gentlemen further remarks to make?

HUNGERGURT. Without wishing to contradict our Rektor, I should like to remind him of the fact that the other window has been bricked up since last autumn.

SONNENSTICH. Habebald!

HABEBALD. Yes, Herr Rektor?

SONNENSTICH. Let the other window remain closed! I feel compelled, gentlemen, to put the matter to a vote. May I ask those who are *for* the opening of the only window in question to rise?

He counts.

—One, two, three.—One, two, three.—Habebald!

HABEBALD. Yes, Herr Rektor?

SONNENSTICH. Let window number one likewise remain closed. —I for my part am convinced that the prevailing atmosphere leaves nothing to be desired.—Have any of you gentlemen further remarks to make?——Gentlemen!—In the event of our omitting to apply to the Ministry of Education for the expulsion of this delinquent student, the Ministry of Education will hold *us* responsible for the misfortune which has descended upon us. Of the various schools afflicted with suicide epidemics, those at which twenty-five per cent of the students have fallen victims to the epidemic have been suspended by the Ministry of Education. It is our duty as custodians of this institution to protect it from such a shattering blow. It grieves us that we are in no position to regard the other qualifications of the delinquent student as mitigating circumstances. While a lenient procedure might be justifiable in relation to the delinquent student, in relation to this institution, endangered as it is at the moment in the most serious way, it would *not* be justifiable. We find ourselves under the necessity of judging the guilty lest we, the innocent, should ourselves be judged.—Habebald!

HABEBALD. Yes, Herr Rektor?

SONNENSTICH. Bring him up!

Exit HABEBALD.

ZUNGENSCHLAG. If the p-prevailing a-a-atmosphere is authoritatively regarded as leaving little or nothing to be desired, I would like to propose that during the s-summer vacation the other window be b-b-b-b-b-b-bricked up!

FLIEGENTOD. If our good colleague Zungenschlag considers our premises to be inadequately ventilated I should like to propose that our good colleague Zungenschlag have a ventilator installed in his frontal cavity.

ZUNGENSCHLAG. I d-d-don't have to put up with that sort of thing!—I d-don't have to put up with insolence!—I am master of my f-f-f-f-five senses!

SONNENSTICH. I must ask our colleagues Fliegentod and Zungenschlag to observe a measure of decorum. The delinquent student would seem to be already on the threshold.

HABEBALD *opens the door and* MELCHIOR, *pale but composed, steps before the assembly.*

SONNENSTICH. Come nearer the table!—After Rentier Stiefel had been informed of his son Moritz's impious misdeed, the bewildered father searched his son Moritz's effects in the hope of learning thereby the occasion of this loathsome crime. He thus chanced, in a place which has no bearing upon the matter in hand, on a document which, without entirely explaining the loathsome crime, nevertheless provides an unfortunately all too adequate explanation of the criminal's morally deranged predisposition. The document in question is a treatise twenty pages long in dialogue form, entitled *Copulation,* equipped with life-size illustrations and teeming with shameless indecencies, a document that would meet the most extravagant demands of an abandoned libertine, a connoisseur in pornographic literature.—

MELCHIOR. I . . .

SONNENSTICH. Please hold your tongue!—As soon as Rentier Stiefel had handed over to us the document in question and we had promised the bewildered father to make the author known to him at any cost, the handwriting was compared with the handwriting of all the fellow students of the impious deceased, and in the unanimous judgment of the entire teaching staff, as well as in the expert opinion of our respected colleague in calligraphy, it betrayed the profoundest similarity to your own.—

MELCHIOR. I . . .

SONNENSTICH. Please hold your tongue!—Regardless of the overwhelming fact of such a resemblance, recognized, as it is, by unimpeachable authorities, we feel ourselves entitled to abstain for the time being from taking action in order thoroughly to interrogate the culprit on the crime against decency with which he is charged and on the impulse to self-destruction which arose therefrom.—

MELCHIOR. I . . .

SONNENSTICH. You are to answer the precisely formulated questions which I am about to put to you one by one with a simple and unassuming "yes" or "no."—Habebald!

HABEBALD. Yes, Herr Rektor?

SONNENSTICH. The dossier!——I must ask the secretary, Professor Fliegentod, to transcribe the proceedings, as far as possible word for word, from this point on.

To MELCHIOR.

Are you familiar with this document?

MELCHIOR. Yes.

SONNENSTICH. Do you know what this document contains?

MELCHIOR. Yes.

SONNENSTICH. Is the handwriting of this document yours?

MELCHIOR. Yes.

SONNENSTICH. Was the indecent document born in your brain?

MELCHIOR. Yes.—Please point out to me one indecency, Herr Rektor.

SONNENSTICH. You are to answer the precisely formulated

questions which I put to you with a simple and unassuming "yes" or "no."

MELCHIOR. What I wrote is fact, no more, no less. Facts well known to you.

SONNENSTICH. Scoundrel!!

MELCHIOR. Please show me one offense against morals in the document.

SONNENSTICH. Do you imagine I shall let myself be made a clown of by you?—Habebald . . . !

MELCHIOR. I . . .

SONNENSTICH. You have as little respect for the dignity of your assembled teachers as you have sense of decency! You are flouting the instinctive human feeling for modesty and discretion! You are flouting the moral order itself!—Habebald!

HABEBALD, *placing a volume before him.* Here, Herr Rektor.

SONNENSTICH, *taking the volume up.* But this is Langenscheidt's *Agglutinative Volapuk in Three Hours!*

MELCHIOR. I . . .

SONNENSTICH. I call upon the secretary, Professor Fliegentod, to close the minutes!

MELCHIOR. I . . .

SONNENSTICH. Please hold your tongue!!—Habebald!

HABEBALD. Yes, Herr Rektor?

SONNENSTICH. Take him downstairs!

SCENE 2

A cemetery in streaming rain. PASTOR KAHLBAUCH *stands before an open grave, with his umbrella up. On his right* RENTIER STIEFEL *and the latter's friend* ZIEGENMELKER *and* UNCLE PROBST. *On his left* REKTOR SONNENSTICH *and* PROFESSOR KNOCHENBRUCH. *Boys from the school complete the circle. At a little distance* MARTHA *and* ILSE, *by a half-ruined gravestone.*

PASTOR KAHLBAUCH. . . . For he who denies the grace with which the Eternal Father has blessed those born in sin shall die the death of the spirit!—He who has lived and worked for evil in self-willed carnal denial of the honor which is God's due shall die the death of the body!—But he who lightly casts from him the cross which the All-merciful has laid upon him for his sins, verily, verily I say unto you, he shall die an eternal death!—

He throws a spadeful of earth into the grave.

Let us who dutifully plod the path of thorns praise the Lord, the All-bountiful, and thank him for the inscrutable disposition of His grace. For as surely as this person died a threefold death, as surely will our Lord God lead the righteous to bliss and everlasting life.—Amen.

RENTIER STIEFEL, *his voice strangled with sobs, throws a spadeful of earth into the grave.* The boy was no son of mine!—The boy was no son of mine!—I never liked him—from the beginning.

REKTOR SONNENSTICH *throws a spadeful of earth into the grave.* Suicide, as the weightiest conceivable transgression against the moral order, is the weightiest conceivable proof of the existence of the moral order, in that the suicide, by saving the moral order the necessity of passing judgment, *ipso facto* confirms the existence of the moral order.

PROFESSOR KNOCHENBRUCH *throws a spadeful of earth into the grave.* Debased, deformed, debauched, depraved, and degenerate!

UNCLE PROBST *throws a spadeful of earth into the grave.* I wouldn't have believed my own mother if she'd told me a child could treat his parents so basely!

FRIEND ZIEGENMELKER *throws a spadeful of earth into the grave.* Could treat a father thus who for more than twenty years, early and late, had entertained no thought but the welfare of his child!

PASTOR KAHLBAUCH, *pressing* RENTIER STIEFEL's *hand.* We know that all things work together for good to them that love God. I Corinthians 12:15.—Think of the disconsolate mother, and seek to replace what she has lost with love redoubled.

REKTOR SONNENSTICH, *pressing* RENTIER STIEFEL's *hand.* We'd

probably have been unable to give him his promotion in
any case.

PROFESSOR KNOCHENBRUCH *presses* RENTIER STIEFEL'S *hand.*
And if we *had* given him the promotion he'd have flunked
out next spring sure enough!

UNCLE PROBST, *pressing* RENTIER STIEFEL'S *hand.* Above all,
your duty now is to think of yourself. You are a *pater
familias . . .* !

FRIEND ZIEGENMELKER, *pressing* RENTIER STIEFEL'S *hand.* Entrust yourself to my guidance!—Wretched weather, enough
to make the bowels quake!——If you don't hit back with a
hot grog, and quick, it gets you right in the heart!

RENTIER STIEFEL, *blowing his nose.* The boy was no son of
mine . . . the boy was no son of mine . . .

Exit RENTIER STIEFEL, *accompanied by* PASTOR KAHLBAUCH,
REKTOR SONNENSTICH, PROFESSOR KNOCHENBRUCH, UNCLE
PROBST *and* FRIEND ZIEGENMELKER. *The rain abates.*

HÄNSCHEN RILOW *throws a spadeful of earth into the grave.*
Rest in peace, honest fellow!—Give my greetings to my everlasting brides of sacrificial memory and commend me most
devotedly to God in all His grace, O Simple Simon!—I dare-
say they'll put a scarecrow on your grave in memory of
your angelic simplicity . . .

GEORG. Has the pistol been found?

ROBERT. No need to look for any pistol!

ERNST. Did you see him, Robert?

ROBERT. It's a damned fraud!—Who saw him?—Who?

OTTO. That's just it: they'd thrown a sheet over him.

GEORG. Was his tongue hanging out?

ROBERT. His eyes!—That was why they'd put the sheet over
him.

OTTO. Horrible!

HÄNSCHEN RILOW, *to Robert.* Are you positive he hanged
himself?

ERNST. They say he had no head left at all.

OTTO. Nonsense!—Rubbish!

ROBERT. I had the rope in my hands!—I've never seen a hanged man yet who didn't have to be covered up.

GEORG. He couldn't have taken himself off in a nastier way!

HÄNSCHEN RILOW. Hell, do you expect hanging to be pretty?

OTTO. Matter of fact, he owes me five marks. We made a bet. He swore he could keep his place.

HÄNSCHEN RILOW. It's your fault he's where he is. You called him a show-off.

OTTO. Bosh! I have to grind all night, too. If he'd done his Greek Lit. he wouldn't have needed to hang himself.

ERNST. Done your essay, Otto?

OTTO. Only the introduction.

ERNST. I can't think what to say.

GEORG. Weren't you there when Affenschmalz assigned it?

HÄNSCHEN RILOW. I shall fix myself up with something out of Democritus.

ERNST. I shall see if I can find something in Meyer's *Lexicon.*

OTTO. Have you done the Virgil for tomorrow?———

The Schoolboys leave.—MARTHA *and* ILSE *approach the grave.*

ILSE. Quick, quick!—The gravediggers are coming.

MARTHA. Wouldn't it be better if we waited, Ilse?

ILSE. What for?—We can bring fresh ones. Fresh ones and then more fresh ones.—There are plenty where these came from.

MARTHA. You're right, Ilse!—

She throws a wreath of ivy into the grave. ILSE *opens her apron and lets fall a profusion of fresh anemones on the coffin.*

I shall dig up our roses. I'll get beaten in any case.—Here they'll really grow!

ILSE. I'll water them whenever I come by. I'll bring forget-me-nots from the brook, and irises from home.

MARTHA. It will be a glorious display! Glorious!

ILSE. I was just across the bridge there when I heard the shot.

MARTHA. Poor kid.

ILSE. And I know why he did it too, Martha.

MARTHA. Did he say something?

ILSE. "Parallelepipedon!" But don't tell anyone.

MARTHA. Cross my heart!

ILSE.—Here's the pistol.

MARTHA. So that's why no one could find it.

ILSE. I took it out of his hand when I came by next morning.

MARTHA. Give it to me, Ilse!—Please give it to me!

ILSE. No. I'll keep it as a souvenir.

MARTHA. Ilse, is it true he's in there without a head?

ILSE. He must have loaded it with water.—The king's-tapers were sprinkled all over with blood. His brains were hanging from the willow branches.

SCENE 3

MR. *and* MRS. GABOR.

MRS. GABOR. . . . They needed a scapegoat. They couldn't allow these spreading accusations to fall on themselves. So now that my child has had the misfortune to fall foul of these fogies at the right moment, I, his own mother, am supposed to finish the hangmen's work for them?—Heaven forbid!

MR. GABOR.—For fourteen years I have observed in silence your "intelligent" methods of bringing up children. They were at variance with *my* ideas. My own conviction has always been that a child is not a plaything, that a child is entitled to our most solemn and serious attention, but I told myself that if the charm and intelligence of one parent *could* replace the serious principles of the other, then, possibly, they might deserve to do so.——I'm not reproaching you, Fanny, but do not stand in my way when I seek to make good the wrong that you and I have done our boy!

MRS. GABOR. I shall stand in your way as long as there's a drop of warm blood in my veins! My boy will be lost in a Reformatory. A criminal nature might be improved in such a place, I don't know. I do know this: a good boy would only be turned into a criminal by such a place—as surely as a plant dies without sun and air. I am not aware of having done wrong. Today, as always, I thank Heaven for having shown me the way to give my child an upright character and a noble mind. What has he done that's so terrible?— It would not occur to me to try to excuse a fault—but it wasn't his fault they turned him out of school. Even if it *was,* he's atoned for it. Maybe you understand all this better than I do. Theoretically you may be right. But I can't let my only child be hounded to death!

MR. GABOR. That doesn't depend on us, Fanny.—It's a risk we have accepted, just like our happiness. Whoever's not strong enough for the march falls by the wayside. And it isn't the worst thing, after all, if what's inevitable comes in good time. Leave it to Heaven to protect us from it! Our duty is to strengthen the weak of will as long as reason can find a way.

—"It's not his fault he was thrown out of school." If he had *not* been thrown out, that wouldn't have been his fault either, I suppose.—You are too lighthearted. You only see childish naughtiness when it's a case of a fundamental flaw in the character. You women are not qualified to judge of such matters. Anyone who could write what Melchior wrote must be rotten to the core; the very marrow is affected; a halfway healthy nature would be incapable of such a thing. None of us are saints, each one of us strays from the straight and narrow path, but there's a principle involved. This was no unintentional lapse, but the documentation, with horrifying clarity, of a purpose openly entertained, a natural drive toward immorality for its own sake. This piece of writing is evidence of that extreme degree of spiritual corruption which we lawyers describe as "moral depravity."—Whether anything can be done for such a state of mind I cannot say, but if we are to keep alive the last ray of hope, if we are to keep our consciences as parents of the person in question unstained, it is time to take a stand. We must be serious at long last.

—Let's not go on quarreling, Fanny. I know how hard it will be for you. I know that you idolize him because your own great gifts are mirrored in his. Be stronger than

yourself! Show yourself selfless for once where your son is
concerned!

MRS. GABOR. How can I get anywhere against an attitude like
that?—It takes a man to talk like that! It takes a man to let
himself be fooled by dead words! It takes a man to see no
further than his nose this way!—Melchior has always been
impressionable, I saw that from the start, and acted according to my conscience and my best judgment. But are we
responsible for accidents? Suppose a tile should fall on your
head tomorrow and a friend of yours—your father, say—
should walk all over you instead of tending your wounds?
—I'll not see my child murdered before my very eyes. What
is a mother for?—It's just outrageous, I can't believe it! What
has he written, for heaven's sake? That he should write
such things—doesn't it prove how utterly artless he is, how
childlike, how stupid, how innocent? To find moral corruption here, one must have the soul of a bureaucrat, one
must be wholly ignorant of human nature, one must . . .
Say what you want. If you put Melchior in a Reformatory,
it is over between us. Then let me see if—somewhere in the
world—I can't find a way to snatch my son from his de-
struction!

MR. GABOR. You'll have to resign yourself to it—if not today,
tomorrow. Coming to terms with misfortune isn't easy for
anyone. I'll be at your side. If your courage threatens to
give out, I'll do everything in my power to comfort you.
The future looks so gray and overcast. If I lost you too, it
would be the end.

MRS. GABOR. Never to see him again! Never again! He can't
stand crudity, he'll never get used to the filth of it, he'll cut
himself loose—with the ghastly example of Moritz always
before him!—And if I see him again—the joy of spring in his
heart—his bright laughter—everything about him—his child's
determination to fight for the right and the good—oh, his
heart was pure and clear as the morning sky—it was my
most precious possession . . . If there's an injustice here
that cries out for expiation, turn against me, do what you
like with me, I'll take the blame, but keep your frightful
hands off my child!

MR. GABOR. He has gone wrong.

MRS. GABOR. He has not gone wrong!

MR. GABOR. He has gone wrong!!——I'd have given anything to spare you this, I know how you love him.——This morning a woman came to see me. She was beside herself. She could hardly speak. She held this letter in her hand. It's addressed to her fifteen-year-old daughter. She told me she'd opened it out of foolish curiosity, the girl not being home. In this letter Melchior tells the fifteen-year-old child that what he's done is leaving him no peace, he has sinned against her, et cetera, et cetera, but that naturally he'll answer for everything, she mustn't take it to heart even if there are consequences, he's already taking steps to help her, his expulsion will make things easier, what was an error at the time may yet turn out for the best—and a lot more.

MRS. GABOR. Impossible!

MR. GABOR. The letter was written *for* him. It's a forgery—a fraud. His expulsion is the talk of the town, and someone's helping him to exploit that fact. I haven't spoken yet with the boy—but look at the handwriting! Look at the style!

MRS. GABOR. What a rotten, shameless trick!

MR. GABOR. I'm afraid you're right.

Pause.

MRS. GABOR. No. No! Never!!

MR. GABOR. It'll be better for us.—The woman wrung her hands and asked me what she should do. I suggested she might stop her fifteen-year-old daughter from hanging around haylofts. Luckily she left the letter with me.—If we now send Melchior to another school where he's not even under parental supervision, we'll have a repetition of the same case in three weeks: another expulsion—he'll make a habit of it—the "joy of spring" can be lasting.—So what should I do with the boy, Fanny? Tell me.

MRS. GABOR. The Reformatory.

MR. GABOR. The . . . ?

MRS. GABOR. Reformatory.

MR. GABOR. There above all he will find what was wrongly withheld from him at home: iron discipline, principles, and a moral compulsion to which he must in all circumstances submit.—What's more, a House of Correction isn't the abode of horror that you imagine: the emphasis is laid on developing Christian thoughts and Christian feelings. There at last the boy will learn to desire the good, not just the interesting. As for conduct, he will learn to ask what is lawful, not just what is natural.——Half an hour ago I got a letter from my brother confirming this woman's statement: Melchior confided in him and asked for 200 marks to flee to England . . .

MRS. GABOR, *covering her face.* Merciful heaven!

SCENE 4

Reformatory—a corridor.—DIETHELM, REINHOLD, RUPRECHT, HELMUTH, GASTON, *and* MELCHIOR.

DIETHELM. Here's a twenty-pfennig piece.

REINHOLD. What of it?

DIETHELM. I put it on the floor. You all stand round it in a circle. The one that hits it, gets it.

RUPRECHT. Aren't you joining in, Melchior?

MELCHIOR. No, thank you.

HELMUTH. The Joseph!

GASTON. He couldn't, oh no! He's here for a vacation!

MELCHIOR, *to himself.* It's not smart of me to stay out. They all watch me. I'll have to join in. You crack up if you don't. —They're killing themselves, that's what prison's done for them.—If I break my neck, good. If I make a getaway, also good. I can't lose.—Ruprecht is getting to be my friend. He knows the ropes here.—I'll reward him with the story of Thamar, daughter-in-law of Judah, Moab, Lot and his daughters, Queen Vashti, Abishag the Shunammite . . . He has the sorriest face in the outfit.

RUPRECHT. I've got it.

HELMUTH. Here *I* come!

GASTON. Day after tomorrow maybe.

HELMUTH. Look!——Now!——O God, O God . . .

ALL. Summa cum laude! Summa cum laude!

RUPRECHT, *taking the coin.* Thank you very much!

HELMUTH. Give it here, you bastard.

RUPRECHT. You pig!

HELMUTH. You jailbird!

RUPRECHT *strikes him in the face.* There!

He runs away.

HELMUTH, *running after him.* I'll kill him!

THE REST, *on their trail.* After him! Give it to him! Get going! Get going!

MELCHIOR, *alone, turning toward the window.*—That's where the lightning conductor comes down.—You have to wrap a handkerchief around it.—When I think of *her,* the blood rushes to my head. And Moritz—it's as if I had lead in my shoes.———I'll go to a newspaper office. "Pay me by the hundred, I'll sell papers—collect news—write—local stuff—ethical questions—psycho-physical . . ." It's not so easy to starve any more. Luncheonettes, temperance cafés.—The building is sixty feet high and the stucco's coming off . . . She hates me—she hates me because I took her freedom away. Whatever I do about it now, it remains rape.—I can only hope, gradually, over the years . . . In one week's time it's a new moon. Tomorrow I'll grease the hinges. By Saturday I must somehow find out who has the key.—Sunday evening, during the service, a cataleptic fit—God grant no one else falls sick!—It all stretches out before me as if it had already happened. I can get over the window sill without trouble—swing—hold—but you have to wrap a handkerchief round it.——Here comes the Grand Inquisitor.

Exit left. Enter DR. PROCRUSTES *at right with a* LOCKSMITH.

DR. PROCRUSTES. . . . I know the windows are on the fourth floor and that nettles have been planted underneath. But what do degenerates care about nettles?—Last winter one climbed out of a skylight on us, and we had all the trouble of picking him up, carting him off, interring him . . .

THE LOCKSMITH. Do you want the grating of wrought iron?

DR. PROCRUSTES. Wrought iron, yes. And, since it can't be set in, riveted.

SCENE 5

A *bedroom.*—MRS. BERGMANN, INA MÜLLER, *and* DR. VON BRAUSEPULVER.—WENDLA *in bed.*

DR. VON BRAUSEPULVER. How old are you actually?

WENDLA. Fourteen and a half.

DR. VON BRAUSEPULVER. I've been prescribing Blaud's pills for fifteen years, and in a large number of cases I've had the most striking successes. I prefer them to cod-liver oil or iron tonics. Begin with three or four pills a day and increase the dose as rapidly as you can stand it. In the case of Fräulein Elfriede Baroness von Witzleben I ordered the dose in- creased by one pill every three days. The baroness mis- understood me and increased the dose by three pills every day. After scarcely three weeks she was able to accompany her mama to Pyrmont for an after-cure. From tiring walks and extra meals I shall excuse you. In return for which, my dear child, you must be all the more diligent in taking exer- cise, and you must ask for food as soon as your appetite returns. Soon thereafter the palpitations will cease, not to mention the headaches, shivering, giddiness—and these ter- rible digestive disturbances of ours. Eight days after the cure began, Fräulein Elfriede Baroness von Witzleben ate a whole roast chicken garnished with potatoes in their jackets—for breakfast.

MRS. BERGMANN. May I offer you a glass of wine, Herr Doktor?

DR. VON BRAUSEPULVER. Thank you, my dear Mrs. Bergmann. My carriage is waiting. Don't take it to heart. In a few weeks our little patient will be as fresh and lively as a gazelle. So take comfort!—Good day, Mrs. Bergmann. Good day, dear child. Good day, ladies. Good day!

MRS. BERGMANN *escorts him to the door.*

INA, *at the window.*—Your plane tree is changing color again already.—Can you see it from your bed? A short-lived splen- dor, hardly worth the joy we feel to see it come and go.—I must be going soon too. Müller'll be waiting for me outside the post office, and I have to go to the dressmaker first. Mucki is getting his first pair of trousers, and Karl's going to have a new woolen suit for the winter.

WENDLA. Sometimes I feel so happy—all joy and sunshine. I never dreamt one's heart could be so light. I want to go out and walk in the meadows in the evening sun, look for primroses by the river, sit down on the bank and dream . . . And then I get the toothache and feel as if I must be going to die tomorrow. I go hot and cold, it gets black in front of my eyes, and the monster flies in again.——Every time I wake up I see Mother crying. Oh, that hurts so much—I can't tell you, Ina!

INA.—Shall I put your pillow a little higher for you?

MRS. BERGMANN, *coming back.* He thinks the vomiting will die down, and then it will be all right to get up again . . . I think it would be better for you to get up soon, too, Wendla.

INA. The next time I drop in, you'll be bouncing about the house again, I'm sure.—Good-by, Mother. I simply must go to the dressmaker's. God bless you, Wendla, dear.

Kisses her.

Get better quickly!

WENDLA. Good-by, Ina.—Bring me some primroses when you come again. Good-by! Give my love to the boys.

Exit INA.

What did he say when he was outside, Mother?

MRS. BERGMANN. He didn't say anything.—He said Baroness von Witzleben had a tendency to faint, too. He said it was usual with anemia.

WENDLA. Did he say I had anemia, Mother?

MRS. BERGMANN. You're to drink milk and eat meat and vegetables as soon as your appetite comes back.

WENDLA. Mother, I don't think I have anemia . . .

MRS. BERGMANN. You have anemia, child. Calm yourself, you have anemia.

WENDLA. No, Mother. I know it, I feel it, it's not anemia, it's dropsy . . .

MRS. BERGMANN. You have anemia. Didn't he say you had anemia? Calm yourself, child. You'll get better.

WENDLA. I won't get better. I've got dropsy. Oh, Mother, I'm going to die!

MRS. BERGMANN. You're not going to die, child . . . Merciful Heavens, you're not going to die!

WENDLA. Then why do you cry so terribly?

MRS. BERGMANN. You're not going to die! It's not dropsy! You're going to have a baby, Wendla! A baby! Why have you done this to me?

WENDLA.—I haven't done anything to you.—

MRS. BERGMANN. On top of all, don't deny it, Wendla!—I know everything, I just didn't have it in me to speak about it.— Wendla, my Wendla . . . !

WENDLA. But it's impossible, Mother: I'm not married.

MRS. BERGMANN. Great God above—that's just it, you're not married. That's the dreadful thing!—Wendla, Wendla, Wendla, what have you done?

WENDLA. I don't know, Heaven knows I don't know. We were in the hay. . . . I never loved anyone but you, Mother, you!

MRS. BERGMANN. My precious—

WENDLA. Why didn't you tell me everything, Mother?

MRS. BERGMANN. Child, child, let us not make each other's hearts any heavier! Pull yourself together. Don't despair! How could I tell such things to a fourteen-year-old girl? It'd have been the end of the world. I've treated you no different than my mother treated me.—Let's place our trust in God, Wendla, let's hope for mercy, and do our part. Look, *nothing* has happened yet, and if we're not faint-hearted God won't forsake us.—Be brave, Wendla, be brave! ——One may be sitting by the window with one's hands in one's lap because everything has turned out for the best after all, and then trouble comes, and you feel your heart breaking inside you . . . Why are you trembling, Wendla?

WENDLA. Someone's at the door.

MRS. BERGMANN. I didn't hear anything, dear.

Goes to the door and opens it.

WENDLA. I did. Very clearly.——Who can it be?

MRS. BERGMANN.—No one——Schmidt's mother, from Garden
Street.——You've come at the right time, Mother Schmidt.

SCENE 6²

VINTAGERS—*men and women alike—in the vineyard.—In the
west the sun is sinking behind the mountain peaks. The
clear sound of bells from the valley below.* HÄNSCHEN RILOW
and ERNST RÖBEL, *at the uppermost vine trellis, beneath the
over-hanging cliffs, rolling in the drying grass.*

ERNST.—I've been overworking.

HÄNSCHEN. Let's not be sad.—Pity, the way time flies.

ERNST. You see them hanging there and can't do anything
about it. And tomorrow they're in the wine press.

HÄNSCHEN. I find hunger unbearable, but fatigue is just as bad!

ERNST. I can't manage any more.

HÄNSCHEN. Just this one shining muscatel!

ERNST. I can stretch my stomach just so much.

HÄNSCHEN. When I bend the spray, it swings from my mouth

---

² Another Wedekind translator, Eric Vaughn, points out that
there is an analogy between this scene and Act II, Scene 4. The
sexual activity of the two boys is indicated by much the same
method as that of Wendla and Melchior. But Wedekind, it seems
to me, has respected the taboos of bourgeois society to this extent—
that there is much more symbolism in the homo- than in the
heterosexual scene. Then again, the scene-on-stage begins toward
the end of the actual drama in the vineyard: the kiss is not a
climax but something closer to an aftermath. Mr. Vaughn thinks
the Pastor is no Pastor but a Reverend Father of the Roman
Church, the little lady being, not a wife, but a housekeeper. This
interpretation would make of Wedekind a highly clinical observer
of a certain type of homosexual fantasy. I myself am prepared to
believe that Ernst will not turn out a homosexual at all, but that
summer and autumn will leave spring quite far behind. E.B.

to yours. Neither of us need move—just bite the grapes off and let the stalk spring back to the vine.

ERNST. You make a good resolution. "But lo! the strength that fled is renewed again."

HÄNSCHEN. Add the flaming firmament—and the evening bells —I don't ask much more of the future.

ERNST. I sometimes see myself as already a worthy pastor with a good-natured homebody for a wife, a voluminous library, and duties to perform—positions to hold—in every sphere of society. Six days for meditation; on the seventh, one opens one's mouth. When you take your walk, schoolboys and girls shake hands with you. And when you return home, the coffee is steaming, a big cake is served, and girls bring apples in through the garden door.—Can you imagine anything finer?

HÄNSCHEN. What *I* imagine is half-closed eyelashes, half-opened lips, and Turkish draperies!—Look, I don't believe in their grand manner: our elders pull their long faces to hide their stupidities from us. Among themselves they call each other dunderheads just like us. I know that.—When I'm a millionaire, I'll build a monument to the Lord God.— Think of the future as a bowl of milk with sugar and cinnamon on it. One man knocks it over and bawls, another churns it up and sweats. Why not skim it? Or don't you believe one can learn to?

ERNST.—Let's skim it!

HÄNSCHEN. And leave what's left for the hens.—I've got my head out of many a noose before . . .

ERNST. Let's skim it, Hänschen!—How can you laugh?

HÄNSCHEN. Are you starting over?

ERNST. Somebody has to start.

HÄNSCHEN. When we think back in thirty years to an evening like this maybe it will seem indescribably beautiful.

ERNST. How does it get this way—all by itself?

HÄNSCHEN. Why shouldn't it?

ERNST. If one were alone—one might burst out crying.

HÄNSCHEN. Let's not be sad!

He kisses him on the mouth.

ERNST *kisses him.* I left the house thinking I'd just speak to you and go right back.

HÄNSCHEN. I was waiting for you.—Virtue's not a bad suit of clothes, but you need quite a figure to fill it.

ERNST. It still hangs pretty loose on *us.*—I wouldn't have known contentment if I hadn't met you.—I love you, Hänschen, as I have never loved a living soul . . .

HÄNSCHEN. Let's not be sad.—When we think back in thirty years, maybe we'll just make a joke of it.—And it's all so beautiful now. The mountains glow, grapes hang down into our mouths, and the evening wind caresses the cliffs like a playful little flirt . . .

SCENE 7

A clear November night. Dry leaves rustle on bushes and trees. Ragged clouds race across the moon.—MELCHIOR *climbs over the graveyard wall.*

MELCHIOR, *jumping down inside the wall.* The wolves won't follow me here.—While they're searching the brothels I can catch my breath and see how I'm doing. . . . My coat's in rags, my pockets are empty, just about everything is a threat to me . . . I must try to push on through the forest by day . . .

I've stepped on a cross.—The flowers would have frozen anyhow. The ground is bare all around.—In the kingdom of the dead!

Climbing through that skylight wasn't as hard as the journey: this was the one thing I was unprepared for.

I'm suspended over the abyss—the ground has fallen away beneath my feet, it's faded clear away.—I wish I'd stayed there!

Why must it be she?—Why not the one who was to blame? —Inscrutable Providence!—I would have broken stones and starved . . . !

—What keeps me going?—Crime follows crime. Deeper and

deeper in the mire. Not even the strength left to put an end to it . . .

I wasn't bad!—I wasn't bad!—I wasn't bad . . .

No mortal ever wandered among graves so full of envy—Pah—I wouldn't have the courage! Oh, if only madness would overtake me—this very night!

I must look over there among the most recent ones.—The wind whistles a different note against every stone—a symphony of distress.—The decaying wreaths are torn in half. They dangle in pieces by their long ribbons around the marble crosses—a forest of scarecrows. Scarecrows on every grave. Each more horrible than the last. Tall as houses. The very devils run from them.—How coldly the gilt letters glitter! . . . The weeping willow groans and runs over the inscription with giant fingers . . .

A praying cherub—A tablet—

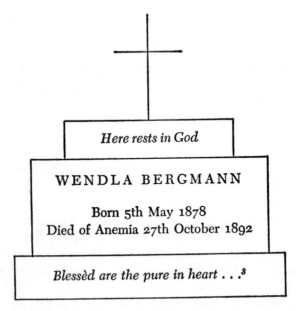

Here rests in God

WENDLA BERGMANN

**Born 5th May 1878
Died of Anemia 27th October 1892**

Blessèd are the pure in heart . . .[3]

[3] This is how the German editions, presumably following Wedekind's MS., have presented these lines. As no audience could be expected to read such an inscription, we must imagine either that Melchior reads it aloud or that (in a highly expressionistic production)

A cloud casts its shadow on the earth—how it rushes and howls—it is massing in the east like an army on the march. —Not a star in the sky.

—Evergreen around that little plot. Evergreen?—— Wendla . . .

And I am her murderer.—I am her murderer!—Nothing is left but despair.—I mustn't cry *here*. I must get away— away—

MORITZ STIEFEL *comes stomping over the graves, his head under his arm.* One moment, Melchior. This opportunity will not be repeated in a hurry. You've no idea how everything is bound up with time and place . . .

MELCHIOR. Where have *you* come from?

MORITZ. By the wall there. You knocked my cross over. I lie by the wall.—Give me your hand, Melchior . . .

MELCHIOR. You are *not* Moritz Stiefel!

MORITZ. Give me your hand. You'll live to thank me. Things aren't going to be easy for you. It is a strangely lucky encounter.—I came over on purpose . . .

MELCHIOR. Don't you sleep, then?

MORITZ. Not what you people call sleeping.—We sit on church steeples and rooftops . . . anywhere . . .

MELCHIOR. Without rest?

MORITZ. For the fun of it.—We haunt Maypoles and solitary forest shrines.—We hover over crowds, gardens, public fairgrounds, places where disasters happen.—Indoors, we cower in the chimney corner or behind the bed curtains.—Give me your hand.—We have no truck with each other, but we see and hear all that goes on in the world. We know that what men do and strive for is folly, and we laugh about it.

MELCHIOR. What good does that do?

MORITZ. What good does it have to do?—We can't be got at— not by anything—not by good, not by bad. We are 'way high

---

the inscription is suddenly made legible to the public by enlargement and projection. Another oddity is the date of Wendla's death in view of the fact that Wedekind says he wrote the play "Autumn 1890 to Easter 1891." E. B.

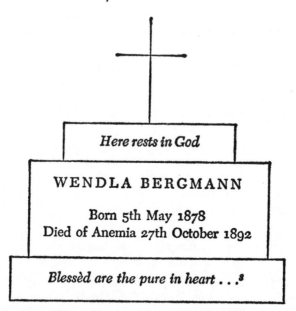

Here rests in God

WENDLA BERGMANN

Born 5th May 1878
Died of Anemia 27th October 1892

Blessèd are the pure in heart . . .³

MORITZ. Not what you people call sleeping.—We sit on church steeples and rooftops . . . anywhere . . .

MELCHIOR. Without rest?

MORITZ. For the fun of it.—We haunt Maypoles and solitary forest shrines.—We hover over crowds, gardens, public fairgrounds, places where disasters happen.—Indoors, we cower in the chimney corner or behind the bed curtains.—Give me your hand.—We have no truck with each other, but we see and hear all that goes on in the world. We know that what men do and strive for is folly, and we laugh about it.

MELCHIOR. What good does that do?

MORITZ. What good does it have to do?—We can't be got at—not by anything—not by good, not by bad. We are 'way high

³ This is how the German editions, presumably following Wedekind's MS., have presented these lines. As no audience could be expected to read such an inscription, we must imagine either that Melchior reads it aloud or that (in a highly expressionistic production) the inscription is suddenly made legible to the public by enlargement and projection. Another oddity is the date of Wendla's death in view of the fact that Wedekind says he wrote the play "Autumn 1890 to Easter 1891." E. B.

above all earthly goings-on, each for himself alone. We have
nothing to do with each other because it's boring to do so.
We none of us still cherish anything that we might lose
later. We are above the battle—both the weeping and the
laughter. We are satisfied with ourselves, and that's the
whole story.—The living we despise unspeakably, we can
hardly even pity them. Their doings cheer us up. Being
alive, they are not really to be pitied. We smile at their
tragedies, each of us for himself, and make our observations
on the subject.—Give me your hand. If you give me your
hand, you'll fall down laughing at the emotion with which
you give me your hand.

MELCHIOR. Doesn't that disgust you?

MORITZ. We're above such disgust. We smile.—I was among
the mourners at my funeral. A most entertaining experience!
That's what being above it all means, Melchior. I bawled
with the best of them, and then slipped over to the cemetery
wall to hold my sides laughing. Only by being above it all
like us are you in a position to swallow all the hogwash . . .
There must have been quite a bit of laughter at *my* expense
before I soared aloft.

MELCHIOR. I have no wish to laugh at myself.

MORITZ. . . . The living are truly not to be pitied.—I admit
this would never have occurred to *me* either, but now it's
inconceivable to me that men can be so naïve. I've seen
right through the whole swindle. Not the smallest cloud
remains.——How can you even hesitate, Melchior? Give me
your hand. Before you can turn round, you'll be sky-high
above yourself.—Your life is a sin of omission.

MELCHIOR.—Can you forget, you people?

MORITZ. We can do anything.—Give me your hand.—We can
deplore youth that takes its timidity for idealism and age
that dies of a broken heart rather than surrender its superi-
ority. We see emperors tremble at a street ballad, and beg-
gars at the mention of the last trump. We look through the
actor's mask and watch the poet putting his mask on in the
dark. We see that this man is contented in his beggary. In
the weary and heavy-laden we descry the capitalist. We
observe lovers and see that they blush before each other,

sensing that they are deceived deceivers. We see parents bringing children into the world in order to be able to shout at them: "How lucky you are to have such parents!" and we see the children go and do likewise. We can eavesdrop on the innocent in their love-starved loneliness, on the two-bit whore reading Schiller . . . We see God and the Devil trying to put each other out of countenance, and in our hearts we cherish the unshakable awareness that they're both drunk . . . This is peace, Melchior, contentment.— You need only offer me your little finger.—Your hair may be white as snow before another such opportunity presents itself.

MELCHIOR. If I agree, Moritz, it will be from self-contempt. I see myself as a pariah. All that gave me courage is in the grave. I can no longer regard myself as deserving of noble emotions. I can't conceive of anything that could stand between me and doom. To myself I am the most execrable creature on earth . . .

MORITZ. Why do you hesitate . . . ?

Enter a MAN IN A MASK.

THE MAN IN THE MASK, *to* MELCHIOR. You're trembling with hunger. You're in no position to judge.

To MORITZ.

Go away!

MELCHIOR. Who are you?

THE MAN IN THE MASK. That will become clear.

To MORITZ.

Get going!—What do you think *you're* doing here?—Why don't you have your head on?

MORITZ. I shot myself.

THE MAN IN THE MASK. Then stay where you belong. Your time is past. Don't molest us with the stench of your grave. How can you? Just look at your fingers. Pah! They're crumbling already.

MORITZ. Please don't send me away . . .

MELCHIOR. Who are *you*, sir?

MORITZ. Don't send me away. Please! Let me join you for a

while. I won't cross you in any way.——It's so gruesome down below.

THE MAN IN THE MASK. Then why do you prate about being above it all?—You know quite well that's all humbug—sour grapes. Why do you lie so assiduously, you bogy?——Well, if it's such a priceless boon, stay for all I care. But refrain from empty boasting, my friend—and please leave your dead hand out of the game.

MELCHIOR. Are you going to tell me who you are, or not?

THE MAN IN THE MASK. Not.—I suggest that you place yourself in my hands. I would give your survival my best attention.

MELCHIOR. You are—my father?

THE MAN IN THE MASK. Wouldn't you know your father by his voice?

MELCHIOR. No.

THE MAN IN THE MASK.—At the moment your father is seeking solace in the doughty arms of your mother.—I will unlock the world to you. Your loss of equilibrium arises from the misery of your present position. With a warm dinner in your belly you'll laugh at it.

MELCHIOR, *aside*. They can't both be the devil.

Aloud.

After what I am guilty of, a warm dinner cannot give me back my peace of mind.

THE MAN IN THE MASK. That depends on the dinner!—I can tell you this much: that little girl would have given birth splendidly. She was superbly built. It was Mother Schmidt's abortion pills that did for her.——I will take you among men. I will give you the opportunity to enlarge your horizon in the most amazing way. I will acquaint you, without exception, with everything of interest that the world has to offer.

MELCHIOR. Who *are* you? Who *are* you?—I can't entrust myself to a man I don't know.

THE MAN IN THE MASK. You can't get to know me unless you entrust yourself to me.

MELCHIOR. You think so?

THE MAN IN THE MASK. It *is* so.—Anyhow, you have no choice.

MELCHIOR. At any moment I can give my friend here my hand.

THE MAN IN THE MASK. Your friend is a charlatan. "We are above the battle, we smile." Put a penny in a man's pocket, and he'll stop smiling. Your humorist friend is the most pitiful creature in all creation. And the most deplorable.

MELCHIOR. Whatever *he* may be, you tell me who *you* are or I give this humorist my hand.

THE MAN IN THE MASK. Well?

MORITZ. He's right, Melchior. I was bragging. Accept his guidance. Make use of him. If he's masked, he's masked, you know where you are with him.

MELCHIOR. Do you believe in God?

THE MAN IN THE MASK. It all depends.

MELCHIOR. Could you tell me who invented gunpowder?

THE MAN IN THE MASK. Berthold Schwarz—alias Konstantin Anklitzen, a Franciscan monk, in about 1330, at Freiburg im Breisgau.

MORITZ. If only he hadn't!

THE MAN IN THE MASK. Then you'd have hanged yourself.

MELCHIOR. Where do you stand on morality?

THE MAN IN THE MASK. Fellow!—You take me for some little pupil of yours?

MELCHIOR. What *should* I take you for?

MORITZ. Don't quarrel!—Please don't quarrel. What good does it do?—What's the point of our sitting together, two alive and one dead, here in the churchyard at two o'clock in the morning, if we're going to quarrel like a bunch of drunks?— It should be a pleasure to me to be present at these negotiations.—If you want to quarrel, I'll put my head under my arm and go.

MELCHIOR. Still the same timid old Moritz!

THE MAN IN THE MASK. The ghost is not wrong. One should not leave one's dignity out of account.—I take our morality to be the real product of two imaginary factors. The imagi-

nary factors are "I ought to" and "I want to." The product
is called "morality." Its reality is undeniable.

MORITZ. If only you'd told me that before!—My morality drove
me to my death. I took up the murderous weapon for my
parents' sake. "Honor thy father and thy mother that thy
days may be long." In my case, the old saying has been
made to look rather silly.

THE MAN IN THE MASK. Don't permit yourself illusions, my
friend! Your parents would no more have died of it than
you need have. Strictly considered, they would have raged
and thundered solely from physical need.

MELCHIOR. That may be true as far as it goes.—But I can
assure you, sir, that if I'd gone ahead and given Moritz
my hand just now, only my morality would have been
responsible.

THE MAN IN THE MASK. You didn't—because you're not Moritz!

MORITZ. I don't believe the difference is so essential. You might
have happened on me too, honored stranger, as I was trudg-
ing through the alder plantations with the pistol in my
pocket.

THE MAN IN THE MASK. Then you don't remember me? Even
at the last moment you were hesitating between death and
. . . life.—Incidentally, in my opinion this is hardly the
place to prolong so searching a debate.

MORITZ. It's certainly getting cold, gentlemen.—They may
have dressed me in my Sunday suit, but I'm wearing neither
shirt nor shorts.

MELCHIOR. Farewell, dear Moritz. Where this man is taking
me I don't know. But he *is* a man . . .

MORITZ. Don't hold it against me that I tried to kill you, Melchior. Put it down to lingering affection.—I'd gladly moan
and groan for the rest of my life if I could go out with you
one more time.

THE MAN IN THE MASK. To each his own: to you the soothing
consciousness that you possess *nothing*, to you the enervat-
ing doubts about *everything*.—Farewell.

MELCHIOR. Farewell, Moritz! Thank you very much for ap-
pearing to me. How many untroubled, happy days we've

had in the fourteen years! In the years ahead, things may go well with me or badly, I may become a different man ten times over, but, come what may, I shall never forget *you* . . .

MORITZ. Thanks, thanks, dear heart!

MELCHIOR. . . . though I live to be an old man with gray hair, you may still be closer to me, Moritz, than all the living.

MORITZ. Thank you.—Good luck on your journey, gentlemen. —Don't let me keep you.

THE MAN IN THE MASK. Come, my boy!

He puts his arm in MELCHIOR's *and withdraws with him over the graves.*

MORITZ, *alone.*—So here I sit with my head on my arm.—— The moon hides her face, unveils herself again, and looks not a bit the smarter.——So I shall go back to my little plot, set up my cross that that madcap trampled down, and, when everything is in order, I shall lie on my back again, warm myself with the putrefaction, and smile . . .

LA RONDE

Ten Dialogues
by

ARTHUR SCHNITZLER

English version by
Eric Bentley

Characters

THE WHORE
THE SOLDIER
THE PARLOR MAID
THE YOUNG GENTLEMAN
THE YOUNG WIFE
THE HUSBAND
THE LITTLE MISS
THE POET
THE ACTRESS
THE COUNT

THE TIME: *The eighteen-nineties.*

THE PLACE: *Vienna.*

1 THE WHORE AND THE SOLDIER

Late in the evening. On the Augarten Bridge.

SOLDIER, *on his way home, whistling.*

WHORE. Want to come with me, Angel Face?

SOLDIER *turns round, then walks on.*

WHORE. Wouldn't you like to come with me?

SOLDIER. You mean me? Angel Face?!

WHORE. Who do you think? Come on. Come with me. I live near here.

SOLDIER. I got no time. Have to get back to the barracks.

WHORE. You'll get back to the barracks all right. But it's nicer with me.

SOLDIER, *near her now.* Yeah. Could be.

WHORE. Uh, uh! A cop might come.

SOLDIER. Nonsense! What's a cop? I got my sword on.

WHORE. Come on with me!

SOLDIER. Leave me alone. I got no money anyhow.

WHORE. I don't need no money.

SOLDIER *stops. They are under a street lamp.* You don't need no money? Who are you for God's sake?

WHORE. Civilians have to pay, sure. A guy like you can get it from me for nothing.

SOLDIER. So you're the one Huber told me about. . . .

WHORE. I don't know any Huber.

SOLDIER. You'd be it. That's right. The cafe in the Schiff Gasse. Then he went home with you.

WHORE. The cafe in the Schiff Gasse! I've taken plenty of guys home from there. Eh!
Her eyes tell how many.

SOLDIER. Let's go then, let's go.

WHORE. What? You're in a hurry now?

SOLDIER. Well, what are we waiting for? I gotta be back in the barracks at ten.

WHORE. How long you been in the army?

SOLDIER. What business is that of yours? Live far from here?

WHORE. Ten minutes' walk.

SOLDIER. Too far. How about a kiss?

WHORE *kisses him.* I figure that's the best part of it. When I like a guy.

SOLDIER. I don't. No. I can't go with you. Too far.

WHORE. Tell you what. Come tomorrow. In the afternoon.

SOLDIER. Okay. Give me the address.

WHORE. Only—I bet you won't come.

SOLDIER. I told you I would, didn't I?

WHORE. Tell you what—if it's too far tonight—how about over there?
She points toward the Danube.

SOLDIER. What's over there?

WHORE. Lovely and quiet there too. No one around this late.

SOLDIER. Aw, that's no good.

WHORE. It's always good—with me. Come on, stick around with me. How long do we have to live?

SOLDIER. Okay, then. But let's make it snappy.

WHORE. Easy. It's so dark there. One slip, and you're in the Danube.

SOLDIER. Might be the best thing.

WHORE. Pst! Hey, wait a second. We're just coming to a bench.

SOLDIER. You know your way around.

WHORE. Wish I had a guy like you for a boy friend.

SOLDIER. I'd make you jealous too much.

WHORE. I'd know how to take care of that.

SOLDIER. Think so?

WHORE. Not so loud. Could be a cop around at that—he might be lost. You wouldn't think we were right in the middle of Vienna, would you?

SOLDIER. Over here. Come on over here!

WHORE. What's eating you? If we slip, we're in the river!

SOLDIER *has grabbed hold of her.* Ah! now . . .

WHORE. Hold on tight now.

SOLDIER. Don't worry . . .

❋   ❋   ❋   ❋   ❋

WHORE. It'd have been a lot better on the bench.

SOLDIER. On the bench, off the bench . . . Well, you getting up?

WHORE. Where are you rushing off—

SOLDIER. Got to get back to the barracks. I'm late anyhow.

WHORE. Tell me, soldier—what's your name?

SOLDIER. What's my name got to do with you?

WHORE. Mine's—Leocadia.

SOLDIER. Ha! That's a new one!

WHORE. Soldier . . .

SOLDIER. Well, what do you want?

WHORE. How about a dime for the janitor?

SOLDIER. Ha! . . . What do you think *I* am? Goodby! Leocadia . . .

WHORE. You crook! You son of a bitch!
    He is gone.

2 THE SOLDIER AND THE PARLOR MAID

The Prater. Sunday evening. A path leading from the WURSTELPRATER—*or amusement park—out into dark avenues of trees. The din of the amusement park is audible. So is the sound of the* FÜNFKREUZERTANZ—*a banal polka—played by a brass band. The Soldier. The Parlor Maid.*

PARLOR MAID. Yes, but now you must tell me. What were you wanting to leave for all the time?

SOLDIER *laughs stupidly; he is embarrassed.*

PARLOR MAID. I thought it was marvellous. I love dancing.

SOLDIER *takes her by the waist.*

PARLOR MAID, *letting him.* But we're not dancing *now.* Why are you holding me so tight?

SOLDIER. What's your name? Kathi?

PARLOR MAID. You've got a Kathi on your mind.

SOLDIER. I know. I've got it: Marie.

PARLOR MAID. Look, it's dark here. I get so scared.

SOLDIER. Nothing to be afraid of with me around. Just leave it to uncle.

PARLOR MAID. But where are we going to, through? There's no one around at all. Let's go back, come on! How *dark* it is!

SOLDIER, *pulling at his Virginia cigar till the tip glows.* See it get lighter? Ha! My little treasure!

PARLOR MAID. Ooh! What are you doing? If I'd known *this.* . . .

SOLDIER. Nice and soft! Damned if you're not the nicest and softest one in the whole bunch, Fräulein!

PARLOR MAID. What whole bunch?

SOLDIER. In there—in the Swoboda.

PARLOR MAID. You tried all of them?

SOLDIER. Oh, you notice. Dancing. You notice a lot of things. Ha!

PARLOR MAID. You danced with that blonde more than with me. The one with the face.

SOLDIER. Friend of a buddy of mine. An old friend of his.

PARLOR MAID. The corporal with the turned-up mustache?

SOLDIER. Nah. The civilian. You know—the one at the table with me before. With the hoarse voice?

PARLOR MAID. Oh, yes. I know. He's pretty fresh.

SOLDIER. Did *he* try something with you? I'll show the bastard. What did he try?

PARLOR MAID. Oh, nothing. I just saw how he was with the other girls.

SOLDIER. Now, Fräulein, tell me . . .

PARLOR MAID. Ooh! You'll burn me with that cigar.

SOLDIER. Oh, pardon me, Fräulein—or can I call you . . . Marie?

PARLOR MAID. We haven't known each other very long.

SOLDIER. Hell, there's lots of people use first names and don't even like each other.

PARLOR MAID. Let's make it next time, when . . . You see, Herr Franz . . .

SOLDIER. You got my name!

PARLOR MAID. You see, Herr Franz . . .

SOLDIER. Make it just—Franz, Fräulein.

PARLOR MAID. *You* mustn't be so fresh. Sh! What if somebody comes!

SOLDIER. What if they do? You can't see six feet in front of you.

PARLOR MAID. But, heavens, where are we getting to?

SOLDIER. Look! There's two just like us.

PARLOR MAID. Where? I can't see a thing.

SOLDIER. There. Right up there.

PARLOR MAID. What do you say like *us* for?

SOLDIER. Oh, I only mean—they kinda like each other.

PARLOR MAID. Hey, watch out! What was that? I nearly fell.

SOLDIER. It's these railings they put round the grass.

PARLOR MAID. Don't push so hard. I'll fall right over.

SOLDIER. Sh! Not so loud!

PARLOR MAID. Look now I'm *really* going to scream! What are you doing . . . hey . . .

SOLDIER. There's no one for miles around.

PARLOR MAID. Let's go back with the rest of them.

SOLDIER. But we don't need them, Marie, what we need is . . . uh, huh . . .

PARLOR MAID. Herr Franz, please! For Heaven's sake!! Now listen, if I'd had . . . any idea . . . oh! . . . oh!! . . . yes . . .

❀   ❀   ❀   ❀   ❀

SOLDIER (*blissfully*). Jesus Christ Almighty! . . . Ah-h! . . .

PARLOR MAID. . . . I can't see your face at all.

SOLDIER. My face? . . . Hell!

❀   ❀   ❀   ❀   ❀

SOLDIER. Now look, Fräulein, you can't stay in the grass all night.

PARLOR MAID. Oh, come on, Franz, help me up!

SOLDIER. Okay.
He grabs her.
Oops!

PARLOR MAID. Oh dear, Franz!

SOLDIER. Yes, yes? What's the matter with Franz?

PARLOR MAID. You're a bad man, Franz.

SOLDIER. Oh, so that's it? Hey, wait for me!

PARLOR MAID. What do you let me go for?

SOLDIER. Can't I get this cigar lit for God's sake?

PARLOR MAID. It's so dark.

SOLDIER. Well, tomorrow it'll be light again.

PARLOR MAID. Tell me something—do you like me?

SOLDIER. I thought you might have noticed!
He laughs.

PARLOR MAID. Where are we going?

SOLDIER. Why, back!

PARLOR MAID. Oh, please, Franz, not so quick!

SOLDIER. What's the matter? I don't like running around in the dark.

PARLOR MAID. Tell me, Franz, do you . . . like me?

SOLDIER. I just told you I liked you.

PARLOR MAID. Come on then, give me little kiss.

SOLDIER, *condescending.* Here . . . listen! You can hear that music again.

SOLDIER. Sure. What's wrong with that?

PARLOR MAID. Well, Franz, look, I must be getting back. They'll gripe anyhow, the lady of the house is such a . . . she'd like it best if we never went out at all.

SOLDIER. Sure. You go home then.

PARLOR MAID. Herr Franz! I thought . . . you might take me.

SOLDIER. Home? Eh!
The open vowel indicating disgust.

PARLOR MAID. Oh, please, it's so dreary—going home alone!

SOLDIER. Where do you live?

PARLOR MAID. It's not far—Porzellan Gasse.

SOLDIER. Oh! Then we go the same way . . . But it's too early for me! I want some fun. I got a late pass tonight. Don't have to be back in the barracks till twelve. I'm going dancing.

PARLOR MAID. *I* see how it is. It's that blonde. The one with the face.

SOLDIER. Ha! . . . Her face ain't so bad.

PARLOR MAID. Heavens, you men are wicked! I bet you do this to every girl.

SOLDIER. That might be *too* many.

PARLOR MAID. Franz, do me a favor. Not tonight—stay just with me tonight, look. . . .

SOLDIER. Okay, okay. But I can dance for a while first, I suppose?

PARLOR MAID. Tonight I'm not dancing with anyone but you.

SOLDIER. Here it is.

PARLOR MAID. What?

SOLDIER. The Swoboda, quick work, huh? And they're still playing *that* thing.
Singing with the band.
Tatatatum, tatatatum! . . . All right, if you want to wait, I'll take you home. If you don't, I'll be saying good night . . .

PARLOR MAID. I think I'll wait.

SOLDIER. Why don't you get yourself a glass of beer?
Turning to a blonde, dancing by with her boy, putting on a "refined" accent.
May I have the pleasure?

3 THE PARLOR MAID AND THE YOUNG GENTLEMAN

A hot summer afternoon. His parents are off in the country. The cook is having her half-day. In the kitchen, the Parlor Maid is writing the Soldier a letter; he is her lover. There is a ring from the Young Gentleman's room. She gets up and goes into the Young Gentleman's room. The Young Gentleman is lying on the sofa with cigarette and French novel.

PARLOR MAID. You rang, Herr Alfred?

YOUNG GENTLEMAN. Oh, Yes . . . Marie . . . yes, I did ring as a
matter of fact. . . . Now what was it? . . . Oh, I know, let the
blinds down, Marie, will you? . . . It's cooler with the blinds
down . . . don't you think? . . .

PARLOR MAID *goes to the window and lets the Venetian
blinds down.*

YOUNG GENTLEMAN, *going on reading.* What are you doing,
Marie? That's right. Oh, but now I can't see to read.

PARLOR MAID. The way you always study so, Herr Alfred!

YOUNG GENTLEMAN, *passing over this loftily.* That'll be all,
thanks.

The PARLOR MAID *goes out.*

The YOUNG GENTLEMAN *tries to go on reading; soon lets the
book fall; rings again.*

The PARLOR MAID *is in the doorway.*

YOUNG GENTLEMAN. Look, Marie . . . now, um, what I was going to say . . . well . . . yes, is there any cognac in the house?

PARLOR MAID. Yes, Herr Alfred. But it's locked up.

YOUNG GENTLEMAN. Oh. Well, who has the key?

PARLOR MAID. Lini has the key.

YOUNG GENTLEMAN. Who's Lini?

PARLOR MAID. The cook, Herr Alfred.

YOUNG GENTLEMAN. Oh. Then go and tell Lini.

PARLOR MAID. Well . . . Lini's having her half-day.

YOUNG GENTLEMAN. Oh.

PARLOR MAID. Shall I run over to the cafe for you, Herr Alfred?

YOUNG GENTLEMAN. Oh, no . . . hot enough as it is. I don't need
cognac anyway. Listen, Marie, just bring me a glass of water.
Wait, Marie—let it run, hm? Till it's quite cold?

The PARLOR MAID *goes.*

The YOUNG GENTLEMAN *is watching her go when the* PARLOR

MAID *turns round at the door. The* YOUNG GENTLEMAN *stares into space. The* PARLOR MAID *turns the faucet on and lets the water run. Meanwhile, she goes to her little room, washes her hands, and arranges her curls in the mirror. Then she brings the* YOUNG GENTLEMAN *the glass of water. She walks to the sofa.*

The YOUNG GENTLEMAN *raises himself part way. The* PARLOR MAID *puts the glass in his hand. Their fingers touch.*

YOUNG GENTLEMAN. Oh. Thanks. . . . Well, what is it? Now be careful. Put the glass back on the tray. . . .

He lies back and stretches out.

What's the time?

PARLOR MAID. Five o'clock, Herr Alfred.

YOUNG GENTLEMAN. I see. Five. Thank you.

The PARLOR MAID *goes; at the door, she turns; the* YOUNG GENTLEMAN *is looking; she notices and smiles.*

The YOUNG GENTLEMAN *lies where he is for a while, then suddenly gets up. He walks to the door; then returns and lies down on the sofa. He tries to read again. In a couple of minutes, he again rings.*

The PARLOR MAID *enters with a smile which she makes no attempt to hide.*

YOUNG GENTLEMAN. Look, Marie, what I was going to ask you . . . didn't Dr. Schueller call by this morning?

PARLOR MAID. No. No one called this morning.

YOUNG GENTLEMAN. Well. that's strange. So Dr. Schueller didn't call? You know him—Dr. Schueller?

PARLOR MAID. Oh, yes. The tall gentleman with the big black beard.

YOUNG GENTLEMAN. Yes. Maybe he *did* call?

PARLOR MAID. No. No one called, Herr Alfred.

YOUNG GENTLEMAN, *taking the plunge.* Come here, Marie.

PARLOR MAID, *coming a little closer.* Yes, Herr Alfred?

YOUNG GENTLEMAN. Closer . . . yes . . . um . . . I only thought . . .

PARLOR MAID. Yes, Herr Alfred?

YOUNG GENTLEMAN. Thought . . . I thought . . . about that
blouse. What kind is it? . . .Oh, come on, closer. I won't bite
you.

PARLOR MAID *comes*. What's this about my blouse? You don't
like it, Herr Alfred?

YOUNG GENTLEMAN *takes hold of the blouse and, in so doing,
pulls the* PARLOR MAID *down on him.* Blue, is it? Yes, what a
lovely blue!
Simply.
You're very nicely dressed, Marie.

PARLOR MAID. Oh, Herr Alfred!

YOUNG GENTLEMAN. Well, you are!
He's opened the blouse. Matter-of-fact.
You've got lovely white skin, Marie.

PARLOR MAID. I think you're flattering me, Herr Alfred.

YOUNG GENTLEMAN, *kissing her bosom*. This can't hurt you, can
it?

PARLOR MAID. Oh no!

YOUNG GENTLEMAN. How you're sighing! Why do you sigh like
that?

PARLOR MAID. Oh, Herr Alfred . . .

YOUNG GENTLEMAN. And what nice slippers you have on . . .

PARLOR MAID. . . . but . . . Herr Alfred . . . if the doorbell
rings . . .

YOUNG GENTLEMAN. Who'd ring at this hour?

PARLOR MAID. But, Herr Alfred . . . you see, it's so light!

YOUNG GENTLEMAN. Oho, you needn't be embarrassed with me!
You needn't be embarrassed with anybody . . . pretty as you
are! I swear you *are*, Marie! You know, your hair has such a
pleasant smell.

PARLOR MAID. Herr Alfred . . .

YOUNG GENTLEMAN. Don't make such a fuss, Marie. I've seen you . . . quite different. When I came in late the other night, and went for a glass of water, the door to your room was open . . . yes . . .

PARLOR MAID *hides her face.* Heavens, I'd no idea you could be so naughty, Herr Alfred.

YOUNG GENTLEMAN. I saw a great, great deal . . . this . . . and this . . . and this . . . and . . .

PARLOR MAID. Herr Alfred!!

YOUNG GENTLEMAN. Come on . . . here . . . that's right, yes . . .

PARLOR MAID. But if anyone rings . . .

YOUNG GENTLEMAN. Now stop it, for Heaven's sake. We won't go to the door. . . .

❀　　❀　　❀　　❀　　❀

The doorbell rings.

YOUNG GENTLEMAN. Christ Almighty! . . . What a racket the man makes! Maybe he rang before and we just didn't pay attention.

PARLOR MAID. Oh, I kept my ears open the whole time.

YOUNG GENTLEMAN. Well, now, go and see—through the peephole.

PARLOR MAID. Herr Alfred . . . You *are* . . . No! . . . a naughty man!

YOUNG GENTLEMAN. Now please, go take a look.

The PARLOR MAID *goes. The* YOUNG GENTLEMAN *quickly pulls up the Venetian blinds.*

PARLOR MAID *comes back.* Whoever it was, he's gone away again. There's no one there. Maybe it was Dr. Schueller.

YOUNG GENTLEMAN, *disagreeably affected.* That'll be all, thanks.

The PARLOR MAID *comes closer.*

YOUNG GENTLEMAN, *retreating.* Look, Marie, I'm going. To the café.

PARLOR MAID, *tenderly.* So soon . . . Herr Alfred?

YOUNG GENTLEMAN, *severely.* I'm going to the café. If Dr. Schueller should come here . . .

PARLOR MAID. He won't be here today.

YOUNG GENTLEMAN, *more severely.* If Dr. Schueller should come here, I . . . I . . . I'm—in the café.

He goes into the next room.

The PARLOR MAID *takes a cigar from the smoking-table, slips it in her pocket, and goes out.*

4   THE YOUNG GENTLEMAN AND THE
YOUNG WIFE

Evening. A drawing-room in a house in the SCHWIND GASSE, *furnished with cheap elegance.*

The YOUNG GENTLEMAN *has just come in and, still in hat and overcoat, lights the candles. Then he opens the door into the next room and glances in. The glow of the candles in the drawing room falls on the parquet floor and makes its way to the four-poster against the rear wall; a reddish glow from the fireplace in a corner of the bedroom is thrown on the bed curtains.*

The YOUNG GENTLEMAN *also inspects the bedroom. He takes an atomizer from the dressing table and sprays the pillows with a fine stream of violet perfume. Then he goes with the spray through both rooms, squeezing the little bulb the whole time, so that soon the whole place smells of violets. He takes off hat and overcoat, sits down in a blue velvet armchair, lights a cigarette, and smokes. After a short while he gets up to make sure that the green shutters are drawn. Suddenly he goes back to the bedroom, opens the drawer of the bedside table, feels around till he finds a tortoise shell hairpin. He looks round for a place to hide it, and finally puts it in his overcoat pocket. Then he opens a cupboard in the drawing room, takes out a silver tray, a cognac bottle, and two liqueur glasses, and puts it all on the table. He goes back to his overcoat and fishes out a small white parcel, which he opens and puts next to the cognac bottle. He returns to the cupboard and takes out two dessert plates, knives, and forks. From the small parcel he extracts a mar-*

*ron glacé and eats it. Then he pours himself a glass of cognac
and quickly drinks it down. He looks at his watch. He paces
the room. In front of the large mirror on the wall he stops
for a while, smoothing his hair and little moustache with a
pocket comb. He goes to the door to the hall and listens—not
a sound. He draws the blue curtains screening the door to
the bedroom. The doorbell rings. The* YOUNG GENTLEMAN
*gives a start. He drops into an armchair and only rises when
the door opens and the* YOUNG WIFE *enters.*
The YOUNG WIFE *thickly veiled, shuts the door behind her
and stands for a moment with her left hand on her heart, as
though she had to master intense emotion.*

YOUNG GENTLEMAN *goes to her, takes her left hand, and im-
prints a kiss on the white, black-trimmed glove; softly.* I
thank you.

YOUNG WIFE. Alfred—Alfred!

YOUNG GENTLEMAN. Come in, dear lady . . . come in, Frau
Emma.

YOUNG WIFE. Let me alone for a moment, please—oh, please,
Alfred!
She stays close by the door.
The YOUNG GENTLEMAN *stands before her, holding her hand.*

YOUNG WIFE. But where am I, actually?

YOUNG GENTLEMAN. In my house.

YOUNG WIFE. This place is a horror, Alfred.

YOUNG GENTLEMAN. Why? It's very dignified.

YOUNG WIFE. I met two men on the stairs.

YOUNG GENTLEMAN. People you know?

YOUNG WIFE. They may be. I'm not sure.

YOUNG GENTLEMAN. Forgive me—you must know who you
know!

YOUNG WIFE. But I didn't see a thing.

YOUNG GENTLEMAN. Even if they'd been your best friends, they
couldn't have recognized you. Even I . . . if I didn't know
it was you . . . this veil . . .

YOUNG WIFE. There are two.

YOUNG GENTLEMAN. Won't you come a bit farther in? And anyway do take off your hat.

YOUNG WIFE. What are you thinking of, Alfred? I told you— five minutes. No, not a second more! I swear . . .

YOUNG GENTLEMAN. Then the veil!

YOUNG WIFE. There are two.

YOUNG GENTLEMAN. Oh, well, both veils then—at least I'm allowed to see you!

YOUNG WIFE. Do you really love me, Alfred?

YOUNG GENTLEMAN, *deeply hurt.* Emma, can you ask . . . ?

YOUNG WIFE. It's so hot in here.

YOUNG GENTLEMAN. But you still have your fur cape on—you're going to catch cold!

YOUNG WIFE *at last steps into the room, throwing herself into an armchair.* I'm dead tired.

YOUNG GENTLEMAN. Permit me.
He takes her veils off, takes out the hatpin, puts hat, pin, and veils down side by side on the sofa.
The YOUNG WIFE *lets it happen.*
The YOUNG GENTLEMAN *stands before her, shaking his head.*

YOUNG WIFE. What's the matter with you?

YOUNG GENTLEMAN. Never were you so beautiful!

YOUNG WIFE. How's that?

YOUNG GENTLEMAN. Alone . . . alone with you . . . Emma . . .
He sinks on one knee beside the armchair, takes both her hands and covers them with kisses.

YOUNG WIFE. And now . . . let me go. I have done what you asked.
The YOUNG GENTLEMAN *drops his head on to her lap.*

YOUNG WIFE. You promised me to be good.

YOUNG GENTLEMAN. Yes.

YOUNG WIFE. This room's stifling.

YOUNG GENTLEMAN *gets up.* You still have your cape on.

YOUNG WIFE. Put it with my hat.

The YOUNG GENTLEMAN *takes off her cape and puts it on the sofa along with the hat and the other things.*

YOUNG WIFE. And now—adieu——

YOUNG GENTLEMAN. Emma!

YOUNG WIFE. The five minutes are up.

YOUNG GENTLEMAN. No, no! You haven't been here one minute yet!

YOUNG WIFE. Alfred, please, tell me exactly what time it is.

YOUNG GENTLEMAN. Quarter past six, on the nose.

YOUNG WIFE. I should have been at my sister's long ago.

YOUNG GENTLEMAN. You can see your sister any time . . .

YOUNG WIFE. Oh God, Alfred, why did you get me to do this?

YOUNG GENTLEMAN. Because I . . . worship you, Emma.

YOUNG WIFE. How many women have you said that to?

YOUNG GENTLEMAN. Since I saw you, to none.

YOUNG WIFE. What a frivolous woman I am! If anyone had told me—a week ago . . . or even yesterday . . .

YOUNG GENTLEMAN. It was the day before yesterday you promised . . .

YOUNG WIFE. Because you kept tormenting me. But I didn't want to, God is my witness—I didn't want to. Yesterday I'd made up my mind. . . . Do you know I even wrote you a long letter last night?

YOUNG GENTLEMAN. I didn't get it.

YOUNG WIFE. I tore it up. I should have sent it after all!

YOUNG GENTLEMAN. It's better like this.

YOUNG WIFE. No, it's scandalous . . . of me. I can't understand myself. Good-bye, Alfred, let me go.

The YOUNG GENTLEMAN *takes her in his arms and covers her face with hot kisses.*

YOUNG WIFE. So this is . . . how you keep your promise?

YOUNG GENTLEMAN. One more kiss! Just one.

YOUNG WIFE. The last!
He kisses her, she reciprocates, and their lips stay together a long time.

YOUNG GENTLEMAN. May I tell you something, Emma? Now I know what happiness is.
The YOUNG WIFE *sinks back in an armchair.*

YOUNG GENTLEMAN *sits on the arm of the chair, putting his arm gently round her neck. . . . Or rather, now I know what happiness* might *be.*
The YOUNG WIFE *gives a profound sigh.*
The YOUNG GENTLEMAN *kisses her again.*

YOUNG WIFE. Alfred, Alfred, what are you making of me?

YOUNG GENTLEMAN. It's not really so uncomfortable here, is it? And we are so safe. It's a thousand times better than meeting in the open air.

YOUNG WIFE. Oh, don't remind me.

YOUNG GENTLEMAN. Even those meetings I shall think of with delight! Every minute I've had the privilege of spending at your side will linger forever in the memory.

YOUNG WIFE. You remember the Industrial Ball?

YOUNG GENTLEMAN. Do I remember? . . . But didn't I sit next to you during supper—right up close? The champagne your husband——
The YOUNG WIFE *gives him a look of protest.*

YOUNG GENTLEMAN. I was only going to mention the champagne! Tell me, Emma, wouldn't you like a glass of cognac?

YOUNG WIFE. Maybe just a drop. But first let me have a glass of water.

YOUNG GENTLEMAN. Yes . . . now, where is . . . Oh yes.

*He draws the curtains back from the door and goes into the
bedroom.*

The YOUNG WIFE *looks after him.*

The YOUNG GENTLEMAN *returns with a filled decanter and
two glasses.*

YOUNG WIFE. Where were you?

YOUNG GENTLEMAN. In the—next room.

He pours a glass of water for her.

YOUNG WIFE. Now I'm going to ask you something, Alfred, and
you must swear to tell the truth.

YOUNG GENTLEMAN. I swear . . .

YOUNG WIFE. Was there ever another woman in these rooms?

YOUNG GENTLEMAN. But, Emma, this house has been around
for twenty years!

YOUNG WIFE. You know what I mean, Alfred . . . with you . . .

YOUNG GENTLEMAN. With me, here? Emma! You couldn't think
such a thing!

YOUNG WIFE. Then you have . . . how shall I . . . ? But no, I'd
better not ask you. It's better if I don't ask. It's my own
fault. We pay for everything!

YOUNG GENTLEMAN. But what is it? What's the matter with
you? *What* do we pay for?

YOUNG WIFE. No, no, no, I mustn't return to consciousness—or
I'd sink into the ground for very shame.

YOUNG GENTLEMAN, *still with the decanter in his hand, sadly
shakes his head.* Emma, if only you had any idea how you
hurt me!

The YOUNG WIFE *pours herself a glass of cognac.*

YOUNG GENTLEMAN. I'll tell you something, Emma. If you're
ashamed to be here—that's to say, if I'm nothing to you—if
you don't feel that for me you're all the bliss in the world—
then leave. Leave.

YOUNG WIFE. That is just what I'll do.

YOUNG GENTLEMAN, *seizing her hand.* But if you realize that

I can't live without you, that to kiss your hand means more
to me than all the caresses of all the women in the whole
world. Emma, I'm not like the other young men who know
how . . . this sort of thing is done . . . call me naïve if you
wish . . . I . . .

YOUNG WIFE. But what if you *were* like the other young men?

YOUNG GENTLEMAN. Then you wouldn't be here now: you aren't
like the other young women.

YOUNG WIFE. How do you know?

YOUNG GENTLEMAN *has drawn her on to the sofa and sits down
close beside her.* I've thought a lot about you. I know you're
unhappy.
The YOUNG WIFE *looks pleased.*

YOUNG GENTLEMAN. Life is so empty, so trivial. And so short.
. . . Isn't life frightfully short, Emma? There is only one
happiness: to find someone who loves you.
The YOUNG WIFE *has taken a candied pear from the table
and puts it into her mouth.*

YOUNG GENTLEMAN. Give me half!
She offers it to him with her lips.

YOUNG WIFE *takes the* YOUNG GENTLEMAN'S *hands, which
threaten to go astray.* What are you doing, Alfred? Is this
your promise?

YOUNG GENTLEMAN *swallows the candied fruit, then says more
boldly.* Life is so short!

YOUNG WIFE, *feebly.* But that's no reason . . .

YOUNG GENTLEMAN, *mechanically.* Oh, but it is.

YOUNG WIFE, *more feebly.* Now look, Alfred, you promised to
be good. . . . And it's so light . . .

YOUNG GENTLEMAN. Come, come, my only one, my only . . .
He lifts her off the sofa.

YOUNG WIFE. What are you doing?

YOUNG GENTLEMAN. It's not light in there.

YOUNG WIFE. Is there another room?

YOUNG GENTLEMAN, *taking her with him.* A lovely one . . . and quite dark.

YOUNG WIFE. I'd rather stay here.
The YOUNG GENTLEMAN *has already got her through the curtains and in the bedroom; he begins to unhook her dress at the waist.*

YOUNG WIFE. You're so . . . Oh God, what are you doing to me? . . . Alfred!

YOUNG GENTLEMAN. Emma, I worship you!

YOUNG WIFE. Wait, please, at least wait . . .
weakly
Go, I'll call for you . . .

YOUNG GENTLEMAN. Let me . . . let you help me . . . let . . . me . . . help . . . you . . .

YOUNG WIFE. But you're tearing everything!

YOUNG GENTLEMAN. Don't you wear a corset?

YOUNG WIFE. I never wear a corset. Neither does Duse, incidentally. You can unbutton my boots.
The YOUNG GENTLEMAN *unbuttons her boots, kisses her feet.*

YOUNG WIFE, *slipping into the bed.* Oooh, I'm cold.

YOUNG GENTLEMAN. It'll get warm.

YOUNG WIFE, *laughing softly.* You think so?

YOUNG GENTLEMAN, *not liking this, to himself.* She shouldn't have said that!
He undresses in the dark.

YOUNG WIFE, *tenderly.* Come, come, come.

YOUNG GENTLEMAN, *in a better mood at once.* At once . . .

YOUNG WIFE. It smells of violets here.

YOUNG GENTLEMAN. It's you . . . yes
Close by her.
. . . you.

YOUNG WIFE. Alfred . . . Alfred!!!!

YOUNG GENTLEMAN. Emma . . .

    ❊   ❊   ❊   ❊   ❊

YOUNG GENTLEMAN. I must be too much in love with you . . .
that's why . . . I'm nearly out of my senses.

YOUNG WIFE. . . .

YOUNG GENTLEMAN. All these past days I've been going crazy.
I felt it coming.

YOUNG WIFE. Don't worry your head about it.

YOUNG GENTLEMAN. Of course not, you can almost take it for
granted when a man . . .

YOUNG WIFE. Don't . . . don't . . . You're nervous. Just relax . . .

YOUNG GENTLEMAN. You know Stendhal?

YOUNG WIFE. Stendhal?

YOUNG GENTLEMAN. His book *De l'amour.*

YOUNG WIFE. No. Why do you ask?

YOUNG GENTLEMAN. There's a story in it that's most significant.

YOUNG WIFE. What sort of story?

YOUNG GENTLEMAN. A bunch of officers have gotten together . . .

YOUNG WIFE. Oh.

YOUNG GENTLEMAN. And they talk about their love affairs. And
every one says that with the woman he loved most . . . most
passionately, you know . . . she made him . . . with her he
. . . well, the fact is, it happened to every one of them . . .
what happened to me with you.

YOUNG WIFE. I see.

YOUNG GENTLEMAN. This is very indicative.

YOUNG WIFE. Yes.

YOUNG GENTLEMAN. But that's not all. One of them claims . . .
it has never happened to him in all his life. But—Stendhal
adds—this man was a notorious show-off.

YOUNG WIFE. Oh.

YOUNG GENTLEMAN. All the same it kind of throws you, that's the stupid thing about it, even if it doesn't really matter.

YOUNG WIFE. Naturally. Anyway . . . you promised to be good.

YOUNG GENTLEMAN. Please don't laugh! That won't improve things.

YOUNG WIFE. I'm not laughing. This Stendhal story's very interesting. I'd always thought it happened only with older men . . . or with very . . . well, you know, men who've been too fast.

YOUNG GENTLEMAN. What an idea! That has nothing to do with it. By the way, I forgot the most charming story in the Stendhal. A lieutenant of hussars even says that he spent three nights—or was it six? I can't remember—with a woman he'd been wanting for weeks—*désiré* and all that—and all those nights they didn't do a thing but cry with happiness— both of them . . .*

YOUNG WIFE. Both of them?

YOUNG GENTLEMAN. Both of them. Does that surprise you? I find it so understandable. Specially when you're in love.

YOUNG WIFE. But there must be a lot who don't cry.

YOUNG GENTLEMAN, *nervously.* Surely . . . after all, it was an exceptional case.

YOUNG WIFE. Oh . . . I thought Stendhal says all hussars cry on these occasions.

YOUNG GENTLEMAN. There, you're just making fun . . .

YOUNG WIFE. Not in the least. Don't be so childish, Alfred.

YOUNG GENTLEMAN. I can't help it, it makes me nervous . . . and I have the feeling you're thinking of it the whole time. I'm embarrassed.

YOUNG WIFE. I am not thinking about it.

YOUNG GENTLEMAN. You are. If I could only be sure you love me!

YOUNG WIFE. Do you want better proof than . . . ?

* The Young Gentleman's stories are based on *De l'amour,* Chapter 60: "Failures."

YOUNG GENTLEMAN. You see! You're always making fun of me.

YOUNG WIFE. Not at all! Come, give me your sweet little head.

YOUNG GENTLEMAN. Oh, this is *good.*

YOUNG WIFE. Do you love me?

YOUNG GENTLEMAN. Oh, I'm so happy!

YOUNG WIFE. But you don't have to cry as well!

YOUNG GENTLEMAN *moves away, highly irritated.* Again, again! Didn't I beg you?

YOUNG WIFE. I said you shouldn't cry, that was all . . .

YOUNG GENTLEMAN. You said "Cry *as well.*"

YOUNG WIFE. You're nervous, my dear.

YOUNG GENTLEMAN. I know that.

YOUNG WIFE. You shouldn't be. It's rather nice that . . . that we —that we—we're . . . comrades, as you might say . . .

YOUNG GENTLEMAN. Now you're starting over.

YOUNG WIFE. Don't you remember? It was one of our very first talks: we wanted to be . . . "just comrades. . . ." Oh, it was lovely that time . . . at my sister's, in January, at the great ball . . . during the quadrille. . . . For Heaven's sake, I should have left long ago! My sister will be waiting—what shall I tell her? Adieu, Alfred. . . .

YOUNG GENTLEMAN. Emma! You're going to leave me like this?

YOUNG WIFE. Yes. Like this!

YOUNG GENTLEMAN. Just another five minutes . . .

YOUNG WIFE. All right, five minutes. But you must promise me to keep quite still . . . Yes? . . . I'm going to give you a good-bye kiss . . . Ssh . . . keep still, as I told you, or I'll get right up. My sweet . . . sweet . . .

YOUNG GENTLEMAN. Emma . . . I worsh . . .

❋   ❋   ❋   ❋   ❋

YOUNG WIFE. Darling Alfred . . .

YOUNG GENTLEMAN. Oh, it's heaven with you!

YOUNG WIFE. But now I really must go.

YOUNG GENTLEMAN. Oh, let your sister wait.

YOUNG WIFE. I must go *home*. It's too late for my sister. What time is it now?

YOUNG GENTLEMAN. How'd I find *that* out?

YOUNG WIFE. By looking at your watch!

YOUNG GENTLEMAN. But it's in my waistcoat.

YOUNG WIFE. Well, get it.

YOUNG GENTLEMAN *get up with a mighty heave*. Eight.

YOUNG WIFE, *rising hastily*. For Heaven's sake! Quick, Alfred, my stockings—whatever shall I say? They'll be waiting for me . . . at home . . . eight o'clock!

YOUNG GENTLEMAN. When do I see you next?

YOUNG WIFE. Never.

YOUNG GENTLEMAN. Emma! Don't you still love me?

YOUNG WIFE. That's why. Give me my boots.

YOUNG GENTLEMAN. Never again? . . . Here are the boots.

YOUNG WIFE. There's a buttonhook in my pocket book. Please hurry . . .

YOUNG GENTLEMAN. Here's the buttonhook.

YOUNG WIFE. Alfred, this can cost us both our necks!

YOUNG GENTLEMAN, *not liking this at all*. Why?!

YOUNG WIFE. Well, what can I tell him when he asks me where I've been?

YOUNG GENTLEMAN. At your sister's.

YOUNG WIFE. Yes, if only I were a good liar.

YOUNG GENTLEMAN. You'll just have to be.

YOUNG WIFE. All this for a man like you . . . Come here. Let me give you another kiss.
She embraces him.

And now leave me alone, go in the other room, I can't dress with you around.

The YOUNG GENTLEMAN *goes to the drawing room and gets dressed. He eats a little of the pastry, drinks a glass of cognac.*

YOUNG WIFE, *after a while, calling out.* Alfred!

YOUNG GENTLEMAN. Yes, my treasure?

YOUNG WIFE. Maybe it's good we didn't just cry.

YOUNG GENTLEMAN *smiles, not without pride.* You're a very naughty girl.

YOUNG WIFE. What will it be like if we meet at a party one day —by chance?

YOUNG GENTLEMAN. One day? By chance? Surely you'll be at the Lobheimers' tomorrow?

YOUNG WIFE. Yes. Will you?

YOUNG GENTLEMAN. Of course. May I ask for the cotillion?

YOUNG WIFE. Oh, I won't go. How can you think . . . ? Why . . . *She enters the drawing room, fully dressed, and takes a chocolate pastry.* . . . I'd sink into the ground!

YOUNG GENTLEMAN. Well, tomorrow at the Lobheimers'. That's lovely.

YOUNG WIFE. No, no, I'll send word I can't come. . . . Definitely. . . .

YOUNG GENTLEMAN. Then the day after tomorrow—here.

YOUNG WIFE. What an idea!

YOUNG GENTLEMAN. At six.

YOUNG WIFE. There are cabs at the corner, aren't there?

YOUNG GENTLEMAN. As many as you like. Then it's day after tomorrow, six o'clock, here. Say yes, my dearest treasure.

YOUNG WIFE. . . . We'll talk it over tomorrow—during the cotillion.

YOUNG GENTLEMAN, *embracing her.* Angel!

YOUNG WIFE. Don't spoil my hair-do again.

YOUNG GENTLEMAN. So it's tomorrow at the Lobheimers' and the day after—in my arms.

YOUNG WIFE. Good-bye . . .

YOUNG GENTLEMAN, *suddenly worried again*. And what are you going to tell *him* tonight?

YOUNG WIFE. Don't ask . . . don't ask . . . it's too dreadful. Why do I love you so? Good-bye. If I meet people on the stairs again I shall have a stroke.

The YOUNG GENTLEMAN *kisses her hand yet again.*

The YOUNG WIFE *goes.*

YOUNG GENTLEMAN *left alone. He sits down on the sofa. Then he smiles away to himself.* An affair with a respectable woman!

5   THE YOUNG WIFE AND THE HUSBAND

A comfortable bedroom. It is 10:30 *at night. The* YOUNG WIFE *is lying in bed, reading. The* HUSBAND *comes into the room in his bathrobe.*

YOUNG WIFE, *without looking up.* You've stopped working?

HUSBAND. Yes. I'm too tired. And besides . . .

YOUNG WIFE. Yes?

HUSBAND. I suddenly felt so lonely at my desk. I began longing for you.

YOUNG WIFE *looks up.* Really?

HUSBAND *sits by her on her bed.* Don't read any more tonight. You'll ruin your eyes.

YOUNG WIFE *closes the book.* What is it then?

HUSBAND. Nothing, my child. I'm in love with you. But you know that.

YOUNG WIFE. One might almost forget it sometimes.

HUSBAND. One even *has* to forget it sometimes.

YOUNG WIFE. Why?

HUSBAND. Marriage would be imperfect otherwise. It would—how shall I put it? it would lose its sanctity.

YOUNG WIFE. Oh . . .

HUSBAND. Believe me—it's true. . . . If in the course of the five years we've been married we hadn't sometimes forgotten we're in love with one another, we probably *wouldn't* be in love any more.

YOUNG WIFE. That's over my head.

HUSBAND. The fact is simply this: we've had something like ten or twelve different love affairs with one another . . . isn't that how it seems to you?

YOUNG WIFE. I haven't kept count.

HUSBAND. If we'd pushed our first affair to the limit, if I'd blindly surrendered myself to my passion for you from the beginning, we'd have gone the way of millions of others. We'd be through by now.

YOUNG WIFE. I see what you mean.

HUSBAND. Believe me—Emma—in the first days of our marriage I was afraid it would turn out that way.

YOUNG WIFE. So was I.

HUSBAND. You see? Wasn't I right? That's why it's best—from time to time—to live together just as friends.

YOUNG WIFE. Oh, I see.

HUSBAND. That way we can always keep having new honeymoons, because I never risk letting the weeks of the honeymoon . . .

YOUNG WIFE. . . . run into months.

HUSBAND. Exactly.

YOUNG WIFE. And now it seems . . . another of those periods of friendship has come to an end?

HUSBAND, *tenderly pressing her to him*. It could be so!

YOUNG WIFE. But suppose it was different—with me?

HUSBAND. It isn't different with you. You're the cleverest creature alive—*and* the most bewitching. I'm very happy to have found you.

YOUNG WIFE. So you do know how to court a woman—from time to time. I'm glad.

HUSBAND *has got into bed*. For a man who's seen the world a bit—come, put your head on my shoulder—seen the world a bit, marriage means something far more mysterious than to girls from good families like you. You come to us pure and—at least to a certain degree—ignorant, and so you have in reality a much clearer view of the true nature of love than we have.

YOUNG WIFE, *laughing*. Oh!

HUSBAND. Certainly. Because we're insecure—confused by the various experiences we have before marriage—unavoidably. You women hear a lot, and know too much, I'm afraid you read too much too, but you can never have an accurate conception of what we men have to go through. What's commonly called love is made utterly repellent to us—because, after all, what *are* the poor creatures we have to resort to?

YOUNG WIFE. Yes, what *are* the poor creatures you have to resort to?

HUSBAND *kisses her on the forehead*. Be glad, my child, that you never had a glimpse of their condition. Most of them are rather pitiable beings, incidentally. Let us not cast the first stone!

YOUNG WIFE. You pity them? That doesn't seem quite right . . .

HUSBAND, *with fine mildness*. They deserve it. You girls from good families, who can quietly wait beneath the parental roof till a decent man proposes to you—you don't know the misery that drives those poor creatures into the arms of sin.

YOUNG WIFE. They all sell themselves, then?

HUSBAND. I wouldn't quite say *that*. And I'm not thinking merely of material misery. There is also—one might say—a moral misery: an insufficient grasp of what is . . . proper, and especially of what is noble.

YOUNG WIFE. But why should we pity them? Don't they have rather a nice time of it?

HUSBAND. You have peculiar opinions, my child. Don't forget that these creatures are destined by nature to sink forever lower and lower and lower. There is no stopping it.

YOUNG WIFE, *snuggles up to him.* Sinking sounds rather nice!

HUSBAND *pained.* How can you say such a thing, Emma? I should have thought there could be nothing more repellent to a decent woman than the thought of . . .

YOUNG WIFE. Yes, that's true, Karl, of course. I said it without thinking. Tell me more. It's so nice when you talk like this. Tell me more.

HUSBAND. What about?

YOUNG WIFE. About—those creatures!

HUSBAND. But what an idea!

YOUNG WIFE. Look, I asked you before, didn't I, right at the beginning I kept asking you to tell me about your youth.

HUSBAND. Why does *that* interest you?

YOUNG WIFE. Aren't you my husband? And isn't it positively unfair that I know absolutely nothing about your past?

HUSBAND. I hope you don't think I'd . . . in such bad taste . . . No, Emma! It would be profanation!

YOUNG WIFE. And yet you've . . . held any number of other young ladies in your arms, the way you're holding me now.

HUSBAND. "Young ladies!" *They* are . . .

YOUNG WIFE. There's one question you *must* answer. Or else . . . or else . . . no honeymoon.

HUSBAND. You've a way of talking . . . remember, my child, you're a mother—our little girl is sleeping in there.

YOUNG WIFE, *pressing herself to him.* But I want a boy too.

HUSBAND. Emma!

YOUNG WIFE. Oh, don't be so . . . Of course I'm your wife, but I'd like to be—your mistress, sort of.

HUSBAND. You would?

YOUNG WIFE. First, my question!

HUSBAND, *submissive*. What is it?

YOUNG WIFE. Was there a—a married woman—among them?

HUSBAND. What? How do you mean?

YOUNG WIFE. *You* know.

HUSBAND, *somewhat disturbed*. What makes you ask?

YOUNG WIFE. I'd like to know if there . . . I mean . . . there *are* women like that, I know . . . But have *you* . . .

HUSBAND, *gravely*. Do you know any such woman?

YOUNG WIFE. Well, I can't tell.

HUSBAND. Is there such a woman among your friends?

YOUNG WIFE. Well, how could I say yes—or no—and be sure?

HUSBAND. Has one of your women friends . . . People talk a lot when they . . . women among themselves . . . has one of them confessed . . . ?

YOUNG WIFE, *uncertainly*. No.

HUSBAND. Do you *suspect* that one of your friends . . .

YOUNG WIFE. Suspect . . . well . . . suspect . . .

HUSBAND. You do!

YOUNG WIFE. Definitely not, Karl. Most certainly not. Now I think it over, I wouldn't believe it of one of them.

HUSBAND. Not one?

YOUNG WIFE. Of friends—not one.

HUSBAND. Promise me something, Emma.

YOUNG WIFE. Well?

HUSBAND. Promise you'll never go around with a woman if you have the slightest suspicion that . . . her life is not beyond reproach.

YOUNG WIFE. You need a promise for that?

HUSBAND. I know, of course, that you would never *seek* contact with such women. But by *chance* you might. . . . It frequently happens that women who don't enjoy the best reputation seek the company of respectable women, partly for contrast and partly out of a certain—how shall I put it?—out of a certain nostalgia for virtue.

YOUNG WIFE. I see.

HUSBAND. Yes, I believe it's very true, what I just said. Nostalgia for virtue! For there's one thing you can be sure of: in reality all these women are very unhappy.

YOUNG WIFE. Why?

HUSBAND. How can you ask, Emma? Only imagine what sort of existence they have to lead. Full of meanness, lies, treachery—and full of danger!

YOUNG WIFE. Oh yes. I'm sure you're right.

HUSBAND. Indeed, they pay for that bit of happiness . . . that bit of . . .

YOUNG WIFE. . . . pleasure.

HUSBAND. Pleasure? What makes you call it pleasure?

YOUNG WIFE. Well, it's something, or they wouldn't do it.

HUSBAND. It's nothing. Mere intoxication.

YOUNG WIFE, *thoughtfully*. Mere intoxication.

HUSBAND. Not even intoxication. But one thing is certain—it's bought at a price!

YOUNG WIFE. Then . . . you do know what you're talking about?

HUSBAND. Yes, Emma. It's my saddest memory.

YOUNG WIFE. Who was it? Tell me. Do I know her?

HUSBAND. Emma! What are you thinking of?

YOUNG WIFE. Was it long ago? Very long? Before you married me?

HUSBAND. Don't ask. Please, don't ask.

YOUNG WIFE. But Karl!

HUSBAND. She is dead.

YOUNG WIFE. Honestly?

HUSBAND. Yes . . . It may sound ridiculous, but I have the feeling that all these women die young.

YOUNG WIFE. Did you love her very much?

HUSBAND. Can a man love a liar?

YOUNG WIFE. Then, why . . . ?

HUSBAND. Intoxication . . .

YOUNG WIFE. So it *is* . . .

HUSBAND. Please, don't talk about it. All that is long past. I've only loved one woman: you. A man can only love where he finds purity and truth.

YOUNG WIFE. Karl!

HUSBAND. Oh how safe, how good a man feels in these arms! Why didn't I know you as a child? I'm sure I'd never have looked at another woman.

YOUNG WIFE. Karl!

HUSBAND. You're beautiful . . . beautiful . . . Oh! *He puts the light out.*

❋   ❋   ❋   ❋   ❋

YOUNG WIFE. You know what I can't help thinking of tonight?

HUSBAND. What, my treasure?

YOUNG WIFE. Of . . . of . . . of Venice.

HUSBAND. The first night . . .

YOUNG WIFE. Yes . . . Like that . . .

HUSBAND. What is it? Tell me.

YOUNG WIFE. Tonight . . . you love me like that.

HUSBAND. Like that.

YOUNG WIFE. Ah . . . if you could always . . .

HUSBAND, *in her arms.* Yes?

YOUNG WIFE. Oh Karl dear!

HUSBAND. What was it you wanted to say? If I could always . . . ?

YOUNG WIFE. Well, yes.

HUSBAND. Well, what would happen if I could always . . . ?

YOUNG WIFE. Then I'd always know you love me.

HUSBAND. Yes. But you know it anyhow. A man can't always be the loving husband, he must go out into a hostile world and fight the good fight! Always remember this, my child. In marriage there's a time for everything—that's the beauty of it. There aren't many who still remember their Venice after five years.

YOUNG WIFE. No.

HUSBAND. And now . . . good-night, my child.

YOUNG WIFE. Good-night!

6 THE HUSBAND AND THE LITTLE MISS

A private room in the RIEDHOF RESTAURANT; *comfortable, unobtrusive elegance; the gas stove is lit. On the table the remains of a meal: meringues with much whipped cream, fruit, cheese. White Hungarian wine in the glasses.*

The HUSBAND *smokes a Havana cigar, leans back on the corner of the sofa.*
The LITTLE MISS *sits on a chair beside him, scoops the whipped cream out of a meringue and sucks it up with satisfaction.*

HUSBAND. It's good?

LITTLE MISS, *uninterruptible.* Mm!

HUSBAND. Like another?

LITTLE MISS. No, I've eaten too much already.

HUSBAND. You've no wine left.
He fills up her glass.

LITTLE MISS. No . . . I'll only leave it, sir.

HUSBAND. Sir? Don't be so stiff with me.

LITTLE MISS. Well, you're not so easy to get used to, sir.

HUSBAND. Sir!

LITTLE MISS. What?

HUSBAND. You said "sir" again. Come and sit by me.

LITTLE MISS. One moment—I'm not through.
The HUSBAND *gets up, stands behind her chair and puts his arms round her, turning her head towards him.*

LITTLE MISS. What is it now?

HUSBAND. I'd like to have a kiss.

LITTLE MISS *gives him a kiss.* You're pretty fresh, you are.

HUSBAND. You only just noticed it?

LITTLE MISS. Oh, I noticed before . . . in the street. You must have quite an opinion of me.

HUSBAND. How's that?

LITTLE MISS. Going straight to a private room with you.

HUSBAND. You didn't go "straight" to the private room.

LITTLE MISS. You've a nice way of asking.

HUSBAND. You think so?

LITTLE MISS. And after all, what's wrong about it?

HUSBAND. Precisely.

LITTLE MISS. Whether you go for a walk or . . .

HUSBAND. It's much too cold for a walk, isn't it?

LITTLE MISS. It was much too cold.

HUSBAND. But in here it's nice and warm, don't you think?
He has sat down again and puts his arm round the LITTLE MISS, *pulling her over to his side.*

LITTLE MISS, *weakly.* Hey!

HUSBAND. Now tell me . . . You'd noticed me before, hadn't you?

LITTLE MISS. Sure. In the Singer Strasse.

HUSBAND. I don't mean today. The day before yesterday and the day before that. I was following you.

LITTLE MISS. There's plenty follow me!

HUSBAND. I can imagine. But did you notice me?

LITTLE MISS. Well . . . um . . . you know what happened to me the other day? My cousin's husband followed me in the dark, and didn't recognize me.

HUSBAND. Did he speak to you?

LITTLE MISS. The idea! You think everybody's as fresh as you?

HUSBAND. It happens.

LITTLE MISS. Sure it happens.

HUSBAND. Well, what do you do?

LITTLE MISS. Me? Nothing. I just don't answer.

HUSBAND. Hm . . . you answered me.

LITTLE MISS. Well, are you mad at me?

HUSBAND *kisses her violently.* Your lips taste of whipped cream.

LITTLE MISS. Oh, they're sweet by nature.

HUSBAND. Many men have told you that, have they?

LITTLE MISS. Many men! The ideas you get!

HUSBAND. Be honest with me. How many have kissed these lips?

LITTLE MISS. Why ask? If I tell you, you won't believe me.

HUSBAND. Why not?

LITTLE MISS. Guess.

HUSBAND. Let's say—um—but you mustn't be angry!

LITTLE MISS. Why should I be?

HUSBAND. Well, at a guess . . . twenty.

LITTLE MISS *breaking away from him.* Why not a hundred while you're at it?

HUSBAND. It was only a guess.

LITTLE MISS. It was a bad guess.

HUSBAND. Let's say—ten.

LITTLE MISS, *offended.* Oh sure! A girl who lets you talk to her in the street and goes straight to a private dining room!

HUSBAND. Don't be a child. Whether people run around in the streets or sit together in a room. . . . Here we're in a restaurant, the waiter can come in any time—there's nothing to it.

LITTLE MISS. That's just what *I* thought.

HUSBAND. Have you ever been in a private dining room before?

LITTLE MISS. Well, if I must tell you the truth: yes.

HUSBAND. Well, I like that: you're honest.

LITTLE MISS. It wasn't like you think. I was with my girl friend and her fiancé, during the last Carnival.

HUSBAND. Well, it wouldn't be a tragedy if you'd been—with your boyfriend . . .

LITTLE MISS. Sure it wouldn't be a tragedy. But I haven't got a boy friend.

HUSBAND. Go on!

LITTLE MISS. Cross my heart, I haven't.

HUSBAND. You don't mean to tell me I . . .

LITTLE MISS. What? . . . There hasn't been anyone—for more than six months.

HUSBAND. I see . . . And before that? Who was it?

LITTLE MISS. What are you so inquisitive for?

HUSBAND. Because . . . I'm in love with you.

LITTLE MISS. Really?

HUSBAND. Of course. Hadn't you noticed? Come on, tell me. *He pulls her close to him.*

LITTLE MISS. Tell you what?

HUSBAND. Don't keep me begging. I'd like to know who he was.

LITTLE MISS, *laughing.* Oh, a man.

HUSBAND. Come on, come one, who was he?

LITTLE MISS. He was a little bit like you.

HUSBAND. Indeed.

LITTLE MISS. If you hadn't been so much like him . . .

HUSBAND. Well, what then?

LITTLE MISS. Now don't ask. You know what . . .

HUSBAND. So that's why you let me speak to you!

LITTLE MISS. Well, yes.

HUSBAND. Now I don't know whether to be glad or annoyed.

LITTLE MISS. If I was you, I'd be glad.

HUSBAND. Oh, surely.

LITTLE MISS. The way you talk reminds me of him too . . . and the way you look at a girl . . .

HUSBAND. What was he?

LITTLE MISS. Really, your eyes . . .

HUSBAND. What was his name?

LITTLE MISS. Don't look at me like that, no, please!
The HUSBAND *takes her in his arms. A long, hot kiss.
The* LITTLE MISS *shakes herself free and tries to get up.*

HUSBAND. What's the matter?

LITTLE MISS. Time to go home.

HUSBAND. Later.

LITTLE MISS. No, I *must* go home. Really. What do you think mother will say?

HUSBAND. You're living with your mother?

LITTLE MISS. Sure I am. What did you think?

HUSBAND. I see . . . with your mother. Just the two of you?

LITTLE MISS. Just the two . . . ?! There's five of us. Two boys and three girls.

HUSBAND. Don't sit so far away. Are you the eldest?

LITTLE MISS. No. I'm the second. First there's Kathi, she goes out to work. In a flower shop. Then there's me.

HUSBAND. What do you do?

LITTLE MISS. I'm at home.

HUSBAND. All the time?

LITTLE MISS. Well, one of us has got to be at home.

HUSBAND. Naturally. Well—and what do you tell your mother when you—come home late?

LITTLE MISS. It doesn't often happen.

HUSBAND. Tonight for example. Your mother does ask you?

LITTLE MISS. Oh, sure she does. It doesn't matter how careful I am when I get home, she wakes up every time.

HUSBAND. What will you tell her tonight?

LITTLE MISS. Oh well, I guess I'll have been to the theater.

HUSBAND. Will she believe you?

LITTLE MISS. Why shouldn't she? I often go to the theater. Only last Sunday I was at the Opera with my girl friend and her fiancé—and my older brother.

HUSBAND. Where do you get the tickets from?

LITTLE MISS. My brother's a barber.

HUSBAND. Of course, barbers . . . I suppose he's a theatrical barber?

LITTLE MISS. Why are you pumping me like this?

HUSBAND. I'm interested. And what's your other brother?

LITTLE MISS. He's still at school. He wants to be a teacher. Imagine!

HUSBAND. And you've a younger sister too?

LITTLE MISS. Yes, she's only a brat, but at that you've got to keep an eye on her. You've no idea what these girls learn at school. Do you know, the other day I caught her having a date!

HUSBAND. What?

LITTLE MISS. I did. With a boy from the school opposite. She was out walking with him in the Strozzi Gasse at half-past seven. The brat!

HUSBAND. What did you do?

LITTLE MISS. Well, she got a spanking.

HUSBAND. You are as strict as all that?

LITTLE MISS. There's no one else to do it. My older sister's in the shop, Mother does nothing but grumble—and so everything falls on me.

HUSBAND. God, you're sweet!
He kisses her and grows more tender.
And you remind me of someone, too.

LITTLE MISS. Do I? Who is she?

HUSBAND. No one in particular . . . you remind me of the time when . . . well, my youth! Come, drink up, child.

LITTLE MISS. How old are you? . . . Um . . . I don't even know your name.

HUSBAND. Karl.

LITTLE MISS. Honest? Your name's Karl?

HUSBAND. He was called Karl?

LITTLE MISS. Really, it's a miracle . . . it's too . . . No, those eyes! . . . That look!
She shakes her head.

HUSBAND. You still haven't told me who he was.

LITTLE MISS. A bad man, that's what he was, or he wouldn't have dropped me.

HUSBAND. Did you like him a lot?

LITTLE MISS. Sure I liked him a lot.

HUSBAND. I know what he was: a lieutenant.

LITTLE MISS. No, he wasn't in the Army. They wouldn't take him. His father's got a house in the . . . but what do you want to know for?

HUSBAND *kisses her.* Your eyes are gray really. At first I thought they were black.

LITTLE MISS. Well, aren't they nice enough for you?
The HUSBAND *kisses her eyes.*

LITTLE MISS. Oh, no—that's something I can't stand—please, please. . . . Oh God . . . No, let me get up . . . just for a minute, oh please!

HUSBAND, *increasingly tender.* Oh, no! No!

LITTLE MISS. But, Karl, please!

HUSBAND. How old are you? Eighteen, is it?

LITTLE MISS. Nineteen now.

HUSBAND. Nineteen . . . and I . . .

LITTLE MISS. You're thirty . . .

HUSBAND. And . . . a little more. . . . Don't let's talk of it.

LITTLE MISS. At that, he was thirty-two when I met him!

HUSBAND. How long ago?

LITTLE MISS. I can't remember. . . . You know what, there was something in the wine!

HUSBAND. How so?

LITTLE MISS. I'm quite . . . you know . . . everything's turning round.

HUSBAND. Hold on to me. Like this . . .
He pulls her to him and becomes more and more tender; she scarcely defends herself.
I'll tell you something, treasure, now we might really go.

LITTLE MISS. Yes—home.

HUSBAND. Not home exactly.

LITTLE MISS. What do you mean? . . . Oh no, no! . . . I wouldn't . . . What an idea!

HUSBAND. Now, listen to me, my child, next time we meet, you know, we'll arrange it so. . . .

He has slipped to the floor, his head in her lap.

That's good; oh, that's good!

LITTLE MISS. What are you doing?

She kisses his hair.

See, there *must* have been something in the wine . . . so sleepy . . . Hey, what happens if I can't get up? But . . . but look, Karl! . . . If somebody comes in . . . Please . . . the waiter!

HUSBAND. No waiter'll . . . come in here . . . not in . . . your life-time.

*   *   *   *   *

The LITTLE MISS *leans back in a corner of the sofa, her eyes shut.*

The HUSBAND *walks up and down the small room, after lighting a cigar.*

A longish silence.

HUSBAND *looks at the girl for a long time, then says to himself.* Who knows what sort of person she really is——God in heaven! . . . So quickly . . . Wasn't very careful of me . . . Hm . . .

LITTLE MISS, *without opening her eyes.* There must have been something in that wine.

HUSBAND. How's that?

LITTLE MISS. Otherwise . . .

HUSBAND. Why blame everything on the wine?

LITTLE MISS. Where are you? Why are you so far away? Come here to me.

The HUSBAND *goes to her, sits down.*

LITTLE MISS. Now, tell me if you really like me.

HUSBAND. But you *know*. . . .
Interrupting himself quickly.
Of course I do.

LITTLE MISS. You see . . . there *is* . . . Come on, tell me the truth, what was in that wine?

HUSBAND. You think I go around poisoning people?

LITTLE MISS. Look, I just don't understand. I'm not like that. . . . We've only known each other for . . . Listen, I'm not like that, cross my heart—if you believe that of me . . .

HUSBAND. There, there, don't fret so! I don't think anything bad of you. I just think you like me.

LITTLE MISS. Yes . . .

HUSBAND. After all, if two young people are alone together, and have supper, and drink wine—there doesn't have to be anything in the wine.

LITTLE MISS. Oh, I was just gabbing.

HUSBAND. But why?

LITTLE MISS, *somewhat defiantly*. Because I was ashamed!

HUSBAND. That's ridiculous. There's no reason for it. Especially since I remind you of your first lover.

LITTLE MISS. Yes.

HUSBAND. Your first.

LITTLE MISS. Oh sure . . .

HUSBAND. Now it would interest me to know who the others were.

LITTLE MISS. There weren't any.

HUSBAND. That isn't true. It can't be true.

LITTLE MISS. Please don't nag me!

HUSBAND. A cigarette?

LITTLE MISS. No. Thank you.

HUSBAND. Do you know what time it is?

LITTLE MISS. What?

HUSBAND. Half-past eleven.

LITTLE MISS. Really.

HUSBAND. Well . . . what about your mother? Used to it, is she?

LITTLE MISS. You want to send me home already?

HUSBAND. But you wanted—yourself . . .

LITTLE MISS. Look, you're different now. What have I done to you?

HUSBAND. My dear child, what's wrong? Wᴌat are you thinking of?

LITTLE MISS. It was . . . the look in your eyes, honest, cross my heart. But for that you could have gone down on your knees. . . . A lot of men have *begged* me to go to a private room with them!

HUSBAND. Well, would you like to . . . to come here again . . . soon? Or some other place . . . ?

LITTLE MISS. I don't know.

HUSBAND. Now what's *that* mean: you don't know?

LITTLE MISS. Why do you have to ask?

HUSBAND. All right—when? But first I must explain that I don't live in Vienna. I . . . just come here now and then. For a couple of days.

LITTLE MISS. Go on—you aren't Viennese?

HUSBAND. Well, yes, I'm Viennese, but I live . . . out of town.

LITTLE MISS. Where?

HUSBAND. Goodness, *that* doesn't matter, does it?

LITTLE MISS. Don't worry, I won't go there.

HUSBAND. Heavens, you can go there as much as you want. I live in Graz.

LITTLE MISS. Really?

HUSBAND. Yes. What's so astonishing about that?

LITTLE MISS. You're married, aren't you?

HUSBAND, *greatly surprised.* Whatever makes you think so?

LITTLE MISS. It looks that way to me.

HUSBAND. And if I were, it wouldn't bother you any?

LITTLE MISS. Oh, I'd like it better if you were single. But you're married. I know.

HUSBAND. Now tell me, what makes you think so?

LITTLE MISS. Oh, if a man says he doesn't live in town and hasn't always got time . . .

HUSBAND. That isn't so unlikely, is it?

LITTLE MISS. I don't believe it.

HUSBAND. And it wouldn't give you a bad conscience to seduce a married man? Make him unfaithful?

LITTLE MISS. Never mind about that—I bet your wife is no different.

HUSBAND, *very indignant.* That's enough! Such observations . . .

LITTLE MISS. I thought you didn't have a wife.

HUSBAND. Whether I have a wife or not, such observations are beyond the pale!
He has risen.

LITTLE MISS. But, Karl, what is it, Karl? Are you mad at me? Look, I didn't know you were married. I was just gabbing. Come on, let's be friends.

HUSBAND *goes to her after a couple of seconds.* You really are strange creatures.
At her side, he begins to caress her again.
Oh, the female of the species!

LITTLE MISS. No . . . don't . . . and it's so late . . .

HUSBAND. Now listen to me. We must have a serious talk. I want to see you again—many times.

LITTLE MISS. Honest?

HUSBAND. But if so, it's essential. . . . I must be able to rely on you. I can't be watching all the time.

LITTLE MISS. Oh, I can look after myself.

HUSBAND. You're . . . well, not inexperienced exactly, but you're young, and—men in general are an unscrupulous bunch.

LITTLE MISS. And how!

HUSBAND. I don't mean just in morals. . . . Well, *you* know what I mean.

LITTLE MISS. Now, really, what sort of girl do you take me for?

HUSBAND. So, if you want to love me—only me—we'll be able to fix things up somehow, even if I do live in Graz. This place isn't the right thing—someone could come in at any moment!
The LITTLE MISS *snuggles up to him.*

HUSBAND. Next time let's make it somewhere else, okay?

LITTLE MISS. Okay.

HUSBAND. Where we can't be disturbed.

LITTLE MISS. Right.

HUSBAND *embraces her with fervor.* The rest we can talk over on the way home.
He gets up, opens the door.
Waiter . . . the check!

7 THE LITTLE MISS AND THE POET

A small room, comfortably furnished, in good taste. Drapes leave it in semi-darkness. Red net curtains. A big desk littered with papers and books. Against the wall, an upright piano.

The LITTLE MISS *and the* POET *enter together. The* POET *locks the door.*

POET. Here we are, sweetheart.
He kisses her.

LITTLE MISS, *in hat and cloak.* Oh, what a nice room! Only you can't see anything!

POET. Your eyes will have to get used to semi-darkness. These sweet eyes!
He kisses her eyelids.

LITTLE MISS. These sweet eyes won't have time to get used to it.

POET. How's that?

LITTLE MISS. Because I can't stay for more than one minute.

POET. Do take your hat off.

LITTLE MISS. For one minute?

POET *pulls out her hatpin, takes the hat, puts it on one side.* And your cloak.

LITTLE MISS. What are you up to? I've got to go!

POET. First you must rest. We've been walking three hours.

LITTLE MISS. We were in the carriage.

POET. Coming home, yes. But in Weidling-am-Bach we were three solid hours on foot. Now do sit down, child . . . wherever you like . . . at the desk. . . . No, that isn't comfortable. Sit down on the sofa. Here.
He puts her down on the sofa.
If you're very tired, you can stretch out. Like this.
He makes her lie down.
With your little head on the cushion.

LITTLE MISS, *laughing.* But I'm not a bit tired!

POET. You *think* you aren't. Right, and now if you feel sleepy, you can go to sleep. I'll keep perfectly quiet. Or I can play you a lullaby . . . one of my own.
He goes to the piano.

LITTLE MISS. Your own?

POET. Yes.

LITTLE MISS. But, Robert, I thought you were a doctor.

POET. How's that? I told you I was a writer.

LITTLE MISS. Well, writers *are* doctors, aren't they?

POET. Of philosophy? Not all writers. Not me, for instance. Why did you bring *that* up?

LITTLE MISS. Because you said the piece you were going to play was your own.

POET. Oh well . . . maybe it isn't. It doesn't matter. Does it? It never matters who's done a thing—just so long as it's beautiful—you agree?

LITTLE MISS. Oh sure . . . as long as it's beautiful!

POET. Do you know what I meant by that?

LITTLE MISS. By what?

POET. What I said just now.

LITTLE MISS, *drowsily*. Oh, sure.

POET *gets up, goes to her and strokes her hair.* You didn't understand a word.

LITTLE MISS. Now look, I'm *not* stupid.

POET. Of course you are. That's why I love you. It's a fine thing for women to be stupid. In *your* way, that is.

LITTLE MISS. Hey, don't be rude!

POET. Little angel! Isn't it nice just to lie there on a soft Persian rug?

LITTLE MISS. Oh yes. Won't you go on playing the piano?

POET. I'd rather stay with you.
He strokes her.

LITTLE MISS. Look, can't we have the light on?

POET. Oh no . . . twilight is so comforting. Today we were bathing in sunshine all day long. Now we've come out of the bath, so to speak, and we're wrapping the twilight round us like a bathrobe.
He laughs.
No, it'll have to be put a little differently . . . won't it?

LITTLE MISS. Will it?

POET, *edging away from her.* It's divine, this stupidity!
He takes out a notebook and writes a few words in it.

LITTLE MISS. What are you doing?
Turns round to look at him.
What are you writing down?

POET, *in an undertone.* Sun—bath—twilight—robe . . . That's it.
He puts the notebook in his pocket, laughs.
Nothing. And now tell me, treasure, wouldn't you like
something to eat or drink?

LITTLE MISS. I guess I'm not thirsty. But I *am* hungry.

POET. Hm . . . now, I'd rather you were thirsty. The cognac's
right here, but if it's food I'll have to go out and get it.

LITTLE MISS. Can't they bring it up for you?

POET. That's the difficulty. My maid isn't around any more . . .
Never mind. I'll go. What would you like?

LITTLE MISS. It isn't worth it, I've got to go home anyway.

POET. Oho, no you don't! I'll tell you what: when we leave, we'll
go and have supper somewhere.

LITTLE MISS. I haven't got time. And—where could we go?
We'd be seen.

POET. You know so many people?

LITTLE MISS. It's enough if *one* of them sees us.

POET. How so?

LITTLE MISS. What do you think? If Mother heard anything . . .

POET. We could go to a place where nobody *could* see us. There
are restaurants with private rooms after all . . .

LITTLE MISS *sings.* "Just to share a private room with you . . ."

POET. Have you ever been to a private dining room?

LITTLE MISS. As a matter of fact I have.

POET. Who was the lucky man?

LITTLE MISS. Oh, it wasn't what you think . . . I was with my
girl friend and her fiancé. They took me.

POET. Really? Am I supposed to believe that?

LITTLE MISS. Suit yourself.

POET, *close to her*. Did you blush? It's dark in here. I can't make
out your features.
He touches her cheek with his hand.
Even so—I recognize you.

LITTLE MISS. Well, take care you don't mix me up with another
girl.

POET. Peculiar! I can't remember what you look like.

LITTLE MISS. Thank you very much.

POET, *seriously*. Do you know, it's rather spooky—I can't visual-
ize your face—in a certain sense I've *forgotten* you. Now, if
I couldn't recognize your voice either . . . what would you
be? So near and yet so far—rather spooky, what?

LITTLE MISS. What are *you* talking about?

POET. Nothing, angel, nothing. Where are your lips?
He kisses her.

LITTLE MISS. Won't you put the light on?

POET. No . . .
He grows very tender.
Tell me if you love me!

LITTLE MISS. Oh, I do. I do!

POET. Have you ever loved anyone else as much?

LITTLE MISS. I told you I haven't.

POET. But . . .
He sighs.

LITTLE MISS. Well—*he* was my fiancé.

POET. I'd rather you didn't think of him.

LITTLE MISS. Oh . . . what are you doing . . . now look . . .

POET. Let's imagine we're in a castle in India.

LITTLE MISS. I'm sure people there couldn't be as naughty as you.

POET. How idiotic! Divine! If only you had an inkling of what you mean to me . . .

LITTLE MISS. Well, what?

POET. Don't push me away all the time. I'm not doing anything —yet.

LITTLE MISS. Listen, my corset hurts.

POET, *simply.* Take it off.

LITTLE MISS. Okay, but you mustn't be naughty.

POET. Okay.

LITTLE MISS *rises and takes off her corset in the dark.*

POET, *sitting on the sofa in the meanwhile.* Tell me, doesn't it interest you at all to know my last name?

LITTLE MISS. Oh, yes—what is it?

POET. I'd better not tell you my name. I'll tell you what I call myself.

LITTLE MISS. What's the difference?

POET. Well, what I call myself—as a writer.

LITTLE MISS. You don't write under your real name?

POET, *close to her.*

LITTLE MISS. Ah . . . please! . . . Don't!

POET. O the sweet odor that rises from you!
   He kisses her bosom.

LITTLE MISS. You're tearing my chemise.

POET. Off with it all! Away with these . . . superfluities!

LITTLE MISS. *Robert!*

POET. Let's enter our Indian castle!

LITTLE MISS. First tell me if you really love me.

POET. I worship you!

He kisses her hotly.

My treasure, I worship you, my springtime . . . my . . .

LITTLE MISS. Robert . . . Robert . . .

❋   ❋   ❋   ❋   ❋

POET. That was bliss supernal . . . I call myself . . .

LITTLE MISS. Robert. *My* Robert!

POET. I call myself Biebitz.

LITTLE MISS. Why do you call yourself Biebitz?

POET. Biebitz isn't my name, it's what I call myself. You know the name?

LITTLE MISS. No.

POET. You don't know the name Biebitz? How divine! Really? But you're just pretending?

LITTLE MISS. Cross my heart, I've never heard it.

POET. You never go to the theatre?

LITTLE MISS. Oh, yes. Just the other day I got taken—by my girl friend's uncle—and my girl friend—and we went to the Opera—*Cavalleria Rusticana!*

POET. Hmm, but you don't go to the Burg Theater?

LITTLE MISS. Nobody ever gave me a ticket.

POET. I'll send you a ticket one day soon.

LITTLE MISS. Oh please! But don't forget. Make it something funny.

POET. Yes . . . funny . . . well . . . you wouldn't like something sad?

LITTLE MISS. Not as much.

POET. Even if it's by me?

LITTLE MISS. A play—by you? You write for the theatre?!

POET. Excuse me, I just want to light a candle. I haven't seen you since you became mine. Angel!

He lights a candle.

LITTLE MISS. Hey, don't! I feel ashamed. Give me a blanket anyway!

POET. Later!
He walks up to her with the light and contemplates her for a long while.

LITTLE MISS *covers her face with her hands.* Robert!

POET. You're beautiful. You *are* Beauty! You are Nature herself perhaps! You are Sacred Simplicity!

LITTLE MISS. Ouch! You're dripping wax on me! Why can't you be more careful?

POET *puts the candlestick down.* You're what I've been looking for all this time. You love me—just me—you'd love me the same if I were a shop assistant. It does me good. I'll confess that up till now I couldn't get rid of a certain suspicion. Tell me, hadn't you the least idea I was Biebitz?

LITTLE MISS. Look, I don't know what you want with me. I don't know any Biebitz.

POET. Such is fame! Never mind, forget what I told you, forget even the name I told you. I'm Robert for you, and I want to remain Robert. I was joking!
Gaily.
I'm not a writer at all, I'm a shop assistant. In the evenings I play the piano for folk singers!

LITTLE MISS. Now you have me all mixed up . . . and the way you look at a girl! What's the matter, what's eating you?

POET. It's strange—it's hardly ever happened to me, my treasure —I feel like crying. You've got under my skin. Let's stay together, hm? We're going to love one another very much.

LITTLE MISS. Listen, is that true about the folk singing?

POET. Yes, but don't ask any more. If you love me, don't ask. Tell me, could you make yourself quite free for a couple of weeks?

LITTLE MISS. What do you mean, quite free?

POET. Well, away from home.

LITTLE MISS. What! How could I? What would Mother say?
Anyway, everything would go wrong at home without me.

POET. I'd been thinking how lovely it would be to live with you
for a few weeks quite alone, somewhere, in distant solitude,
in the depths of Nature's forests. Thou Nature art my Goddess! And then, one day, farewell—to go who knows
whither?

LITTLE MISS. Now you're talking of good-bye. And I thought
you liked me a lot.

POET. That's just it!
He bends down and kisses her on the forehead.
Sweet creature!

LITTLE MISS. Hold me tight, I'm cold.

POET. It's time to get dressed. Wait, I'll light some more candles.

LITTLE MISS *gets up*. Don't look!

POET. No.
At the window.
Tell me, child, are you happy?

LITTLE MISS. How do you mean?

POET. In general I mean: are you happy?

LITTLE MISS. Things could be better.

POET. You don't understand me. You've told me quite enough
of the state of affairs at home, I know you aren't exactly a
princess. I mean, setting all that aside, do you feel you're
alive? Do you feel you are really alive?

LITTLE MISS. You got a comb?

POET *goes to the dressing-table, gives her the comb, contemplates the* LITTLE MISS. God, you're enchanting to look at!

LITTLE MISS. No . . . don't!

POET. Come, stay here with me a little longer, stay and let me
get something for our supper, and . . .

LITTLE MISS. But it's much too late.

POET. It's not nine yet.

LITTLE MISS. Oh well, but I've got to hurry.

POET. When shall we meet next?

LITTLE MISS. When would you like to see me?

POET. Tomorrow?

LITTLE MISS. What's tomorrow?

POET. Saturday.

LITTLE MISS. Oh, I can't make it. I've got to go see our guardian. With my little sister.

POET. Sunday, then . . . hm . . . Sunday . . . on Sunday . . . I must explain something to you. I'm not Biebitz, Biebitz is a friend of mine. One day I'll introduce you to him. His play is on next Sunday. I'll send you a ticket, and come to the theatre to get you. You'll tell me how you like the play, won't you?

LITTLE MISS. This Biebitz thing . . . well, I may be stupid but . . .

POET. When I know how you felt about the play, I'll really know you.

LITTLE MISS. Okay . . . I'm ready.

POET. Let's go, then, my treasure.
They leave.

8   THE POET AND THE ACTRESS

A room in a country inn. It is an evening in spring; meadows and hills are lit by the moon; the windows are open. All is still.

The POET *and the* ACTRESS *enters; as they come in, the flame of the candle which the* POET *is carrying goes out.*

POET. Oh!

ACTRESS. What's the matter?

POET. The candle. But we don't need it. Look, it's quite light! Marvelous!
The ACTRESS *suddenly sinks on her knees at the window, folding her hands.*

POET. What's the matter with you?
ACTRESS *remains silent.*

POET *goes to her.* What are you doing?

ACTRESS, *indignant.* Can't you see I'm praying?

POET. You believe in God?

ACTRESS. What do you think I am—an anarchist?

POET. Oh.

ACTRESS. Come here, kneel down beside me. You could use a prayer once in a while.
The POET *kneels down beside her and puts his arms round her.*
ACTRESS. You lecher!
She gets up.
And do you know to whom I was praying?

POET. To God, I presume.

ACTRESS, *with great scorn.* Oh yes? It was to you I prayed.

POET. Then why look out of the window?

ACTRESS. Tell me where you've dragged me off to, seducer.

POET. It was your own idea, my child. You wanted to go to the country. You wanted to come here.

ACTRESS. Well, wasn't I right?

POET. Yes, it's enchanting. To think it's only two hours from Vienna—and perfect solitude! What a landscape!

ACTRESS. Isn't it? You could write poetry here, if you had any talent.

POET. Have you been here before?

ACTRESS. Have I been here before? I lived here for years.

POET. With whom?

ACTRESS. Oh, with Fritz, of course.

POET. I see.

ACTRESS. I worshiped that man.

POET. You told me.

ACTRESS. Oh, I beg your pardon—I can leave if I bore you.

POET. *You* bore me? . . . You have no idea what you mean to me. . . . You're a world in yourself. . . . You're the Divine Spark, you're Genius . . . You are . . . The truth is, you're Sacred Simplicity. . . . Yes, you . . . But you shouldn't talk about Fritz—now.

ACTRESS. He was an aberration, yes . . . Oh well . . .

POET. It's good you see that.

ACTRESS. Come over and kiss me.
The POET *kisses her.*

ACTRESS. And now we're going to say good-night. Good-bye, my treasure.

POET. What do you mean?

ACTRESS. I'm going to bed.

POET. Yes—that's all right, but this "good-night" business . . . where am *I* going to sleep?

ACTRESS. I'm sure there are other rooms in this inn.

POET. For me the other rooms have singularly little attraction. By the way, I'd better light up, hadn't I?

ACTRESS. Yes.

POET *lights the candle on the bedside table.* What a pretty room . . . They're religious here, nothing but saints' pictures. . . . Wouldn't it be interesting to spend some time among these people—another world! How little we know of our fellow men!

ACTRESS. Stop talking bosh, and give me my pocketbook, will you, it's on the table.

POET. Here, my own!

The ACTRESS *takes from the pocket book a small framed picture and puts it on the bedside table.*

POET. What's that?

ACTRESS. Our Lady.

POET. I beg your pardon?

ACTRESS. The Blessed Virgin.

POET. I see. You never travel without it?

ACTRESS. Never. It's my mascot. Now go, Robert.

POET. What sort of a joke is this? Don't you want me to help you?

ACTRESS. I want you to go.

POET. Will you ever take me back?

ACTRESS. Perhaps.

POET. When?

ACTRESS. Oh, in about ten minutes.

POET *kisses her.* Darling! See you in ten minutes.

ACTRESS. Where will you be?

POET. I shall walk up and down in front of the window. I love to walk at night in the open air. I get my best ideas that way. Especially when you're nearby. Wafted by your longings, as it were, floating on your art . . .

ACTRESS. You talk like an idiot.

POET, *sorrowfully.* Some women might have said—like a poet.

ACTRESS. Now go. And don't start anything with the waitress. *The* POET *departs.*

ACTRESS *undresses. She listens to the* POET *going down the wooden stairs and then to his steps beneath the open window. As soon as she is undressed, she goes to the window, looks down, sees him standing there; she calls to him in a whisper.* Come!

The POET *comes up in a hurry; rushes to her. In the meantime she has gone to bed and put out the light. He locks the door.*

ACTRESS. Well, now you may sit down by me and tell me a story.

POET *sits by her on the bed.* Shouldn't I close the window? Aren't you cold?

ACTRESS. Oh, no.

POET. What would you like me to tell you?

ACTRESS. Tell me—who are you being unfaithful to—at this moment?

POET. But I'm not being unfaithful—at this moment.

ACTRESS. Don't worry, I'm being unfaithful too.

POET. I can imagine.

ACTRESS. And who do you think it is?

POET. My dear child, I wouldn't have a notion.

ACTRESS. Guess, then.

POET. Wait a moment . . . Well, your producer.

ACTRESS. My dear, I'm not a chorus girl.

POET. Oh, it was just an idea.

ACTRESS. Guess again.

POET. Your leading man—Benno.

ACTRESS. Pooh, that man doesn't like women, didn't you know? He's having an affair with the postman.

POET. Who would have thought it?

ACTRESS. So come and kiss me.
    The POET *embraces her.*

ACTRESS. What are you doing?

POET. Don't torture me like this!

ACTRESS. Listen, Robert, I'll make a suggestion. Get in bed with me.

POET. I accept.

ACTRESS. Quickly.

POET. Well . . . if *I'd* had my way, I'd have been . . . Listen!

ACTRESS. What?

POET. The crickets are chirping outside.

ACTRESS. You must be mad, my dear, there are no crickets in these parts.

POET. But you can hear them!

ACTRESS. Oh, come on!

POET. I'm here.
He goes to her.

ACTRESS. And now lie still . . . Uh! . . . Don't move!

POET. What's the idea?

ACTRESS. I suppose you'd like to have an affair with me?

POET. I thought you might realize that sooner or later.

ACTRESS. A lot of men would like an affair with me.

POET. But at this particular moment the odds are rather strongly in my favor.

ACTRESS. Come, my cricket. From now on I'm going to call you Cricket.

POET. Fine . . .

ACTRESS. Now—who am I deceiving?

POET. Huh? Me, maybe.

ACTRESS. My child, you should have your head examined.

POET. Or maybe someone . . . you've never seen . . . someone you don't know . . . He's meant for you, but you can never find him . . .

ACTRESS. Cricket, don't talk such fantastic rot!

POET. . . . Isn't it strange . . . even you . . . and one would have thought——But no, it would just be . . . spoiling all that's best about you if one . . . Come, come, come . . .

   ✿   ✿   ✿   ✿   ✿

ACTRESS. That's better than acting in damn silly plays. You agree?

POET. Well, I think it's as well you have a part in a reasonable play.

ACTRESS. Meaning yours, you conceited pup.

POET. Of course.

ACTRESS, *seriously.* It really is a *wonderful* play.

POET. You see!

ACTRESS. You're a genius!

POET. By the way, why did you cancel your performance two nights ago? There was nothing wrong with you.

ACTRESS. I wanted to annoy you.

POET. Why? What had I done to you?

ACTRESS. You were conceited.

POET. In what way?

ACTRESS. Everybody in the theatre says so.

POET. Really.

ACTRESS. But I told them: that man has a *right* to be conceited.

POET. And what did they say to that?

ACTRESS. What should those people say? I never speak to them.

POET. I see.

ACTRESS. They'd like to poison me.
Pause.
But they won't succeed.

POET. Don't think of them. Just be happy we're here, and tell me you love me.

ACTRESS. You need further proof?

POET. Oh, that kind of thing can't be *proved.*

ACTRESS. This is just lovely! What more do you want?

POET. How many others did you try to prove it to this way? And did you love them all?

ACTRESS. Oh, no. I loved only one.

POET *embracing her.* My . . .

ACTRESS. Fritz.

POET. My name is Robert. What am I to you, if it's Fritz you're thinking of?

ACTRESS. A whim.

POET. Nice to know!

ACTRESS. Tell me, aren't you proud?

POET. Why should I be proud?

ACTRESS. I think you have some reason.

POET. Oh, because of that!

ACTRESS. Yes, because of that, my pale cricket. How about the chirping? Are they still chirping?

POET. All the time. Can't you hear?

ACTRESS. I can hear. But that's frogs, my child.

POET. You're wrong: frogs croak.

ACTRESS. Certainly, they croak.

POET. But not here, my dear child. This is chirping.

ACTRESS. You're the most pigheaded creature I've ever come across. Kiss me, frog.

POET. Please don't call me that. It makes me nervous.

ACTRESS. What do you want me to call you?

POET. I've got a name: Robert.

ACTRESS. Oh, that's too dull.

POET. I must ask you to call me simply by my name.

ACTRESS. All right, Robert, kiss me . . . Ah!
She kisses him.
Are you content now, frog? Ha, ha, ha!

POET. May I light myself a cigarette?

ACTRESS. Give me one.

The POET *takes the cigarette case from the bedside table, takes out two, lights both and hands one to her.*

ACTRESS. By the way, you never said a word about my work last night.

POET. What work?

ACTRESS. Well . . . !

POET. Oh, I see. I wasn't at the theatre.

ACTRESS. I guess you like your little joke.

POET. Not at all. When you canceled your performance the day before yesterday, I assumed that yesterday you couldn't be in full possession of our powers. So I didn't go.

ACTRESS. You missed something.

POET. Indeed?

ACTRESS. I was sensational. People turned pale.

POET. You could see them?

ACTRESS. Benno said to me "You were a goddess, darling."

POET. Hm . . . and so sick one day earlier.

ACTRESS. Yes. And do you know why? Out of longing for you.

POET. You just told me you cancelled the performance to annoy me!

ACTRESS. What do you know of my love for you? That sort of thing leaves you cold. I was in a fever for nights on end. With a temperature of 105.

POET. A high temperature just for a whim!

ACTRESS. A whim, you call it? I die for love of you, and you call it a whim?

POET. What about Fritz?

ACTRESS. What about him? What about him? I've heard too much about that . . . that cheap crook!

9   THE ACTRESS AND THE COUNT

The ACTRESS's *bedroom, luxuriously furnished. It is noon;
the blinds are still down; on the bedside table, a burning
candle; the* ACTRESS *is lying in her fourposter. Numerous
newspapers are strewn about on the covers.*

The COUNT *enters, in the uniform of a captain of Dragoons.
He stops at the door.*

ACTRESS. It's you, Count!

COUNT. Your good mother gave me permission, or of course I
wouldn't . . .

ACTRESS. Please come right in.

COUNT. I kiss your hand. A thousand pardons—coming straight
in from the street—you know, I can't see a thing. Yes . . .
here we are.
Near the bed.
I kiss your hand.

ACTRESS. Sit down, my dear Count.

COUNT. Your mother said you weren't very well, Fräulein. Nothing too serious, I hope?

ACTRESS. Nothing serious? I was dying!

COUNT. Oh dear me! Not really?

ACTRESS. In any case it's very kind of you to . . . trouble to call.

COUNT. Dying! And only last night you played like a goddess!

ACTRESS. It was a great triumph, I believe.

COUNT. Colossal! People were absolutely knocked out. As for
myself, well . . .

ACTRESS. Thanks for the lovely flowers.

COUNT. Not at all, Fräulein.

ACTRESS, *turning her eyes towards a large basket of flowers, which stands on a small table by the window.* There they are!

COUNT. Last night you were positively *strewn* with flowers and garlands!

ACTRESS. I left them all in my dressing room. Your basket was the only thing I brought home.

COUNT *kisses her hand.* You're very kind.

The ACTRESS *suddenly takes his hand and kisses it.*

COUNT. Fräulein!

ACTRESS. Don't be afraid, Count. It commits you to nothing!

COUNT. You're a strange creature . . . a puzzle, one might almost say.

Pause.

ACTRESS. Fräulein Birken is . . . easier to solve?

COUNT. Oh, little Birken is no puzzle. Though . . . I know her only superficially.

ACTRESS. Indeed?

COUNT. Oh, believe me. But *you* are a problem. And I've always longed for one. As a matter of fact, last night I realized what a great pleasure I'd been missing. You see, it was the first time I've seen you act.

ACTRESS. Is that true?

COUNT. Oh, yes. You see, Fräulein, it's so difficult, the theatre. By the time I get there, the best part of the play'd be over, wouldn't it?

ACTRESS. You'll have to dine earlier from now on.

COUNT. I'd thought of that. Or of not dining at all. There's not much pleasure in it, is there—dining?

ACTRESS. What do you still find pleasure in, young fogey?

COUNT. I sometimes ask myself. But I'm no fogey. There must be another reason.

ACTRESS. You think so?

COUNT. Yes. For instance, Lulu always says I'm a philosopher. What he means is: I think too much.

ACTRESS. Lulu?

COUNT. Friend of mine.

ACTRESS. He's right . . . it *is* a misfortune, all that thinking.

COUNT. I've time on my hands, that's why I think. You see, Fräulein, when they transferred me to Vienna, I thought it would be better. It'd be amusing, stimulating, the city. But it's really much the same here as up there.

ACTRESS. And where is "up there"?

COUNT. Well, down there, Fräulein, in Hungary. The small towns I used to be stationed in.

ACTRESS. What were you doing in Hungary?

COUNT. I'm telling you, dear lady—the Army.

ACTRESS. But why stay in Hungary?

COUNT. It happens, that's all.

ACTRESS. Enough to drive anyone mad, I should think!

COUNT. Oh, I don't know. In a way you have more to do there than here. You know, Fräulein, training recruits, exercising horses . . . and the surroundings aren't as bad as people say. It's really rather lovely, the big plain there. Such a sunset! It's a pity I'm not a painter. I often thought I'd paint one, if I were a painter. We had a man in our regiment, young Splany, and he could do it. Why I tell you this boring stuff I don't know, Fräulein.

ACTRESS. Please, Count! I'm highly amused.

COUNT. You know, Fräulein, it's so easy to talk to you. Lulu told me it would be. It's a thing one doesn't often meet.

ACTRESS. In Hungary!

COUNT. Or in Vienna! People are the same everywhere. Where there are more, it gets overcrowded but that's the only difference. Tell me, Fräulein, do you like people, really?

ACTRESS. Like them? I hate them! I don't want to see them. I never do see them. I'm always alone. This house is deserted!

COUNT. Just as I imagined: you're a misanthropist. It's bound to happen with artists. Moving in that more exalted sphere . . . Well, it's all right for you, at least you know why you're alive.

ACTRESS. Who told you that? I haven't the remotest idea why I'm alive!

COUNT. Not really, Fräulein . . . famous . . . celebrated . . .

ACTRESS. Is that—happiness?

COUNT. Happiness? Happiness doesn't exist. None of the things people chatter about really exist. . . . Love, for instance. It's the same with love.

ACTRESS. You may be right there.

COUNT. Enjoyment . . . intoxication . . . there's nothing wrong with them, they're real. I enjoy something, all right, and I know I enjoy it. Or I'm intoxicated, all right. That's real too. And when it's over, it's over, that's all.

ACTRESS, *grandly*. It's over!

COUNT. But as soon as you don't—I don't quite know how to say it—as soon as you stop living for the present moment, as soon as you think of later on or earlier on . . . Well, the whole thing collapses. "Later on" is sad, and "earlier on" is uncertain, in short, you just get mixed up. Don't you think so?

ACTRESS *nods, her eyes very wide open*. You pluck out the heart of the mystery, my dear Count.

COUNT. And you see, Fräulein, once you're clear about that, it doesn't matter if you live in Vienna or on the Hungarian plains or in the tiny town of Steinamanger. For example . . . where can I put my cap? . . . Oh, thanks. What were we talking about?

ACTRESS. The tiny town of Steinamanger.

COUNT. Oh, yes. Well, as I was saying, there isn't much difference. Whether I spend the evening at the Casino or the Club is all one.

ACTRESS. How does this tie in with love?

COUNT. If a man believes in it, there'll always be a girl around who loves him.

ACTRESS. Fräulein Birken, for example.

COUNT. Honestly, dear lady, I can't understand why you're always mentioning little Birken.

ACTRESS. She's your mistress after all.

COUNT. Who says that?

ACTRESS. Everyone knows.

COUNT. Except me. Remarkable.

ACTRESS. But you fought a duel on her behalf!

COUNT. Possibly I was shot dead and didn't notice.

ACTRESS. Count, you *are* a man of honor. Sit a little closer.

COUNT. If I may.

ACTRESS. Here.
She draws him closer, and runs her fingers through his hair.
I knew you would come today.

COUNT. Really? Why?

ACTRESS. I knew it last night. In the theatre.

COUNT. Oh, could you see me from the stage?

ACTRESS. My dear man, didn't you realize I was playing for you alone?

COUNT. How could that be?

ACTRESS. After I saw you in the front row, I was walking on air.

COUNT. Because of me? I'd no idea you'd noticed me.

ACTRESS. Oh, you can drive a woman to despair with that dignity of yours!

COUNT. Fräulein!

ACTRESS. "Fräulein?" At least take your saber off!

COUNT. Permit me.
He unbuckles the belt, leans the saber against the bed.

ACTRESS. And now kiss me at last.
The COUNT *kisses her. She does not let him go.*

ACTRESS. I wish I had never set eyes on you.

COUNT. No, no, it's better as it is.

ACTRESS. Count, you're a *poseur.*

COUNT. I am? Why?

ACTRESS. Many a man'd be happy to be in your shoes right now.

COUNT. *I'm* happy.

ACTRESS. Oh—I thought happiness didn't exist! Why do you look at me like that? I believe you're afraid of me, Count.

COUNT. I told you, Fräulein, you're a problem.

ACTRESS. Oh, don't bother me with philosophy . . . Come here. And ask me for something. You can have whatever you like. You're too handsome.

COUNT. Well, then I beg leave
Kisses her hand.
to return tonight.

ACTRESS. Tonight? . . . But I'm playing tonight.

COUNT. After the theatre.

ACTRESS. You ask for nothing else?

COUNT. I'll ask for everything else. After the theatre.

ACTRESS, *offended.* Then you can ask, you wretched *poseur.*

COUNT. You see, Fräulein . . . you see, my dear . . . We've been frank with each other till now. I'd find it all very much nicer in the evening, after the theatre. . . . It'll be so much more comfortable. . . . At present, you see, I've the feeling the door's going to open at any moment.

ACTRESS. This door doesn't open from the outside.

COUNT. Fräulein, wouldn't it be frivolous to spoil something at the start? When it might just possibly turn out to be beautiful?

ACTRESS. "Just possibly"!

COUNT. And to tell the truth, I find love in the morning pretty frightful.

ACTRESS. You're the craziest man I've ever come across.

COUNT. I'm not talking about ordinary females. After all, in general, it doesn't matter. But women like you, Fräulein —no, you can call me a fool as often as you like, but women like you . . . Well, one shouldn't have them before breakfast, that's all. And so . . . well . . .

ACTRESS. God, you're sweet!

COUNT. Now you see I'm right, don't you? What I have in mind . . .

ACTRESS. Tell me what you have in mind.

COUNT. What I mean is . . . I'll wait for you after the theatre, in my carriage, then we can drive off somewhere, well, and have supper and . . .

ACTRESS. I am not Fräulein Birken!

COUNT. I didn't say you were, my dear. Only, one must be in the mood! I get in the mood at supper. It's lovely to drive home after supper, and then . . .

ACTRESS. And then?

COUNT. Let events take their natural course.

ACTRESS. Come closer. Closer!

COUNT *sits down on the bed.* I must say, the perfume that comes from these pillows—mignonette, is it?

ACTRESS. It's hot in here, don't you think?
The COUNT *bends down and kisses her throat.*

ACTRESS. Oh my dear Count, this isn't on your program.

COUNT. Who says so? I have no program.
The ACTRESS *draws him to her.*

COUNT. It *is* hot.

ACTRESS. You find it so? And dark, like evening . . .
Pulling him to her.

It *is* evening, Count. It's night. . . . Shut your eyes if it's too light for you. Come! Come!

The COUNT *no longer defends himself.*

❋   ❋   ❋   ❋   ❋

ACTRESS. What's that about being in the mood, you *poseur?*

COUNT. You're a little devil.

ACTRESS. Count!

COUNT. All right, a little angel.

ACTRESS. And you should have been an actor. Really! You understand women. Do you know what I'm going to do now?

COUNT. Well?

ACTRESS. I'm going to tell you I never want to see you again.

COUNT. Why?

ACTRESS. You're too dangerous for me. You turn a woman's head. And now you stand there as if nothing has happened.

COUNT. But . . .

ACTRESS. I beg you to remember, my dear Count, that I've just been your mistress.

COUNT. Can I ever forget it?

ACTRESS. So how about tonight?

COUNT. What do you mean exactly?

ACTRESS. You intended to meet me after the theatre?

COUNT. Oh, yes, all right: let's say the day after tomorrow.

ACTRESS. The day after tomorrow? We were talking of tonight.

COUNT. There wouldn't be much sense in that.

ACTRESS. Fogey!

COUNT. You misunderstand me. I mean—how should I say—from the spiritual viewpoint.

ACTRESS. It's not your spirit that interests me.

COUNT. Believe me, it's all part of it. I don't agree that the two can be kept separate.

ACTRESS. Don't talk philosophy at me. When I want that, I read books.

COUNT. But we never learn from books.

ACTRESS. That's true. And that's why you'll be there tonight. We'll come to an agreement about the spiritual viewpoint, you . . . spiritualist!

COUNT. Then—with your permission—I'll wait with my carriage.

ACTRESS. You'll wait here. In my apartment.

COUNT. . . . After the theatre.

ACTRESS. Of course.
The COUNT *buckles on his saber.*

ACTRESS. What are you doing?

COUNT. I think it's time for me to go, Fräulein. I've been staying rather long as it is, for a formal visit.

ACTRESS. Well, it won't be a formal visit tonight!

COUNT. You think not?

ACTRESS. Just leave it to me. And now give me one more kiss, little philosopher. Here, you seducer . . . you . . . sweet thing, you spiritualist, you polecat, you . . .
After several emphatic kisses she emphatically pushes him away.
My dear Count, it was a great honor.

COUNT. I kiss your hand, Fräulein.
At the door.
Au revoir!

ACTRESS. Adieu, tiny town of Steinamanger!

10 THE COUNT AND THE WHORE

*Morning, toward six o'clock. A mean little room, with one
window; the dirty yellow blinds are down; frayed green
curtains. A chest of drawers, with a few photographs on it
and a cheap lady's hat in conspicuously bad taste. Several
cheap Japanese fans behind the mirror. On the table, covered with a reddish cloth, stands a kerosene lamp, still
feebly and odorously alight, with a yellow paper lamp-
shade: next to the lamp, a jug with a little left-over beer,
and a half empty glass. On the floor by the bed, untidy
feminine clothing, apparently thrown off in a hurry.*

The WHORE *is asleep in the bed, breathing evenly. On the
sofa lies the* COUNT, *fully dressed and in a light overcoat;
his hat is on the floor by the head of the sofa.*

COUNT *moves, rubs his eyes, rises with a start and, in a sitting
position, looks round.* However did I get . . . Oh . . . So I did
go home with that female. . . .

He jumps up, sees her bed.

Why, here she is. To think what can happen to a man of
my age! I don't remember a thing—did they carry me up?
No . . . I remember seeing . . . When I got into the room, yes,
I was still awake then, or I woke up, or . . . or perhaps it's
only that the room reminds me of something? . . . Upon my
soul, yes, I saw it last night, that's all. . . .

He looks at his watch.

Last night indeed! A few hours ago. I knew something had
to happen. Yesterday when I started drinking I felt that . . .
And what happened? Nothing . . . Or did I . . . ? Upon my
soul . . . the last time I couldn't remember was ten years
ago. The thing is, I was tight. If I only knew when it
started . . . I remember exactly going into that whores'
cafe with Lulu and . . . No, no . . . First we left the Sacher
. . . and then, on the way, it started. . . . Now I've got it. I
was driving in my carriage with Lulu . . . Silly to rack my
brains. It's all one. I'll be on my way.

He rises. The lamp rocks.

Oh!

He looks at the sleeping girl.

She sleeps soundly, that one. I can't remember a thing, but
I'll put the money on her bedside table—and good-bye.
He stands and looks at her a long while.
If one didn't know what she is. . . .
He again contemplates her.
I've known quite a lot of girls who didn't look so virtuous,
even in their sleep. Upon my soul . . . now Lulu would
say I'm philosophizing, but it's true, sleep does make us
all equal, it seems to me, like his big brother—Death. . . .
Hmm, I'd like to know if . . . No, I'd remember after all . . .
No, no, I dropped down on the sofa right away . . . and
nothing happened. . . . It's incredible how women can all
look alike. . . . Let's go.
He goes to the door.
. . . Oh, there's that.
He takes out his wallet and is about to get a bill.

WHORE *wakes up.* Um . . . Who's here so early?
Recognizing him.
Hiya, son!

COUNT. Good morning. Slept well?

WHORE *stretches.* Come here. Little kiss.

COUNT *bends down, thinks better of it, pulls up short.* I was
just going . . .

WHORE. Going?

COUNT. It's time really.

WHORE. You want to go like this?

COUNT, *almost embarrassed.* Well . . .

WHORE. So long, then. Come back and see us.

COUNT. Yes. Good-bye. Don't you want to shake hands?
The WHORE *pulls her hand from under the blanket and offers
it.*

COUNT *takes her hand, mechanically kisses it, catches himself,
and laughs.* As if she were a princess! Anyway, if one
only . . .

WHORE. Why do you look at me like that?

COUNT. If one only sees the head, as now . . . when they wake up . . . they all look innocent . . . upon my soul, one really could imagine all sorts of things if the place didn't reek so of kerosene. . . .

WHORE. Yes, that lamp's a pest.

COUNT. How old are you, actually?

WHORE. Well, what do you think?

COUNT. Twenty-four.

WHORE. Oh, sure!

COUNT. Older?

WHORE. Nearly twenty.

COUNT. And how long have you been . . .

WHORE. In the business? A year.

COUNT. You did start early.

WHORE. Better too early than too late.

COUNT *sits down on her bed.* Tell me, are you happy?

WHORE. What?

COUNT. Well, I mean—how's it going? Well?

WHORE. Oh, I'm doing all right.

COUNT. I see . . . Tell me, did it ever occur to you to do something different?

WHORE. What could I do?

COUNT. Well . . . you're a pretty girl, after all, you could have a lover, for instance.

WHORE. Think I don't?

COUNT. I know—but I mean, *one,* you know: one lover—who keeps you, so you don't have to go with just any man.

WHORE. I *don't* go with just any man. I can afford to be choosy, thank goodness.
The COUNT *looks round the room.*

WHORE *notices this.* Next month we're moving into town. The Spiegel Gasse.

COUNT. We? Who?

WHORE. Oh, the madam and a couple of the other girls.

COUNT. There are others here?

WHORE. In the next room . . . can't you hear? That's Milli, she was at the café too.

COUNT. Somebody's snoring.

WHORE. That's Milli all right! She'll snore all day till ten in the evening, then she'll get up and go to the café.

COUNT. But that's an appalling sort of life!

WHORE. You said it. And the madam gets fed up with her. I'm always on the streets at twelve noon.

COUNT. What are you doing on the streets at twelve noon?

WHORE. What do you think? I'm on my beat.

COUNT. Oh, yes, I see . . . Of course . . .
He gets up, again takes out his wallet, and puts a bill on her bedside table.
Good-bye.

WHORE. Going already? . . . So long . . . Come again soon.
She turns over on her side.

COUNT *stops again.* Listen, tell me something. It doesn't mean a thing to you by now?

WHORE. What?

COUNT. I mean, you don't have fun with it any more?

WHORE *yawns.* I'm sleepy.

COUNT. It's all the same to you if a man is young or old, or if he . . .

WHORE. What are you asking all this for?

COUNT. Well . . .
Suddenly struck by a thought.

Upon my soul, now I know who you remind me of, it's . . .

WHORE. So I look like somebody, do I?

COUNT. Incredible, quite incredible—now, I beg you, please don't say a word for at least a minute. . . .
He stares at her.
exactly the same face, exactly the same face.
He suddenly kisses her on the eyes.

WHORE. Hey!

COUNT. Upon my soul, it's a pity you aren't . . . something else . . . you could make your fortune.

WHORE. You're like Franz.

COUNT. Who's Franz?

WHORE. Oh, the waiter at our café.

COUNT. How am I just like Franz?

WHORE. He always says I could make my fortune. And I should marry him.

COUNT. Why don't you?

WHORE. Thank you very much . . . I don't want no marriage, not for anything. Maybe later.

COUNT. The eyes . . . exactly the same eyes . . . Lulu'd certainly say I'm a fool—but I'm going to kiss your eyes once more like this. And now good-bye. God bless you. I'm going.

WHORE. So long.

COUNT, *turning at the door.* Listen . . . tell me . . . aren't you a little bit surprised?

WHORE. Why?

COUNT. That I want nothing from you.

WHORE. There's a lot of men don't feel like it in the morning.

COUNT. Well, yes . . .
To himself.

It's too silly that I'd like her to be surprised. . . . Good-bye, then . . .

At the door.

Really, it annoys me. I know such girls are interested in nothing but the money . . . Now why do I say "such girls"? . . . At least it's nice that she doesn't pretend, it's a relief, or should be . . . Listen, I'll come again soon, you know.

WHORE, *with closed eyes.* Good.

COUNT. When are you usually in?

WHORE. I'm always in. Just ask for Leocadia.

COUNT. Leocadia . . . Right. Well, good-bye.

At the door.

I haven't got the wine out of my head yet. Isn't it the limit . . . I spend the night with one of these . . . and all I do is to kiss her eyes because she reminds me of someone. . . .

He turns to her.

Tell me, Leocadia, does it often happen that a man goes away like this?

WHORE. Like what?

COUNT. Like me.

WHORE. In the morning?

COUNT. No . . . I mean, has it occasionally happened that a man was with you—and didn't want anything?

WHORE. No. Never!

COUNT. What's the matter? Do you think I don't like you?

WHORE. Why shouldn't you like me? Last night you liked me all right.

COUNT. I like you now too.

WHORE. Last night you liked me better.

COUNT. What makes you think so?

WHORE. Don't talk silly.

COUNT. Last night . . . Tell me, didn't I drop down on the sofa right away?

WHORE. Sure you did—with me.

COUNT. With you?

WHORE. Sure—you don't remember?

COUNT. I . . . we . . . well . . .

WHORE. But you went right off to sleep after.

COUNT. I went right off . . . I see . . . So that's how it was!

WHORE. Yes, son. You must've been good and drunk if you can't remember.

COUNT. I see . . . All the same, there *is* a faint resemblance . . . Good-bye . . .
He listens.
What's the matter?

WHORE. The chambermaid's started work. Look, give her something as you go out. The front door's open, so you save on the janitor.

COUNT. Right.
In the entrance hall.
So . . . it would have been beautiful if I'd only kissed her eyes. It would almost have been an adventure. . . . Well, I suppose it wasn't to be!
The Chambermaid stands by the door and opens it for him.
Oh . . . here . . . Good-night!

CHAMBERMAID. Good morning!

COUNT. Oh, of course . . . Good morning . . . Good morning!

THE UNDERPANTS

A Middle-Class Comedy
by

CARL STERNHEIM

English version by
Eric Bentley

Characters

THEOBALD MASKE
a petty official

LUISE MASKE
his wife

GERTRUD DEUTER
a neighbor

FRANK SCARRON
a writer

BENJAMIN MANDELSTAM
a barber

A STRANGER

THE TIME: *About* 1910.
THE PLACE: *Germany. Maske's living room.*

A Note on the Style: The German original is deliberately bizarre. Few of the oddities have any exact English equivalent: Any *traduttore* becomes a *traditore* by sheer necessity. All I can plead in self-defense is that I have tried to steer a middle course between the over-literal and the over-free. For while a literal rendering would be grotesque to the point of unreadability, to rewrite Sternheimian rococo into the standard colloquial English of 1959 would be evading the issue. One would earn the praises of those who value fluency—but not of those who value Carl Sternheim.

E. B.

ACT ONE

Enter THEOBALD *and* LUISE.

THEOBALD. I'll go clear out of my mind!

LUISE. Put the stick down.

THEOBALD, *beating her.* Disgraced! The whole neighborhood prattling about it! "Frau Maske's lost her underpants!"

LUISE. Ow! Ouch!

THEOBALD. In the open street. The Kaiser himself might have seen it. And me just a petty official.

LUISE, *screaming.* That's enough!

THEOBALD. Can't you tie your ribbons and button your buttons before you leave home? Your inner life's nothing but dreams and fantasies and excesses, your outer life is lasciviousness and irresponsibility.

LUISE. I tied a good hard double knot.

THEOBALD, *bursting out laughing.* A good hard double knot. What low-down sort of chatter is that? A good hard——all right, *there's* a good hard double smack on the ear! The consequences! Think of the consequences! But I don't dare. Dishonored! Run out of the service, out of my job . . .

LUISE. Oh, cool off.

THEOBALD. I'm furious.

LUISE. You're innocent.

THEOBALD. Guilty! Guilty of having a wife that's a slattern, a trollop, a moon-gazer.

Beside himself.

Where is the world?

He takes her head and beats it on the table.

Down here in the pots and pans! Down on the dusty floor of your room! Not in the sky! Do you hear me? Is this chair unbesmirched? No. Dirt! Has this cup a handle? I touch the world. It breaks open! There are holes in it! Holes in this life of ours! Appalling! Think of that, woman. Auspicious fate gave me a position that brings in 700 thaler.

Shouts.

700 thaler! Enough for a couple of rooms, decent food, to buy clothes, provide heat in winter. We can manage a ticket to the theatre. Good health spares us doctors and druggists. Heaven smiles on our existence. That's where you come in with *your* way of doing things and utterly destroy a life the gods have blessed. Why no heat yet? Why is this door open, that one shut? Why not the other way round? Why isn't the clock going?

He winds it up.

Why do the pots and pans leak? Where is my hat, where has an important document got to, and how can your pants fall down in the open street? How could they?

LUISE. You knew me as a young girl.

THEOBALD. So?

LUISE. And you liked me to be dreaming.

THEOBALD. What else should a young girl do with her time? That's what she's made for. Reality's something she should keep away from. But now you've bumped into it. The dream is over!

LUISE. Yes.

THEOBALD. Look how deeply moved I am, Luise.

LUISE. Oh, I quite believe you, husband.

THEOBALD. In the open street.

LUISE. I still can't understand it.

THEOBALD. Laughter and grimaces! Street urchins! Young bucks! I shall go clear out of my mind.

LUISE. There you go again.

THEOBALD. My heart froze inside me. I am averse to anything sensational—you know that. Do I permit you a hat, a dress in the latest fashion? You have to dress to disadvantage, and why? Because your attractive face is *too* attractive for my modest place in the world. Your eyes, your bosom are too great a challenge. If I could only get you to see that every scandal is caused by the failure of two factors—which should combine in a single phenomenon—to, um, combine.

LUISE. Oh, stop it. I've had as much as I can take.

THEOBALD, *loudly*. Two factors which should combine in a single phenomenon—my position and your appearance—have failed to combine.

LUISE. I can't do anything about that. God made me this way.

THEOBALD. It isn't God's fault. It's the fault of a shameless education that takes a girl's hair and makes it wave, that takes a girl's bosom, which would otherwise be harmless, and pushes it out through her bodice. A plague on match-making mothers!

LUISE. Mother was a very respectable person.

THEOBALD. And if I lose my job?

LUISE. Why should you?

THEOBALD. And the Kaiser riding by, as they say? God in heaven!

LUISE. Theobald!

THEOBALD. One quiver of his eyebrows, and I'm finished. I'd sink into the dust, never to rise again. Misery, shame, hunger would bring me down in sorrow to the grave.

LUISE. You're torturing me.

THEOBALD, *his head in his hands*. Oh, oh, oh!

LUISE, *after a pause*. Would a leg of mutton and string beans be all right?

THEOBALD. On the open street! How lucky we have no children yet. To have this hanging over them!

LUISE. I thought of fixing some raspberries.

THEOBALD. And His Majesty!

LUISE. Father says he's sending some more wine.

THEOBALD. How many bottles?

LUISE. A case.

THEOBALD. Have we any left?

LUISE. Five bottles.

THEOBALD. Hm. Leg of mutton. And just the right amount of salt . . . Woman, demons are forever at work in our souls.

If we don't exert the full force of our will and get the better of them—impossible to tell how far they will go with us . . . Raspberries. With cream. But where will you get the cream at such short notice?

LUISE. Fräulein Deuter will let me have some.

THEOBALD. Think so?—Women and clothes, tsk, tsk, tsk . . .

He sits in an armchair at the window and takes the newspaper. LUISE *is busy at the fireplace.*

Another thing. They say that sea serpent has turned up again—in the Indian Ocean.

LUISE. Gracious heavens above, is it possible?

THEOBALD. It's in the *News.*

LUISE. Tsk, tsk.

THEOBALD. Thank God there are few living things in that part of the world. Few or none.

LUISE. What does such a beast live off?

THEOBALD. Well, the experts disagree. It must be horrible to look at. I prefer places where one's safety is provided for. Like our town. One should restrict oneself to what is one's own, and hold it fast, though the price be unceasing vigilance. What have I in common with this serpent? What can it do to me but excite my imagination? And what's the good of that?

He rises.

If one has one's little apartment, everything in it is familiar. One put it together piece by piece. One came to value it all, to cherish it. Does one have to fear that the bird will burst out of its cage and go for the dog? That the clock will spit fire? No. It strikes seven as it has done for three thousand years whenever it was seven. I call this Order. One likes it. One even *is* it.

LUISE. Surely.

THEOBALD. To ruin a holiday for me with such excitement! Pray that we keep what we have. And see to the roast. I must be off again now to hear the latest gossip about this confounded incident.

LUISE. Are you all right again now?

THEOBALD. The good Lord has put me in mind how fortunate we've been up to now. And remember, the tulips need watering. Pray, Luise!

He disappears through the hall door and down the steps.

LUISE *has followed him onto the landing and looked after him.* Neighbor!

FRÄULEIN DEUTER, *from below*. Is that you, Frau Maske? Good morning.

LUISE. Did you hear about my accident?

DEUTER *appears above*. It couldn't have been much.

LUISE. Will you come in for a moment?

DEUTER. I'll take the liberty.

LUISE *comes back with* FRÄULEIN DEUTER.

From what Frau Kiesewetter says, they were pure linen and looked very nice and quite reputable.

LUISE. Yes—

DEUTER. But you'd sewn on your initials in red, and they're doing them in white these days. Still, only a couple of people even saw it, because the Kaiser was driving by, and everyone was looking at him. Is it true the ribbon broke?

LUISE. When I was straining to see the coachman.

DEUTER *laughs*.

LUISE. What a thing to happen! There was this white hem peeping out from under my skirt. I didn't dare move an inch.

DEUTER. Your dear husband's beside himself?

LUISE. Right off his rocker. The old song and dance about woman's lasciviousness.

DEUTER. They say you looked charming.

LUISE. Who said that?

DEUTER. Frau Kiesewetter. I suppose a few gentlemen turned their heads and were duly astonished.

LUISE. I acquitted myself honorably. One careful pace forward, and I was clear of them. I bent down, and in the twinkling of an eye they were under my shawl.

DEUTER. Of course, by tomorrow they'll be saying the whole thing was a well-planned piece of coquetry.

LUISE. Evil tongues!

DEUTER. But a woman with your looks can just laugh at them.

LUISE. My husband would rather die than hear such gossip.

DEUTER. There are things your husband will have to get used to.

LUISE. Why, Fräulein Deuter?

DEUTER. The sun shines, and mankind wants to take a walk.

LUISE. What?

DEUTER. Dear good little Frau Maske, your husband is someone I simply can't abide.

LUISE. My beloved Theobald!

DEUTER. Oh dear!

LUISE. I mean it.

DEUTER. Oh, all right.

LUISE. Fräulein Deuter, do you think you could spare a little jug of cream?

DEUTER. For you, anything. Isn't your first wedding anniversary coming up this week?

LUISE. The day after tomorrow.

DEUTER. And no sign of life? No little one on the way?

LUISE. Oh . . .

DEUTER. Can that be accidental? From what I know of Herr Theobald . . .

LUISE. Now you be quiet.

DEUTER. I'll get you the cream.

Exit DEUTER. *After a moment* SCARRON *comes very quickly up the stairs.* LUISE, *who had stayed on the landing, cries out.*

SCARRON. Did I frighten you? Do you know me?

LUISE. Who are you looking for?

SCARRON. I'm at the right apartment.

LUISE. This is the house of——

SCARRON. Yes, and who else?

LUISE. My husband will be back at any moment.

SCARRON. Before he comes we must have said everything.

LUISE. Sir!

SCARRON. May I speak in metaphors, lady? Risk a big statement without further circumlocution? No. Forgive me. I got far too excited, too little master of a soul which even now was mine but which at this moment is dancing along the hallway.

LUISE. Someone's coming. They mustn't see us together.

SCARRON *disappears up the stairs.*

DEUTER *comes in with a jug.* There! Your clothes—above all your underwear—count for a great deal. At the same time, a lot can be done with a ribbon, a little bow. Oh, I could show you things. It's not always a matter of clothes when we find favor. You have lovely eyes. So long though, we'll talk another time. Today we'd better not let ourselves be caught at it, little coquette.

She runs laughing back down the stairs. Enter SCARRON.

LUISE. You have a wish?

SCARRON. Lady, if you want to know, I have a pretext.

LUISE. Make it short.

SCARRON. This morning, on the main avenue of the Tiergarten——

LUISE. Oh Heaven!

SCARRON. Rapture came rushing through all my limbs. A young lady——

LUISE *turns away.*

SCARRON. I believe in miracles. For months I have dashed through the streets in a frenzy—in search of miracles. I have turned a hundred street corners, flashed round them, expecting to find a miracle. And now I've found one. Under a linden tree. Bound by untoward circumstance to that bright green trunk, bathed in sunshine, a helpless, brown body beneath bewildered eyes. Amid the foolish, greedy crowd, an enchanting martyrdom. O dazzling jest of God! I quivered, I positively twitched, with life! What I suffered in the three seconds before you reached down, took from me what till then I thought I loved and brought me, lady, to the very threshold of you. I haven't yet learned to speak your lan-

guage. The something that is between us till now is but a
movement of the blood. When are you going to tell me what
the words are that do you good—so that I can speak them?

LUISE *makes a gesture.*

SCARRON. I know: you cannot admit such breathless emotion
into your life till it is licensed by considerable further acquaintance. Permit me a moment of silent worship.

A moment of silence. SCARRON *sits with his eyes closed.*

LUISE. Sir!

SCARRON. You don't know who I am?

LUISE. I think I've seen you.

SCARRON. When?

LUISE. This morning.

SCARRON. When else? Only then?

LUISE. Only then. The places you prefer I am a stranger to.
My life is lived within these four walls.

SCARRON *walks right up to her.* LUISE *retreats.*

SCARRON. Hear one man's fate.

LUISE. I'm afraid to.

SCARRON. From today, I shall desire you with all the strength
of my soul: it is such bliss to say so that I do not even ask
your opinion—whether you'd like to send me to the devil or,
alternatively, invite me back.

LUISE. The gall of the man! Stand up.

SCARRON. I am so full of conviction, even my limbs express
certitude. They refuse to stand up. Kill me, lady. But let
me remain kneeling.

LUISE. For Heaven's sake. What if my husband comes in?

SCARRON. Brown. They're chestnut brown. I'll take the two
rooms announced for rent in your window. You glow like a
chestnut in charcoal. Let us take it as settled. The discussion
is over.

LUISE. A gentleman of such distinction—at our place? Who
would believe it?

SCARRON. Once out of doors again, I promise never to return
except in the attire of the simplest citizen.

LUISE. You stir me to the depths.

SCARRON. As you do me—to depths below depths.

LUISE. Renting those rooms.

SCARRON. If I should wish . . .

LUISE. What if he comes in?

SCARRON. Just introduce me.

LUISE. As who?

SCARRON. Herr Scarron. Between the first sound of his key in
the lock and his actual entrance there are seconds in which
to rise.

LUISE. You at our place!

SCARRON. Where?

LUISE. Bedroom and living room, O God.

SCARRON. Simply, "O God." That is everything. Why do you
tremble?

LUISE. No!

SCARRON. I am a church bell. My clapper hangs limply down.
But just strike me, and I'll sound all the fine sounds you
have in your throat! Enough. I'm going. When shall I return?

LUISE. He's bound to be back soon.

SCARRON. You'll expect me then?

LUISE *is silent*.

SCARRON. You'll expect me then?

LUISE. Yes.

> *They stand before the ladder.* SCARRON *rushes out.* LUISE
> *climbs the ladder as in a dream, stays at the top for a mo-
> ment. Enter* DEUTER.

DEUTER. The door open? Heavens, what are you doing up there
in the sky?

LUISE. The curtains . . .

DEUTER. You couldn't reach the curtains if your arms were
twice as long. Besides, you'll be losing your——No, I'm joking. But that ribbon is hanging, so you're bound to fall over
it when you get down. You are certainly a supersensual
person, I've known it quite a while.

LUISE. Oh, stop scoffing.

DEUTER. Who's the lucky man, little woman? Or rather god among men? You've known a long time I'm not the sort of neighbor that murders reputations. Shall I tell you right out what I want from you?

LUISE. Help me down.

DEUTER. Stay where you are: the position is good for the purpose. I am full of the lust for life, but my face isn't right for it, I know. You, on the other hand, are blessed with such an appearance, I would count it the fullest satisfaction of my desires could I but see or hear at close quarters whatever satisfaction life brings to you.

LUISE. I don't understand.

DEUTER. Do you like me?

LUISE. Certainly.

DEUTER. You instinctively know I'll stand by you forever?

LUISE. You won't do me any harm.

DEUTER. What was he after?

LUISE. Just imagine!

DEUTER. A nobleman! I'd give ten years of my life. What excuse did he have?

LUISE. Oh, he had a real reason. He saw me this morning.

DEUTER. In all your glory?

LUISE. That's right.

DEUTER. What a treat! Oh, you bring joy to many. I suppose he rose to the bait like a tiger?

LUISE. He was quite impetuous.

DEUTER. He shook at the tree of the world and overpowered you!

LUISE. He's renting the rooms from us.

DEUTER. Marvelous! You'll go far, I see that.

LUISE. Catch me.

She jumps down.

DEUTER, *kissing her.* I'll deck you out in a special style. On top you'll still be the old Cinderella—for Herr Theobald. But underneath you'll be a white dream with a pair of brightly colored ruffles he'll never forget—a red one at the knee as a barrier. Now listen. Six meters of fine batiste will make six pairs of pants. I'll borrow a pattern, neat as a new pin, we'll leave no stone unturned. Four meters of fine bobbin lace for the petticoats.

LUISE. What are you dreaming of? I'm an honest wife.

DEUTER. But he's a hero, a stormer of barricades!

LUISE. Oh! You're a regular procuress!

DEUTER. I agree. There are no better jobs available when you're out there with your back to the wall.

LUISE. But what nonsense it all is! You know very well my husband will wring his neck the first time he gives me a look.

DEUTER. O simplicity! A husband can have a dozen eyes, and his wife can just fill them with sand, if she really wants to.

LUISE. Let's drop this.

DEUTER. Too late. In the gray twilight of your domesticity romance sits at the window looking out. The master of the house has had a year at his disposal. Why hasn't he made use of it, and filled your veins with his masculine might? Why aren't you running around twice your normal size and listening to little sounds within? Where is God's blessing on this marriage?

LUISE. We were cheated of it. A child would be beyond our means.

DEUTER. In view of this dereliction of sacred duty a judge has arisen—in you.

LUISE. I came within a hair's breadth of standing before you this day a virgin. It isn't his fault if I'm not.

DEUTER. Barbarian!

LUISE. "On 700 a year?" he says every day.

DEUTER. Lift up your eyes to the throne of grace! Man is entitled to his happiness, so one may help him to it with a quiet heart. Put your hand in mine.

LUISE. Heaven knows, we see eye to eye.

DEUTER. Hoho! Your lord and husband will have to be quite a fellow to change things now.

LUISE. For Heaven's sake, the mutton!

DEUTER. Who?

LUISE. For lunch, I mean.

DEUTER. *You're* having mutton too?

LUISE. I *was* having mutton. I forgot it, talking.

DEUTER. Wait a minute. Suppose *my* mutton strays into *your* oven. Then there's beans. Shall I attend to it?

LUISE. How good you are! What about yourself?

DEUTER. A fried egg will do me. Be right back.

Runs off. LUISE *goes to the window, takes down the Room For Rent board, makes a fire in the grate while humming:* "Früh wann die Hähne krähn."[1] *Then she goes to the mirror and looks at herself, then back to the grate, humming on.* DEUTER *comes back with the pan.*

On the fire, quick. It's almost ready. Add one touch of butter and a pinch of salt.

LUISE. What do I owe you?

DEUTER. Listen. I've often wanted to tell you. Your husband is a machine. If you get in his way you'll be run over. But since, like all steam rollers, he always announces his coming, it's easy to get out of his way. Just to make sure of things, though, I'm offering my services as a signalman, flag in hand. If you want me to hold your husband up, I hold up my flag. In the meanwhile you have time to clear the tracks.

LUISE. The soul is free, I can feel mine stirring within me, and you have talked away my every reservation. No bonds for me, no bridle, no servitude, no upraised finger! Forward to freedom! You help me.

DEUTER. Only if you take what I say to heart, happy little fool. Let your sovereign reason take charge of the abundant opportunities provided by your husband's absence between nine and three. In his hours of leisure, just do your duty. And nothing can go wrong. Your nobleman will have to have his supposed working hours precisely when your hus-

[1] From *The Forsaken Maiden,* words by Mörike, music by Hugo Wolf. C. F. Manney's translation reads: "When crows the cock at morn/ Ere the starbeams dwindle/ Must I arise, forlorn/ Hearthfire to kindle."

band sleeps. In this way you keep them from meeting and avoid embarrassments. That's enough for now. Shall I do the shopping?

LUISE. But bring roses instead of violets, and make it eight meters instead of six.

DEUTER. Theobald will have to be a Cyclops to escape his fate, a veritable giant. What else have you in your heart?

LUISE. Don't judge me.

DEUTER. I wouldn't know how. For me there were always just wishes. For every old unfulfilled wish, two new ones.

LUISE. It's as if a great weight had fallen off my shoulders.

DEUTER. It's as if one were a child again.

LUISE. And nothing had happened yet . . .

DEUTER. As if the young girl were to come . . .

LUISE. And dream . . .

DEUTER. And long . . .

LUISE. And, O miracle! Give . . .

They take each other's hands and dance in a ring, singing: Ring Around a Rosy.[2] *While they're still laughing,* DEUTER *runs out.*

Quick! Raspberries, come forth! What did he say his name was? Two spoonfuls of sugar. What a world he brings with him! I see an image: a woman, in a veil, lying there below, he is bending over her, she is stretching out her foot. . . . Father must give me a pair of shoes. Well, now to lay the table, it's past three o'clock.

She laughs.

THEOBALD, *entering with* MANDELSTAM. Now what's this monkey business with the furnished-room ad in the window?

LUISE. As soon as you approve, the rooms are rented.

THEOBALD. Oho!

To MANDELSTAM.

[2] The German verses could be given this approximate rendering:
Round and round again
Go the children twain
Dancing under the elderbush.
What are they doing? Hush, hush, hush.

What do you say? Oh, don't worry, you have my promise. But the situation *is* critical.

To LUISE.

For how much?

LUISE. Fifteen thaler.

THEOBALD. Inclusive?

LUISE. Exclusive.

THEOBALD, *to* MANDELSTAM. Think of that: fifteen thaler exclusive.

MANDELSTAM. I don't understand.

THEOBALD. Exclusive of coffee. Isn't it enough to make your hair stand on end? If only I hadn't set foot out of doors!

To MANDELSTAM.

Greed of gold is not in my nature, the lodger as a human being weighs equally in the scales, but—are you a barber, Herr—

MANDELSTAM. Mandelstam.

THEOBALD. Semitic?

MANDELSTAM. No, no.

THEOBALD. Would you turn toward the light?

MANDELSTAM. Stam. With one M.

THEOBALD. German, myself. I make no noise about this Jewish thing. It's best to keep the Red Sea between them and me, that's all.

MANDELSTAM. Just what *I* think.

THEOBALD *presses his hand.* Good for you. Now to business. You were prepared to pay five thaler for the smaller room?

MANDELSTAM. With coffee.

THEOBALD. But now there's someone who could use both rooms for fifteen thaler. Let me put it this way: I am Herr Mandelstam and put the question to you, Herr Maske. In your own interest and that of your family, what will you, what can you do?

MANDELSTAM. Your calculations favor the other fellow. But you approved me, and I'm counting on you as a man of your word. To be disappointed in such a matter would be more than a young man like me could bear.

THEOBALD. What are you thinking of? Could the nation that produced Friedrich Schiller produce an apostate?

MANDELSTAM. You like Schiller?

THEOBALD. I make no claim to be a literary expert of course.

MANDELSTAM. Wagner, not Schiller, is the man of our time.

THEOBALD. To remove all possible doubt, I too should like to name a name: Martin Luther.

MANDELSTAM. Very good.

LUISE. Can I serve now?

THEOBALD. May I invite you to a bite of lunch?

MANDELSTAM. I'll take the liberty.

They sit.

THEOBALD. Give me your hand. Well, you look like a fine fellow to me, quite innocent of the trouble you're causing.

MANDELSTAM. I lost my parents at an early age. I live from the work of my hands.

THEOBALD. And that keeps you going?

MANDELSTAM. Three years with the same employer.

THEOBALD. Very good.

MANDELSTAM. In the evenings every penny I've saved goes for Wagner. I've seen *Lohengrin* three times.

THEOBALD. Good God!

MANDELSTAM. A seventh heaven of delight.

THEOBALD. One must also take walks. Stretch one's legs. Health, health . . .

MANDELSTAM. Oh, certainly. Health . . .

THEOBALD. What's this, what's this? Let me have some more beans. Now speak right out.

MANDELSTAM. Oh, I'm sure you can guess the rest. Not that I can have any very specific trouble.

THEOBALD. But?

MANDELSTAM. My mother was always delicate. Undernourished too. My father used to drink a bit more than he could stand.

THEOBALD. The devil!

MANDELSTAM. If I'd brought a completely healthy body into the world, believe me, I should have made other plans for myself.

THEOBALD. Hear that, Luise?

LUISE. Yes.

THEOBALD. Oh yes, health and strength come first. Feel this thigh. The biceps.

MANDELSTAM. Gigantic.

THEOBALD. Life is my horse, young man: I ride it with those biceps. I can lift a hundredweight. I can pick you up with one arm and wave you in the air. If my muscles rub up against someone, oh, he knows it, he knows it! You need feeding and caring for, young fellow. What do you say to boarding with us?

MANDELSTAM. If it isn't beyond my means, I should be glad to.

THEOBALD. What do you think, Luise? Do you feel no emotion? How much must we ask?

LUISE. That is no matter to settle all in a moment.

THEOBALD. Not a word from me, my boy: this is woman's sphere! Talk it over with her, I won't put a spoke in the wheel.

To Luise.

Bring me a cigar to celebrate with, Luise.

LUISE. You were going to bring some home. There are none left.

THEOBALD. All the commotion drove it from my mind. I'll run over and get some. Can the other lodger be relied on to rest content with one fine big room?

LUISE. He's coming by at quarter past three. Talk with him.

THEOBALD. If it's for a period of time one might buy a screen and, so to say, make two rooms out of one. Much could also be done with a curtain. But if he won't?

MANDELSTAM. I have your word.

THEOBALD. By heaven, you'll have your room, O Aryan Mandelstam! I'll be right back.

Exit. A moment of silence.

MANDELSTAM. Pardon me . . .

LUISE. I wonder you don't want to see the room. It seems to mean a lot to you, to live in this particular house. Do you work for Lämmerhirt across the way?

MANDELSTAM. No. I work on the Linden Strasse.

LUISE. That's fifteen minutes' walk from here. Strange. Wouldn't you be smarter to——

MANDELSTAM. I have my reasons.

LUISE. Are you nearsighted? You look at me so.

MANDELSTAM. Oh, Frau Maske!

LUISE. What's the matter with you? You're blushing all over!

MANDELSTAM. Harbor no unjust thoughts about me! Don't find me strange, even!

LUISE. Oh, your secrets don't bother me.

MANDELSTAM. Since this morning I have only one secret. Salvation to be relieved of it!

LUISE. Then confide in my husband.

MANDELSTAM. The last man in the world! I'd forfeit his sympathy forever. It carries no stigma, and concerns, not me, but you . . . yes, you more than anyone else in the world.

LUISE. Me? What do you mean, me?

She has stood up.

MANDELSTAM, *getting up.* Pardon me.

LUISE. Speak.

MANDELSTAM. It wasn't my fault, but . . .

LUISE. Please!

MANDELSTAM. I've never been in a position like this in all my life. Yes, yes, I'll tell you. Your underpants——

LUISE. What?!

MANDELSTAM. This morning—your——

LUISE. Silence!

THEOBALD, *returning.* The decision?

LUISE. I want to talk it over with you.

THEOBALD. Fine.

To MANDELSTAM.

For now, you're in. Would you like a cigar?

MANDELSTAM. I don't smoke.

THEOBALD. Only one lung left? Have you taken a good look
at my chest? Abundant room in it for everything neatly side
by side. Come over here. Stand in front of me. Arms out
sideways. Trunk backwards bend! Slowly. Lower. Just listen. We'll have to have a very serious talk about this.

MANDELSTAM. I'm exhausted.

THEOBALD. Spitting and snorting like a bellows. But, but——

The bell rings. THEOBALD *goes to the door.*

LUISE, *quickly, to* MANDELSTAM. It was an unworthy action,
to come here.

MANDELSTAM. Don't scold.

LUISE. Get out!

SCARRON *enters.* I had the honor of stating my business to
the lady.

THEOBALD. My wife informed me that you need two rooms.
But, knowing nothing of your offer, I gave the smaller room
here to Herr Mandelstam, who in any case comes of a good
German family.

SCARRON. Oh!

LUISE. Herr Mandelstam was just saying, though——

MANDELSTAM. No. No, I've decided to stay.

THEOBALD. Yes, we know.

To SCARRON.

There is a very distinct possibility of your being satisfied
with the fine big room that is left. Six and a half meters by
five! Wouldn't you like to take a good look at it and let us
know your well-considered opinion?

He leads him to the door and into the room.

LUISE, *to* MANDELSTAM. Your conduct is unworthy. I shall have
to tell my husband.

MANDELSTAM. And of course I can't stop you. Still, I request
you not to, or I'll have to ask Herr Maske the following

question: "What can have caused the noble Herr Scarron
to seek lodgings in a house like this except——"

LUISE. You know him?

MANDELSTAM. I had the honor of dyeing his hair. Twice.

LUISE. That's just libel!

MANDELSTAM. He certainly wouldn't remember a thing like
that, but as for me, I know all about him.

LUISE. What causes *you* to do all this?

MANDELSTAM. This morning I was rereading *The Flying
Dutchman*. You remember Senta, the heroine? You are a
dreamer like her, Frau Maske. I was still reading when I
saw you coming with your husband. I sat there, and you
passed by, not six feet in front of me. All of a sudden——

LUISE. Only six feet! Infuriating! Anyway, your behavior is no
concern of mine. I utterly despise you—that is all.

THEOBALD *and* SCARRON *come back.*

THEOBALD. Herr Scarron agrees. He values the room's good
points and will pay twelve thaler. Further, he doesn't expect to use the room for more than a few hours daily.

SCARRON. Yes, indeed.

THEOBALD. For certain important writing assignments which
he cannot complete in all the hubbub of the street where he
lives.

SCARRON. No, indeed.

THEOBALD. I was able to assure him we would do everything
to make his stay with us a pleasant one. My wife, worthy
sir, has the capability, tenderness, and complaisance that
you'd expect of a girl from one of the best middle-class
families. Living in all the certitude of a fine heritage, we
may on occasion give way to pride. At the same time we
would not shrink—especially my wife would not—from the
performance of a kindness.

SCARRON. I'm very, very glad. Yes, indeed.

THEOBALD. To touch, finally, on this question of next-door
neighbors: Herr Mandelstam, who in any case comes of a
good German family, as I think I told you, is out of the
house all day at business. So we can share our attention

between you, giving it without stint during the day to Herr Scarron, and the rest of the time to Herr Mandelstam. Then too: on this side there's an alcove that's lit by a window in our bedroom wall. Whatever Herr Scarron cannot get into his room he can keep there. We'll hang a curtain so you'll know we can't see! The conveniences, gentlemen, are half-way up the stairs. Now, I'm sure, everything must be in beautiful shape. I will forthwith give you your keys—one to the house, one to the apartment—and all is set for you to regard the place as at all times your own. Just for form's sake, I must ask you, Herr Scarron, if the work you'll be doing here would in any way tend to overthrow the government by force? Is it in any way subversive? I am a civil servant.

SCARRON. In no way, sir. You have my word of honor.

THEOBALD. I accept it. I feel it—man to man. For you, as for every German, the word "honor" still has a wealth of meaning.

MANDELSTAM. Till tomorrow morning then.

THEOBALD, *to* SCARRON. The lease is for one year.

SCARRON. Agreed.

THEOBALD. Till tomorrow.

SCARRON, *bowing*. Frau Maske!

THEOBALD. Till tomorrow.

SCARRON *and* MANDELSTAM *leave.*

LUISE. The barber is an unpleasant boor.

THEOBALD. Because he doesn't reek of perfume like the other one?

LUISE. He will bring his sickness into this house and a thousand kinds of uncleanliness!

THEOBALD. I wouldn't say he had any special sickness. He's shiftless, delicate, no marrow, no spunk, if you ask me. From living in hostelries with sufferers from malnutrition. But we'll soon fix that. For the rest, my dear Luise, you keep quiet these next few days, and cut out the tongue work, or I'll whack you so hard on your backside, you won't be able to speak for weeks. Be thankful if the mess you made of things today seems to be without consequences.

It's to be hoped that you fully realize how utterly happy
your life is. What inherited good health means must have
become faintly apparent to you if you took half a look at
that miserable, hollow-cheeked figure of a barber. But for
that matter if you will look the other fellow in the eye, well
combed, immaculately dressed as he is, you can hardly fail
to notice that behind a pretended assurance he only half
conceals a will that has been thoroughly undermined. Believe me, my own, what I said about conscience and honor
revealed in him a man of no convictions. Even so he signed
a lease for a year.

LUISE *breaks out in sobs.*

THEOBALD, *with a loud laugh.* That's choice! We talk of this
funny fellow, and you cry? What's the connection?

He fondles her.

Shall I knock him down for you, you silly thing? Laugh!
These two inferior specimens of masculinity that God has
sent into our house have really put me in a good humor
again. Wasn't he a scream when he stood there saying:
"Frau Maske!"? To my Luise, that loses her underpants!

LUISE *sobs more violently.*

THEOBALD. "Yes, indeed! Yes, indeed! Yes, indeed!" He's a
parrot!

He is shaking with laughter.

And in the other corner, that soapsuds angel gasping for
air! Anyone who wouldn't die laughing at all this simply
doesn't know delicious humor when he sees it!

ACT TWO

THEOBALD, *coming out of the alcove.* So that's that: the curtain is up.

MANDELSTAM, *at the coffee table.* Why didn't you hang it on your side?

THEOBALD. To convince him that no one wants to pry.

MANDELSTAM. If he's of the same school of thought, well and good.

THEOBALD. His short answers to me—his reticence—suggest that he is.

MANDELSTAM. Just his pride in his higher station.

THEOBALD. And *that* brought him here? A quiet workroom could also be found in better-class homes.

MANDELSTAM. What does the man do, actually?

THEOBALD. You avoid calling him by name. To hear him talk, I conclude it's an experience—of the heart . . .

MANDELSTAM. An adventure.

THEOBALD. He called it an experience. You have an unhappy habit of substituting one word for another. It's an intimate experience that he wants to put in writing.

MANDELSTAM. I see. An experience.

THEOBALD. But if you say it that way, you'll get off the track again.

MANDELSTAM. You are very precise.

THEOBALD. It follows. Inexactitude is a detour. From nine in the morning till three in the afternoon I handle official documents. Can I permit myself inexactitude?

MANDELSTAM. Well, a man talks without thinking. I have to entertain my clients as I take the razor to them. Make sure they don't notice when I cut them or slice off the wrong piece of beard. No time for thought. Words are what I need. Any words—just so there's no interruption.

THEOBALD. So you're the victim of your profession!

He laughs.

MANDELSTAM. An experience! Probably a love story.

THEOBALD. Possibly. Do you have to be at work before eight on Saturdays?

MANDELSTAM. Have to be? I choose not to be. The boss himself comes no earlier. The apprentice can shave the riffraff that come before that.

THEOBALD. Hm. Then at least you take an early morning walk. If I were as uncertain of my health as you, I would build up my strength by all possible means.

MANDELSTAM. A lot of walking wears me out.

THEOBALD. At first. I should like you to see your present condition with complete clarity.

MANDELSTAM. Why?

THEOBALD. So that you know where you stand.

MANDELSTAM. If adequate measures are beyond my means, what can the truth do for me?

THEOBALD. A thousand devils, man, what good are lies?

MANDELSTAM. Well, after all, my God, it's all lies—everything.

THEOBALD. You are a card. Ho, ho, ho! A pessimist. Lies? Just lies, eh?

MANDELSTAM. Don't laugh. I'll give you the evidence.

THEOBALD, *laughing.* Fine. Where?

MANDELSTAM. Wherever you like. Everywhere. Everybody.

THEOBALD, *laughing.* Yourself included?

MANDELSTAM, *in a state.* Certainly.

THEOBALD. Herr Scarron?

MANDELSTAM. Him too.

THEOBALD. My wife?

MANDELSTAM. Definitely.

THEOBALD. I myself?

MANDELSTAM. Assuredly.

THEOBALD, *roaring.* You're a fighting cock! A living miracle, and well worth the money! You're no barber! You're a baron in disguise. Sneaking in here to be my wife's lover.

MANDELSTAM, *snorting with rage.* Herr Maske!

THEOBALD. A human bombshell! With intestines like powder kegs!

LUISE *comes out of the bedroom.*

Luise, leave the odors of your middle-class background behind you. Mandelstam is a baron. Your lover. Ho, ho, ho! And the world is all lies. Basta.

MANDELSTAM. At this point, Herr Maske, I must earnestly beg——

THEOBALD. No, no, dear friend. As sure as you're unsteady on your pins and shave men's beards off, as certain as I think of nothing but the fact that both columns in the account book should say the same thing, that Herr Scarron writes love stories, and that my wife belongs to me—so sure is the evidence of my own eyes—so sure is it that your dreams are only lies—of which phenomenon my diagnosis is: liver, lung, or stomach. I shan't rest till I've given you certainty on the point. Are you coming along?

MANDELSTAM. No, thank you. In ten minutes.

THEOBALD. Well, don't be offended. Your hour may yet strike. You may yet convince me. Not in this life, I'm afraid. But no hard feelings on that account. I must be running. You still don't wish . . . ?

MANDELSTAM. Thanks, no.

THEOBALD. Very well. See you soon.

Exit THEOBALD.

MANDELSTAM. He certainly makes it easy for a man.

LUISE, *taking his measure.* He? For a man?

MANDELSTAM. Such credulity is ludicrous.

LUISE. He places his trust where best he can.

MANDELSTAM. One day his eyes will be opened—with a vengeance.

LUISE. To the doings of certain people he brings under his roof.

MANDELSTAM. My meaning exactly.

LUISE. With their transparent pretexts.

MANDELSTAM. Which a child could see through. "To set down a love story far from the noisy street!"

LUISE. If you're going to insult me, I'll call for my husband.

MANDELSTAM. Call away. He's still on the stairs. Get thoroughly on my nerves, I'm not at the end of my resources yet. Why does he laugh at me all the time? Why the contemptuous pity in his tone? By what right, may I ask, do you despise me? For my part, I don't mind admitting I have a certain feeling about you. Not one, however, that would allow me to approach you with anything but the utmost respect.

LUISE. No one's stopping you.

MANDELSTAM. Yes. You are. Do you think I could be a party to such proceedings—an accomplice of such goings-on? Could I stand calmly by while another man makes a conquest of you? At this very table I swear to prevent it with every means in my power!

LUISE. What time was it you have to be at work on Saturdays?

MANDELSTAM. You underestimate me, Frau Maske. An oath has just been taken. As God is my help, you will not reach your goal!

LUISE, *slowly*. You are a child.

MANDELSTAM. Say, rather, a human being in a state of exaltation . . . Heaven is my witness!

LUISE. A regular child. You're getting excited about nothing. Nothing at all.

MANDELSTAM. I permit no man to despise me!

LUISE. You're getting quite out of breath. What about a nice cup of coffee? Honey and roll come with it.

MANDELSTAM. When one has nobody in the wide world.

LUISE. Go ahead with the sugar.

MANDELSTAM. One *has* nobody in the wide world.

LUISE. The honey's from my father's. Two miles from here, he has a little house in the country.

MANDELSTAM. When one has hardly known one's parents.

LUISE. As a rule I'm quite stingy with it.

MANDELSTAM. One is so absurdly alone. No roots in the soil. Nothing to hold a man up.

LUISE. You need caring for a little bit? There's a lot of nervousness around these days. If only you weren't so wild!

MANDELSTAM. I'm not.

LUISE. Violent men I just cannot respect. I like obedient, pliant natures. Well-behaved children.

MANDELSTAM. To a man who never knew a mother, that is the one thing necessary!

LUISE. The *one* thing? I'll believe that when I see it.

MANDELSTAM. This I affirm, Frau Maske, by the memory of my late mother who is looking down on us now: Never shall I overstep the boundary that you prescribe!

LUISE. Not that I'd have anything against you.

MANDELSTAM. After all, it wasn't my fault—what I saw yesterday.

LUISE. I forbid you to mention that ever again. Not a syllable. I was terrified at the way you turned up here. I foresaw unpleasant discussions with my husband.

MANDELSTAM. As if I wouldn't stand by you with my dying breath.

LUISE. Good. With the passage of time, then, we shall perhaps become friends.

MANDELSTAM. And Herr Scarron?

LUISE. What is that fop to me?

MANDELSTAM. A fop. I agree. At that, you might deceive me. Though by no means a novice, I haven't had enough experience of women to judge. Really.

LUISE. He may have his own reason for being here. It is not impossible. But you are reckoning without me, sir. You take for granted an understanding between us. I am outraged. Do you think I'm so blind I can't see what I'd be to this spoiled Don Juan—one more easy conquest that he can set aside in as little time as it took him to think of possessing her? You think I'd sacrifice my reputation and all the advantages of my position to gratify the desires of another?

MANDELSTAM. The looks he gave you permitted me to guess——

LUISE. Looks that are given without our leave are mere presumption.

MANDELSTAM. *I* shall never presume! Grateful for small mercies. Made happy by the lightest breath.

LUISE. Good. Let's leave it all to time.

MANDELSTAM. But don't expect to deceive me.

LUISE. What light clothes you're wearing! Put something else on, it's raining.

MANDELSTAM. When you say that! You make me well and strong in a moment! I don't even notice the weather. I'm going to take my scarf off.

LUISE. No, no! Prevention is better than cure!

MANDELSTAM. The way you say that!

LUISE. Would you like a sandwich to take to work?

MANDELSTAM. You think of everything!

LUISE. I tell myself: it could only do you good.

MANDELSTAM. I don't need to eat. I dream of heaven, and earthly troubles cease to bother me. If the idea appeals to you, sometimes, of an evening, we could read *The Flying Dutchman* together.

LUISE. Is it a love story?

MANDELSTAM. The greatest of love stories. Hear what the Dutchman says about Senta:
>   If in such torment, in such error,
>   Love-longing comes and speaks to me
>   Then can I cry: An end to terror!
>   This is my journey's end! I'm free!

LUISE. Nice. Now be off, or you'll be late.

MANDELSTAM. Wait for the ending:
>   Though without hope, alas, I be,
>   I give myself, O Hope, to Thee!
You should hear that with the music. It goes right through you.

LUISE. See you at noon.

MANDELSTAM. At noon! At noon!

Exit MANDELSTAM.

DEUTER, *entering immediately*. Who's that giddy fellow?

LUISE. A dangerous fellow. A nuisance. Another of those who saw what shouldn't have been on view yesterday. He sneaked in here on the same pretext as our friend. They're sharing the rooms.

DEUTER. Well!

LUISE. And the worst is, he hates Herr Scarron and he's a good guesser. He was just swearing that never would he tolerate ——What do you say?

DEUTER. What a song and dance.

LUISE. I believe he's quite capable of carrying the whole tale to Theobald before anything happened. I'm beside myself. Even before, my husband called out to me: "Mandelstam"—that's this barber boy's name—"Mandelstam is your lover!" It was spoken in jest, but it means Herr Scarron must have mentioned such possibilities in earnest. At least he must have steered the boat into those waters.

DEUTER. How've you been handling him up to now?

LUISE. With flattery. I've tried to build up his confidence.

DEUTER. Very good.

LUISE. But . . .

DEUTER. I shall keep him under observation. You see how lucky you are to have me at your side.

LUISE. What's that you've got there?

DEUTER. Guess.

LUISE. Tell me.

DEUTER. The batiste.

LUISE. It's superfine. You're a dear!

DEUTER. You like it?

LUISE. Marvelous. But expensive?

DEUTER. More dignified than silk!

LUISE. I can imagine how it lies along the skin.

DEUTER. Not like your nasty old twill. Twill is not for a body like yours. I'll measure the waist . . . Lift your skirt . . . Sixty-five centimeters . . . Call it sixty-six.

LUISE. Do you have the ribbon yet?

DEUTER. Here.

LUISE. Divine! You're my very best friend. You do all this for me and still so young yourself.

DEUTER. I've honestly given up all hope. Or, it's true, I wouldn't have so much time to devote to you.

LUISE. We must pray for you.

DEUTER. You think it would help?

LUISE. One must try everything—for the Cause.

DEUTER. You've been making strides.

LUISE. Last night was the hour of decision. A sweet dream . . .

DEUTER. Go on.

LUISE. You poor girl.

DEUTER. Not another word or I'll burst out crying.

LUISE. Surely we can find a man for you. What about the barber?

DEUTER. Pah! I'd rather have your husband!

They laugh heartily.

SCARRON *opens the door from outside and comes in.* Divine cheerfulness! I step out of the rain into a tropical sun!

LUISE, *quietly to* DEUTER. Stay.

DEUTER. One minute—then I must go downstairs.

SCARRON. Uninvited—by means of a latchkey—I invade your gay social life and tear it to shreds! Laugh on, ladies. I will take part only if permitted, only if I really belong. What was it all about?

LUISE. Fräulein Deuter——

SCARRON *bows.*

LUISE.—Fräulein Deuter and I were speaking of the barber.

SCARRON. What barber?

LUISE. Mandelstam, of course.

DEUTER. Frau Maske thought him too ugly for her, but recommended him for the post of *my* lover.

LUISE. The word never passed my lips.

DEUTER. But that was what she meant, Heaven knows.

LUISE. I was joking.

SCARRON. You must have been. He is not what one would call a man.

DEUTER. Yet good enough for an old maid.

SCARRON. Who might that be?

LUISE. She's fishing for a compliment.

DEUTER. Nothing of the kind. But what would you say of this material, Herr Doktor? You like it?

SCARRON. Batiste, isn't it? What's it for?

DEUTER. Pants for the young lady. Pardon me: in your circles they are called lingerie.

LUISE. Fräulein Deuter!

DEUTER. I was measuring her when you interrupted.

LUISE. Fräulein Deuter!

DEUTER. Sixty-six centimeters. I call those slim hips, Herr Doktor.

SCARRON. I certainly shouldn't have held up such a sweet transaction.

LUISE. Herr Scarron?

DEUTER. Now I just need the length.

She bends down and measures.

Sixty-three to just below the knee.

LUISE. Enough. What are you doing?

SCARRON. May I—having so indelicately intruded—may I offer a piece of advice? The ladies who know nothing but fashion and finery, who set the tone in all questions of taste, would not, perhaps, have found their way so far down. They would have come to rest at a point some two or three centimeters above the knee.

DEUTER. Then lend us a hand. I counted on getting such information. I was also wondering if our width of eighteen corresponds to the newest cut?

SCARRON. As wide as possible below. At the top, a closer fit.

DEUTER. Then there was the question——

LUISE, *flying to her bosom.* Trude, be quiet, or I'll be angry with you for life.

SCARRON, *to* DEUTER. This important business has been entrusted to you?

DEUTER. If you have the opportunity to admire the finished product—finished and in place—I believe you may wish to pay me a compliment.

SCARRON. How may I earn your friendship?

DEUTER. Please note that I am already at your service.

SCARRON. It is your wish, then, to be the godmother of a happiness which needs a protecting hand more than the bird that is still unfledged?

DEUTER. But which has the will to fly.

LUISE. And doesn't yet know how.

DEUTER. As for me, I'm only half a bird. When the moment came, my courage failed me, and I stayed under the eaves. I won't be able to provide detailed instructions.

SCARRON. Quite unnecessary, I assure you.

DEUTER. Besides, the nestling is bestirring herself. I found her yesterday with wings aflutter—in intuitive contact with the higher regions.

SCARRON. Let us dare to fly!

DEUTER. A hawk is circling on the horizon. Not the fat old owl who is only to be feared at night. A thin and hungry cloud that swoops down, quick as a flash, into the darkest place of hiding.

SCARRON. Who?

DEUTER. A cloud of soapsuds. A lather beater.

SCARRON. The barber.

LUISE. He's lying in wait. He shouted in my face that he'd be on the watch. And that he'd stand for nothing. I am very unhappy.

DEUTER. Now that it's out, I'll be going. Caution!

SCARRON. Thanks!

DEUTER. I will do my worst against him.

Exit DEUTER.

SCARRON. Luise!

LUISE. I'm afraid.

SCARRON. Sit at the table.

LUISE. My feet are giving way under me.

SCARRON. It doesn't matter if someone comes in—I shan't touch
you. At the other side of this table, but more than two
oceans away, I cower in the shadow of the mountain wall.
Sleeping life off, as it were, in the light of your two blue
suns. You send out beams of will power in my direction.
They singe what is nearer, and kindle what is further away,
with a brilliant, joyous warmth. Your fist is clenched; taking
hold of the idea, it proceeds to enjoy it. An idea to make
the heart melt! Your bosom is heaving now. I see the moving
muslin stiffen. And now, from the tree top to the roots, you
shed your leaves, Luise, 'tis a sweet sort of sorrow. You are
struck down by destiny.

LUISE, *like one sleeping, has buried her head in her arms
on the table.*

With father and mother my life began. Brothers and sisters
moved, beckoning, about me, and from my father issued
almost uninterrupted sound. Where did all that go? I could
see only my mother's arm raised in supplication like a
shadow above me. Then, suddenly, I was alone in a storm
that tore up the ground and brought down the sky on my
head. I ran—with a destination but no path. Stand up,
woman, I am entering upon a false passion! But stay! What
I have to say now is quite different. There are wonderful
women in the world, Luise. Blondes covered with pale-red
birthmarks and brunettes covered with down like young
eagles, whose backs undulate, when you excite them, like
the waves of the sea. Many wear rustling adornments and
stones that shimmer like their own fluidities. Others wear
tight trim skirts, and their temper is cool like their skin.
There are blondes covered with down and brunettes covered with pale birthmarks, some dark and humble, some
flaxen-haired and proud. And there are flaxen-haired, humble maidens with cool skin who tell lies in rustling silk as if
their love were fluid like the words that spring from that
love. The sky is full of stars and the nights are full of women.
The world is sublimely beautiful—but . . . !

Large, broken-off gesture. LUISE *has got up.*

You are the most beautiful woman that ever crossed my path. I expect tempests from you, an explosion to melt down my last remains of earth. Rushing into insanity, I will caress my empty carcass at your uplifted feet.

He has gone close to her.

Before you press your hand into mine, Luise, give it a quick look. It is not impossible that God will make words flow from that hand to our martyred country in fine new songs. I love you ardently, Luise, had you noticed?

LUISE. I am yours.

SCARRON. The formula is classic. A destiny clothed in three words. What humanity! If I could preserve this in my book I should rank with the greatest.

LUISE, *bending forward.* Let me be yours.

SCARRON. Desk, pen, approach your essence! Close to pure, simple Nature, no work of art can fail!

LUISE. Yours.

SCARRON. So be it. In a measure that is greater than either of us. A fire ne'er felt before inflames me. Happiness can elude me no longer. Vibrating with poetic rhythms, I feel myself turn happily away. Turning toward you on my knees. I will preserve your image for mankind. First let me show it to you, and I will claim the full guerdon of your grace.

He runs into his room.

LUISE. Why?

She runs to SCARRON's door and listens. After a moment or two she plucks up courage and knocks.

Heavens!

She breathes, listens, and approaches the table from which she lifts MANDELSTAM's scarf, glancing as she does so at SCARRON's door. She raises the scarf to her face. Just at this moment MANDELSTAM turns up at the hall door. He is seen pressing his face against it. Then he opens it gently and enters.

MANDELSTAM. Gracious, my scarf.

He comes close to LUISE.

LUISE. You frightened me. Where did *you* come from?

MANDELSTAM. Why were you frightened?

LUISE. The way you *crept* in here.

MANDELSTAM. Is that my scarf?

LUISE. God knows.

MANDELSTAM, *kissing her.* Luise!

LUISE, *boxing his ears.* Shameless man!

MANDELSTAM. Forgive me.

LUISE *has gone to* SCARRON's *door and knocked.*

SCARRON'S VOICE. Give me five minutes!

LUISE *is bewildered.*

MANDELSTAM. I implore you. Something came over me, it will
never happen again. I'll kill myself!

LUISE *starts to go to her room.* MANDELSTAM *faints.*

LUISE. Lord have mercy!

Runs to him.

What? Water?

She brings water and gives it to him.

MANDELSTAM. I feel good.

LUISE. Your chin is bleeding. What kind of a point is that?

MANDELSTAM. That? A gimlet.

LUISE. How could you stick *that* in your trouser pocket? It
might have given you a mortal wound!

MANDELSTAM. As long as it touched your heart.

LUISE, *rising.* It would touch anyone's heart. A young man so
full of hopes. What nonsense! Lie down on the sofa for a
minute.

MANDELSTAM, *lying down.* In any event it will reveal to me
what goes on in Herr Scarron's room.

LUISE. You intend to . . .

MANDELSTAM. Bore a hole through the wall. I am crazed with
jealousy, Luise, I don't know myself. What was it brought
you to this wretch's door? Do not misjudge me: despite my
weakness, I will murder him.

LUISE. What right . . . ?

MANDELSTAM. I love you, Luise!

SCARRON, *coming quickly out of his room.* Color, tone, all the
various values realized to the last detail. No one can ever
take them away from me. I come—all love and gratitude——
He sees MANDELSTAM.

Excuse me.

THEOBALD, *entering quickly.* How are you, gentlemen?

ACT THREE

The remains of the evening meal are on the table, about which all are sitting.

THEOBALD, *to* MANDELSTAM. It was very hard for your employer to get through all the work without you this afternoon. He said you might have put your indisposition off to some day other than Saturday.

MANDELSTAM. The first afternoon I've missed in three years.

THEOBALD. He hopes you'll be all right again by the day after tomorrow at the latest. There's all of Sunday in between.

MANDELSTAM. Even a dog wants to rest if anything's not quite kosher with him.

THEOBALD. Kosher? Hm. As you wish. Incidentally, I had a long discussion with a colleague who has the same condition to complain of as yourself. He knows the inside of his poor, ruined body like his account books. He even goes to work with Latin names.

He has stood up and gone to the back.

MANDELSTAM, *eagerly following.* For the life of me, I don't see any basis for the comparison.

SCARRON, *quietly, to* LUISE. I forbid you to stare all the time at that clod.

LUISE. I can't help feeling sorry for him.

SCARRON. All lies. He's an incorrigible ruffian, a highwayman. He deliberately ruined our afternoon and——

THEOBALD. It is first and foremost a matter of the nerves even if the other organs—one more, the other less—are also infected. If I understood him correctly we must regard each nerve as a fine tube surrounded and protected by a second tube. In debilitated persons, this second, protective tube peels off like bark from trees—am I right, Herr Scarron?

SCARRON. More or less. As far as I know.

THEOBALD. Yes. And it is hard beyond all expectation to repair the damage once it is done.

MANDELSTAM. How in the world do you conclude that my nerves—it's outrageous—without having seen more of me . . .

THEOBALD. Be calm. I don't want to excite you. Surely people must have commented on the state of your nerves before now?

MANDELSTAM. Never.

THEOBALD. I will consult a completely unbiased observer. Mr. Scarron: how does our friend strike you?

SCARRON. As typically neurasthenic.

MANDELSTAM. Ha!

THEOBALD. You see? There are of course other factors, as I said. With this other man it's the stomach that's ruined by long years of inadequate nourishment. With you, I would guess it's the lungs.

LUISE. You mustn't scare Herr Mandelstam, Theobald.

THEOBALD. On the contrary, I am trying to arm him against disaster. If possible, to prevent disaster.

LUISE. But he utterly denies having any serious illness.

MANDELSTAM. Absolutely.

THEOBALD. So much the better. I regard it as my simple duty.

MANDELSTAM. And I regard it as inconsiderate to tell such things to a sensitive person. Naturally, they weigh on him, they work away on him . . .

THEOBALD. Even if they have no bearing?

MANDELSTAM. Is there a window open?

THEOBALD. Ever so slightly.

MANDELSTAM. May I close it?

He does so.

LUISE. You'd better put your scarf on.

MANDELSTAM. Many thanks.

SCARRON, *to* THEOBALD. As far as your sick colleague goes, I find this saying extremely helpful: whatever is weak and unfit must yield to the healthy and the strong!

LUISE. Of course it's for the mighty to support the weakling. Religion teaches that.

SCARRON. The religion of other centuries. Not ours.

THEOBALD *hands* MANDELSTAM *a newspaper.* Read!

SCARRON. We are beyond all that. Into the moldy, musty atmosphere of past centuries, heavy with pity as it is, we have brought a good stiff breeze!

MANDELSTAM. Read what? My eyes aren't focused.

THEOBALD, *showing him.* At the bottom there. They say the sea serpent has turned up again in Indian waters.

MANDELSTAM, *furiously.* What do *I* care?

THEOBALD. It may distract you.

SCARRON, *to* THEOBALD. Has the name of Nietzsche reached your ears?

THEOBALD. In what connection?

SCARRON. He teaches the gospel of the age. He shows that the boundless mass of men find a purpose in the individual who is blessed with certain energies. Strength is the highest happiness.

THEOBALD. Strength is certainly a happiness. I learned that in school, and those under me had to suffer for it.

SCARRON. I mean, of course, not only brutal, physical strength. Above all: spiritual energies.

THEOBALD. Yes, of course.

MANDELSTAM. I only noticed this morning that my room faces the northeast.

THEOBALD. One moment. Yes, you are right.

MANDELSTAM. Even for the strongest of men, that would hardly be advantageous.

SCARRON, *to* LUISE. The sloppy dog will have to be taught the Master Morality. Tonight I shall do everything in my power to reach you.

LUISE. For Heaven's sake!

SCARRON. Who do you take me for? Do you think the Evil One Himself is a match for my will power?

LUISE. But wait.

SCARRON. No!

THEOBALD, *who has opened* MANDELSTAM's *door.* Put the bed against the wall opposite the window. Then you'll be sleeping toward the southwest.

MANDELSTAM. I feel the draft on my pillows.

SCARRON, *to* LUISE. This night shalt thou be with me in Paradise.

THEOBALD, *to* MANDELSTAM. Now you exaggerate.

MANDELSTAM *goes into his room. One can see him busy himself with something.*

SCARRON, *to* THEOBALD. Have you never heard of these theories? Do you read so little?

THEOBALD. Hardly at all. Seven hours of official duties. Afterwards I'm tired.

SCARRON. That is deplorable. What are the criteria of your thinking?

THEOBALD. Some of us get along with less thinking than you might imagine.

SCARRON. Yet you live according to a certain scheme?

THEOBALD. Scheme A, Scheme B, Scheme C . . .

SCARRON. That is: you eat, sleep, and copy documents. Where does that lead?

THEOBALD. To a pension—God willing.

SCARRON. Frightful. No interest in politics?

THEOBALD. I was always excited about what Bismarck did.

SCARRON. He's been dead for some time.

THEOBALD. There hasn't been much going on since.

SCARRON. Science?

THEOBALD. Heavens, there isn't much there for the likes of us.

SCARRON. Are you aware that Shakespeare once walked the earth? Do you know Goethe?

THEOBALD. A nodding acquaintance.

SCARRON. For Heaven's sake!

THEOBALD. You take it too hard.

SCARRON. A comfortable philosophy.

THEOBALD. What's wrong with comfort? My life lasts seventy years. With whatever degree of understanding I've managed to acquire, after my own fashion I can enjoy quite a lot of things in that amount of time. As for your higher philosophy and all that, I don't think I could master it if I lived to be a hundred.

LUISE. To think there's to be no more pity in the world!

SCARRON. It simply does not exist.

LUISE. But if I *feel* it . . .

THEOBALD. Don't butt into our conversation.

MANDELSTAM, *returning.* I wonder if Frau Maske could let me have a woolen blanket. I've turned the bed around.

THEOBALD. That was reasonable.

LUISE. I'll go and get one.

She goes into her room.

SCARRON. I judge each man by his contribution to the spiritual development of humanity. The great thinkers, poets, painters, and musicians are our heroes. The layman?—important only insofar as he knows them.

MANDELSTAM. And the great inventors!

SCARRON. Surely—but only to the extent that they enable mankind to circulate the ideas of the geniuses more efficiently.

THEOBALD. And what about sentiment, sir?

SCARRON. What?

THEOBALD. Did I say it wrong? What use have you for the heart?

SCARRON. The heart is a muscle, my dear Maske.

LUISE *returns.*

THEOBALD. Fine. But there's something to it. With females especially.

LUISE, *to* MANDELSTAM. It's big enough to wrap right around you.

MANDELSTAM. Many thanks.

SCARRON. Leave me alone with your simplicity—ultimate problems are under review. Females—women, let us say—are, Heaven knows, a delicious affair, but when a Shakespeare wrestles with the soul of Hamlet, a Goethe struggles for insight into the soul of a Faust, women must stand to one side.

MANDELSTAM. Schwarz wouldn't have been thinking of his wife when he invented the printing press. Neither would Newton. Or Edison. Or Zeppelin.

LUISE. Is that certain?

SCARRON. I'll take my oath on it.

MANDELSTAM. And I'll join you.

THEOBALD. Setting Goethe aside—and Schwarz too, for all I care—even so—if I may put it this way—women have hearts.

SCARRON. A muscle, my dear Maske.

THEOBALD. I know. But they live off that muscle, and make up half the earth's inhabitants.

SCARRON. Well and good. But you are no woman. You should be penetrated with a sense of your dignity as a man. Beside the domestic, friendly element that unites you with your wife, there are also moments in which you feel worlds away from her—moments when sheer masculinity overpowers you and fills you with an almost insane pride!

MANDELSTAM. Wonderfully worded!

LUISE. Not all men are like you.

SCARRON. In their heart of hearts, all, dear lady.

MANDELSTAM. Positively.

THEOBALD. I don't know. There *is* something of the sort, it's true, but, actually, I've always fought against it.

SCARRON. There we have it: he fought against—Nature.

MANDELSTAM. The devil!

SCARRON. What makes man a giant, the gigantic obelisk of creation, whom woman cannot put down, but the transcendent will to knowledge which the profoundest erotic passion cannot paralyze?

MANDELSTAM. "Paralyze" is good.

LUISE. My husband is different.

THEOBALD. Luise, God Almighty, keep away from me with your silly chatter. . . . Speaking from personal experience,

I don't see how it would have helped my marriage if I'd felt more strongly about this difference between the sexes. . . .

SCARRON. Personal gain—we must set aside such considerations. It is incontestable that every step of human progress depends on the strict maintenance of masculinity.

LUISE. Pah!

MANDELSTAM. Who would have thought, ten years ago, that we'd be flying?

THEOBALD. Anyhow, I'm glad to see the two of you so fully in agreement. How pleasant to have lodgers who don't get in each other's hair!

MANDELSTAM. Man stands by man.

SCARRON, *to* MANDELSTAM. Incidentally, you still owe us a statement of your opinion. Up to now you've simply rejected ours.

MANDELSTAM. Zeppelin is no hero then?

SCARRON. Plato and Kant can be dispensed with?

MANDELSTAM. Where should we be without railroad and telephone?

SCARRON. Without his predecessors, Goethe is an absolute impossibility. Would you deny Pontius and Pilate and yet have Goethe stand?

MANDELSTAM. What about Wagner? Mankind's most sacred possession!

THEOBALD, *slowly*. All this aside, there are still a lot of other things. Having children and things like that . . .

MANDELSTAM. Women's affairs yet again!

THEOBALD. Don't shout at me. Have I cast doubt on the accuracy of your facts?

SCARRON. Even a god could not do *that*.

THEOBALD. Yet the two facts I bring from my own experience —that women have hearts and that children are born—get both of you angry.

SCARRON. Incredible! These are platitudes—obvious as . . .

THEOBALD. As what?

SCARRON. No simile comes to mind. Polemics with you are pointless.

THEOBALD. Have a glass of Münchner. Luise, you pour it for Herr Scarron.

SCARRON. Thanks.

THEOBALD. Tomorrow one could go to the Zoological Gardens. They've just acquired a giraffe.

MANDELSTAM *bursts out laughing.* Giraffes!

THEOBALD. What's so funny about it?

MANDELSTAM. I'm having my own thoughts.

THEOBALD. Quite honestly, I'd never have dreamt of taking a look at such a beast. I'm not partial to such freaks and stage tricks of nature. But, since Herr Scarron's put me up to it, I want to do something for my education.

MANDELSTAM *bursts out laughing.*

THEOBALD. Don't get wild, Herr Mandelstam.

SCARRON. You pretend to be so narrow-minded, my friend . . .

MANDELSTAM. When will the scales fall from your eyes?

THEOBALD, *to* MANDELSTAM. Don't overtax your meager resources, Herr Mandelstam.

SCARRON. Should not the presence of a noble young woman be the spur to higher achievement? Raising you above your former station?

THEOBALD. My wife's parents are tailors and have been for generations.

LUISE. Six brothers fell on the field of honor.

MANDELSTAM. Today no one would be so stupid. Getting yourself slaughtered! Ugh!

THEOBALD. The spirit of the age is against it? It isn't modern to love your country?

MANDELSTAM. A while ago you almost made me ill. Now you are making me well again. Despite external handicaps, I feel like another man—strong in the knowledge that there are battalions behind me. That sort of talk leaves us cold. We know the facts: the highest born man in the world descends—like Herr Scarron and myself—from the ape. All men are equal. And anyone can get to the top.

THEOBALD. Anyone who wants to. But there are people for

whom one position is much like another, and the one they already have is the one they prefer. My birth placed me in quite a favorable position, and I feel secure till death in the possession of it—my fellows all over the Fatherland could say the same. Only special merit or extraordinary disgrace could deprive me of this security.

SCARRON. Sir, that is frightful! Slave morality!

THEOBALD, *grinning.* No. It's just that I lose my freedom if the world pays me any particular attention. Inconspicuousness is a magic cloak—under cover of which I give rein to my own real nature.

SCARRON. God forbid this faith of yours should be shared by your fellows!

THEOBALD. As for them, I cannot judge. But I can guarantee that progressive notions are not favored on the higher echelons. One of our bureau chiefs let his wife go off with another man. He wrote later in his deposition that he didn't wish to "take the curb to her"—an expression derived from the stable. Today he sells mineral water at the intersection of Wildenmacher Strasse and Fischer Strasse.

SCARRON. A martyr. His wife must look up to him.

LUISE. His wife looks down on him.

SCARRON. But you are wrong.

LUISE. With all her heart and soul.

MANDELSTAM. I, too, rather doubt it.

THEOBALD. Let's leave it to the two of them, Luise.

MANDELSTAM. I happen to have the evidence in my own past. I lived with little Frau Frühling—they have the restaurant in Ahorn Strasse—the husband permitted the relationship.

THEOBALD. That she is called Frühling and lives on Ahorn Strasse is not to the point.

LUISE *stands up.* Good night.

THEOBALD. You're staying till we all go.

MANDELSTAM. She's worshiped her husband ever since.

THEOBALD. I'll have to drink a schnapps on that. Would anyone like to accompany me to the the Golden Basket for a few minutes?

SCARRON. I am more confused than I can express. I have met this view of life before but never anyone who believed in it!

THEOBALD. Someone of no importance.

SCARRON. And yet someone. And under no circumstances would you cease to believe in it, eh?

THEOBALD. Correct. I don't want to fall off the deep end.

SCARRON. It would be hard, I see that. But one must try!

THEOBALD. Don't trouble yourself about it.

MANDELSTAM. I'm afraid it's a hopeless case.

THEOBALD. Of course, I might see reason over a glass of schnapps in the Golden Basket.

SCARRON. Please! I must beg you to be in earnest about this!

THEOBALD. If I were, I might find many things intolerable that I've been putting up with. I might have to be quite impolite. So come along!

SCARRON. Even if your *point de départ* is a theory of immutable values . . .

THEOBALD. Mandelstam, you come. They have a first-rate Münchner.

MANDELSTAM. Sorry. I must go to bed.

THEOBALD. Each man to his taste.

SCARRON, *gesticulating violently at* THEOBALD's *side.* Even if, with Kant, you assume . . .

THEOBALD *and* SCARRON *exeunt.*

MANDELSTAM. After this conversation, many things will never be the same for me again. To live in the same house with this dolt is hell. True, I have met with dense people before, but such wrongheadedness—disgusting fellow! And his vulgar familiarity because I happened to mention that my constitution wasn't of the strongest! Beside this creature, Herr Scarron seems like God Himself, if the simile is good enough. And what brutality—to take a man whose health one regards as utterly shattered—and saddle him with a room facing northeast!

LUISE. You agreed with Herr Scarron that one should feel pity for nobody.

MANDELSTAM. Pity? Who wants pity? I demand decency, no-

bility of mind—qualities, I must admit, which Herr Scarron
has exemplified in the highest degree.

LUISE. How?

MANDELSTAM. By what he said. Didn't he thrill you? Didn't
you feel what a great, overflowing heart the man has? Isn't
it touching to see how, even now, he tries to knock some
sense into that bonehead? For his pains, he'll get the same
grin that I got when I complained to the master of this
house about the room.

LUISE. We didn't have any other.

MANDELSTAM. Then it was your duty to warn me about this
one.

LUISE. But you demanded it.

MANDELSTAM. In ignorance.

LUISE. You insisted you must have that room to be near my
person.

MANDELSTAM. But if it means my certain death?

LUISE. You exaggerate.

MANDELSTAM *laughs out loud.* Exaggerate! A room facing
northeast—for a man with lung trouble—is like—an adequate
simile does not come to mind. Add to this that the awareness of such a state of affairs cannot but upset my nervous
system. Like the bark on a tree! Peeling away—can't you
see it? You with your sound, solid health—your natural
cheeks look just like make-up.

He runs into his room.

No storm windows! I'll drop dead tonight if I've no woolen
shirt, and mine's in the wash.

He returns.

Do you imagine it takes years to bring a debilitated organ-
ism down to the grave?

He disappears again into his room.

Didn't he say himself his colleague couldn't live more than
three days? In addition to which, the window doesn't close
properly.

He returns.

Now what was that about the tube? It *was* a tube he was
talking about, for Heaven's sake. Say something!

LUISE. You were saying it had to do with the nervous system.

MANDELSTAM. I'm utterly confused. Now I have it: he spoke
of *two* tubes and how it was impossible to patch them up
again.

He again disappears, then shouts.

This hole is contrary to police regulations! Police on every
block, but when it comes to a poor fellow like me, why,
they leave me to rot in a corner like a mad dog.

He appears again.

What was it the doctor always did? Wait a minute. Look
down my throat!

He tears his jaws open.

LUISE. I don't understand such things.

MANDELSTAM. No. This is it.

*He hurls himself into a chair and throws one leg across the
other.*

Hit my knee, here, with the flat of your hand.

When LUISE *does so, and his leg jumps upwards, he shouts.*

I am lost! Obviously, a whole night facing northeast has
been too much for me.

LUISE, *unable to control herself any longer.* But . . .

MANDELSTAM, *beside himself.* And you talk of pity!

LUISE, *close to tears.* You wanted to be near me—more than
anything in the world.

MANDELSTAM, *roaring.* It's the grave I'm near! This is mon-
strous. We must speak further!

*He runs into his room, slamming the door behind him and
locking it on the other side.* LUISE *is motionless.* DEUTER
appears in front of the glass door. LUISE *lets her in.*

DEUTER. The both of them arm in arm down the street?

LUISE. What kept you so late?

DEUTER. I was at the theatre. A superb play—by Sternheim.
I'll tell you about it later. You should have seen *him.* He
simply sparkled!

LUISE. Who?

DEUTER. Not the giant, though he seemed all right. Our hero! Radiating manliness and power!

LUISE. Oh . . . !

DEUTER. Theobald got some of his reflected glory. Seemed livelier than usual. Well, the two of you were together all day. Tell me about it. What happened? I burn.

LUISE. Quiet. Mandelstam is home.

DEUTER. Let me look deep into your eyes. Let me take you by the hands, by the arms.

LUISE. Why, Trude?

DEUTER. To drink in your bliss. This is the sofa he sat on, near you, every moment a little nearer. Pressed, finally, against the sofa back, you could retreat no further, you didn't want to, either. Tell what he did.

LUISE. I don't remember.

DEUTER. That's cheating, you little thief. I want an unexpurgated confession. And don't be shy, Luise. I've done more reading than you think, and I dream about more of the same. I didn't see, but just the same I know. How did it begin? He put his arm around you.

LUISE. He was sitting—somewhere.

DEUTER. What about you?

LUISE. At the table.

DEUTER. He came over to you?

LUISE. He stayed where he was.

DEUTER. And?

LUISE. Spoke.

DEUTER. What? Can you repeat what he said? Splendid things.

LUISE. There was a buzzing in my ear.

DEUTER. He exploded over you like a thunderstorm! Hm? That's what I've read. Your body grew weak at the touch of his manly strength. Your legs wouldn't move.

LUISE. I did feel that way. For a moment there I took leave of my senses.

DEUTER. Happy woman! Then?

LUISE. He came over to me.

DEUTER. Luise! And then?

LUISE. Spoke.

DEUTER. And?

LUISE. Said something.

DEUTER. And?

LUISE. Spoke.

DEUTER. After which?

LUISE. What?

DEUTER. When he was through speaking?

LUISE. He left.

DEUTER. He did what?

LUISE. Left.

DEUTER. He called: "I love you!"

LUISE. Yes.

DEUTER. What about you?

LUISE. Same thing.

DEUTER. "I am yours!"

LUISE. Yes, um . . .

DEUTER. You did?

LUISE. With all my heart.

DEUTER. At last. And then?

LUISE. He left.

DEUTER. Where'd he go?

LUISE. Into his room.

DEUTER. You followed?

LUISE. No.

DEUTER. Unhappy woman!

LUISE. When he shut his door I followed. I even dared to knock.

DEUTER. You knocked?

LUISE. But he didn't open.

DEUTER. He shut himself in? . . . I have it: Mandelstam was around.

LUISE. No.

DEUTER. Are you sure? Without your seeing him, maybe? But *he* saw him?

LUISE. Hm.

DEUTER. Think back,

LUISE. Mandelstam did come in right afterwards.

DEUTER. Ha!

LUISE. I've only just realized.

DEUTER. You see! You see! Misjudging my hero! Carried away with emotion, making large, sweeping gestures, he is suddenly aware of the presence of the creeping fox I have so earnestly warned him against. In an instant, speech and gesture fall to normal. Overcome with feeling, yet sparing the loved one, the tender-hearted man takes his leave. And the intriguer's greedy eyes find the lady, quite properly, alone. How right I was! You are in no position to understand him. Didn't he later take the first opportunity that offered to renew his vows of love?

LUISE. He did. He proved to be jealous of the barber.

DEUTER. I formed a clearer picture of him from afar than you did near at hand.

LUISE. But later, talking with the men . . .

DEUTER. What about?

LUISE. I lost him completely. I went outside. I had to cry.

DEUTER. A false conclusion.

LUISE. It was my aversion to my husband that I felt to be false, and my liking for this other man. The misery that took me by the throat as he talked on made me feel everything about me was false and had been since the day I was born.

DEUTER. You understood him just as little as earlier when he spared you. You simply didn't grasp what he had in mind. Trust to my own deep conviction. He is even now preparing the deed that will finally conquer you.

LUISE. I am plunged in despair. I am forever unhappy.

DEUTER. Fainthearted girl! Not in vain does he draw your husband from your side by night. Not for nothing does he fascinate him with the fire of life, and entangle him inex-

tricably in problems and ideas. Had you been with me at
the theatre, you would know that happiness stands in your
path. There was a man in that play who climbed walls,
burst gates open, and set fire to things—just to be near his
loved one. The conviction that men have us poor creatures
in their power poured forth in a torrent of words. What
shall we do, little fool? Any time that we squander in talk is
stolen from the waiting hero. . . . Good night . . . One
kiss . . . By the bones of the saints, I swear: it shall be . . .
Quiet . . . Lie down, hurry, put all the lights out. He is
coming!

She hurries out.

LUISE. Is it possible?

*She sits motionless for a moment and listens, then goes to
the window and looks out, sits down again, stands up, and
goes into the bedroom where she lights up. Returning, she
begins to get undressed, her face pressed against the hall
door. Sounds are heard on the stairs. She puts out the light
on stage and stands there trembling. The sound is lost again.*

No!

*Mechanically she goes on with her unbuttoning. Then she
approaches* MANDELSTAM'S *door and touches the latch—but
then returns to her own bedroom door, dragging her feet
behind her. And there she stays, lighted from behind, in
slip and pants, slowly and repeatedly combing her hair,
while at intervals* MANDELSTAM'S *regular snoring shakes the
air.*

ACT FOUR

THEOBALD *shouts into the bedroom.* That was a sloppy job you did, mending my suspenders! You can't neglect me just because of these two other fellows!

LUISE *comes in and pours him coffee.*

Luckily neither of them is in. Thank God we needn't expect Scarron before noon. After he'd talked at me till two in the morning like someone with hallucinations, he earnestly requested me to take him to his apartment because the bed there is better. I drank five beers and three schnapps. The result—diarrhea.

LUISE. He's not coming.

THEOBALD. I don't see how anyone can sleep like you with a man running back and forth all the time. Where is the honey?

LUISE. There's none left.

THEOBALD. What housekeeping! Please get some. Also I don't like to find your underwear on my chair. Always something for me to lecture you about!

LUISE. Mandelstam made another scene about facing northeast. After which I sank into bed.

THEOBALD. The man is crazy. What's wrong with the north? Or the east either? Does he consider them inferior points of the compass? The sun rises in the east. Painters like their rooms to face the north. And yet a miserable barber expects to include the west and the south for a miserable five thaler?

LUISE. It's true the south would be easier on his weak chest. And you say Herr Scarron won't come today? How is that?

THEOBALD. Your nose is running, please wipe it. What do you mean: how is that? He was drunk and won't be at his best today.

LUISE. Drunk?

THEOBALD. Plastered. He got to be an awful sight to see. Despite his condition, he never gave up the idea that he must convert me. You'd have thought he'd been stung by a tarantula.

LUISE. Heavens!

THEOBALD. That man is an exotic, ornamental plant in the garden of God. Also, his breath smells.

LUISE. Theobald! He used to have—doesn't he at times have something heroic about him?

THEOBALD. As in a novel, you mean?

LUISE. Yes, as in a novel.

THEOBALD. My Lord! Luise, look: he hasn't much ability. Don't you think he should be a good deal more heroic than he is—to make up for the deficiency?

LUISE. Yes.

THEOBALD. These projects aren't serious that he starts up. I believe he's tired already of the whim that brought him here. Not that it matters to me. He took the room for a year, and it's in writing.

LUISE. May I go to church today? It's almost an emergency.

THEOBALD. Certainly, my dove. A very happy thought. Last week, with your pants falling down, was fraught with danger for us both. It's no less than your duty to thank your Maker. Meanwhile, I shall be following to its logical end a resolve of mine that is fraught with consequences.

LUISE. Tell me.

THEOBALD. You are inquisitive. Rightly . . . When you return, Luise. Leave me an hour to mull it over. You'll be astonished.

LUISE. Will I?

She goes into the alcove.

THEOBALD. What are you doing?

LUISE. The curtain should be on our side. Everyone can see in.

THEOBALD. Don't fall off the window sill.

He follows her. One hears him from inside.

The little woman has pretty good calves.

MANDELSTAM *enters, hurriedly sits at the coffee table, starts greedily to eat, goes to the alcove to shut the door.* What?

Recognizing THEOBALD.

Oh, excuse me.

THEOBALD, *embarrassed.* I didn't hear you come in. We're taking the curtain into our room.

MANDELSTAM. You've had breakfast?

He sits.

THEOBALD. Yes.

LUISE *walks across the stage into her bedroom.*

MANDELSTAM. Good morning, Frau Maske.

THEOBALD. You seem to have slept well.

MANDELSTAM. You got me so excited, I was simply overcome with drowsiness. Yes, I slept wonderfully.

THEOBALD, *laughing.* Despite the northeast . . .

MANDELSTAM. Yes, indeed. Although——

THEOBALD. There's an although?

MANDELSTAM. The bed is a good one.

THEOBALD. Better than the softest belly.

MANDELSTAM. Although——

THEOBALD. You hear the street noises?

MANDELSTAM. Not a sound. Although——

THEOBALD. The morning sun disturbs you . . .

MANDELSTAM. I love nothing so much—and yet . . .

THEOBALD. In view of all these advantages, five thaler is too little. You have my wife to thank.

MANDELSTAM. Not that you'd suddenly raise the price, I'm sure?

THEOBALD. Not at present.

MANDELSTAM. I'm afraid you don't make yourself clear. Why don't we set a date?

THEOBALD. Why bind yourself?

Enter LUISE.

MANDELSTAM. Don't I get any honey today?

LUISE. Honey is extra. All over the world.

MANDELSTAM. I thought it was included.

LUISE. Then you thought wrong. At that, the sugar gets used up anyway in no time at all.

To THEOBALD.

So long.

THEOBALD. And take care.

Exit LUISE.

Why bind yourself? If the doctor discovered something more serious and decided that the northeast outlook is hazardous you'd be in a fix. Yes, the bed is good. The mattress is made of a kind of horsehair not found any more—even on thoroughbreds.

MANDELSTAM. Indisputably.

THEOBALD. Morning sun and perfect quiet . . . It so happens we'd decided to exchange that bed for another—just before you came. Fräulein Deuter, who lives downstairs, offered sixty thaler for it in cash.

MANDELSTAM. Never! You must never do it!

THEOBALD *has gone into* MANDELSTAM's *room.* An eiderdown! And my wife went and added a second pillow expressly against my wishes.

MANDELSTAM. All right, to cut a long story short: one year. We understand each other, Herr Maske.

THEOBALD. The state of your health . . .

MANDELSTAM. I feel as strong as a giant.

THEOBALD. Prices rise in this neighborhood from one day to the next. In three months this room will easily be worth eight thaler and not five.

MANDELSTAM. The more excited you get me the less attractive the proposition!

THEOBALD. I'll name my lowest price. Six thaler.

MANDELSTAM. I can't pay it.

THEOBALD. Very well. Nothing doing.

MANDELSTAM. Oh, all right. Just to put an end to all this. The way you can talk of Bismarck and Luther, I'd never have believed it.

THEOBALD. A deal!

MANDELSTAM. One year. And let's put something in writing at once. "Herr Maske rents to Herr Mandelstam until May 15 . . . one room, morning coffee included."

THEOBALD. But no honey.

MANDELSTAM. "For six thaler. The bed now in the room may not be replaced by another." Now sign.

THEOBALD. Now suppose my wife isn't agreeable. She finds you unsympathetic.

MANDELSTAM. But we needn't have anything to do with each other, for Heaven's sake.

THEOBALD. Even so. As she doesn't like to have you here, she may feel inhibited.

MANDELSTAM. Not by me. I'll swear it to her a thousand times over: she doesn't bother me, she can do and not do as she pleases. Don't throw me out on the street! I admit the bed is good. In view of the appalling state of my health—have mercy on me!

THEOBALD. All right. Since you leave me no alternative. I'm no monster.

He signs.

There: Theobald Maske.

MANDELSTAM. Is there a leftover armchair about the place?

THEOBALD. I'd better tear it up. My wife——

MANDELSTAM, *grabbing the paper out of his hands.* The devil take your wife!

THEOBALD. Here's to our life together!

MANDELSTAM. I'll do *my* part.

He looks into his room.

You should have seen the bed in my previous place. A torture chamber. Uninterrupted noise from all sides. Also a small menagerie . . . oh yes, my dear fellow, fleas, bedbugs. . . . I wrote Richard Wagner's signature on the wallpaper with pins stuck through dead insects.

He laughs.

When I spoke against you last night, I was a little bit carried away. I meant no harm.

THEOBALD. That was more than all right with me. The thing is to agree with Herr Scarron. He pays well. We owe him all kinds of consideration.

MANDELSTAM, *hat on head.* I'll do *my* part.

THEOBALD. Where are you off to today?

MANDELSTAM. The Park Pavilion.

THEOBALD. Wouldn't you be making better use of your day off if you consulted a good doctor?

MANDELSTAM. Not while I feel as I do.

THEOBALD. What's her name?

MANDELSTAM. No one. My last was Frieda. She has an engineer now.

THEOBALD. A fine strapping wench?

MANDELSTAM. Tremendous. Trust me. At the firework display this evening, there'll be more such.

Exit MANDELSTAM.

THEOBALD. It was just an idea in passing—to ask for more rent. A thoroughly feeble brain, that fellow. Eighteen thaler in all. Twelve times eighteen is 180 plus, um . . . 216 thaler for the year. Now I pay 115 for the apartment. 101 are left. I earn 700, that makes 801 thaler and free living quarters. Not bad. It can be done, you see. Great. Excellent. Who's there?

DEUTER *is at the door.*

THEOBALD *lets her in.* Come right in, Fräulein. We were just talking about you.

DEUTER. Who was?

THEOBALD. A barber and I.

DEUTER. A worthless fellow.

THEOBALD. And very much interested in you, it seems.

DEUTER. Leave out the jokes.

THEOBALD. His eyes fluttered gently upwards and he said: "Trude."

DEUTER. How did he know my first name?

THEOBALD. I'm sure I don't know who is lucky enough to be intimate with you.

DEUTER. You're trying to tease me.

THEOBALD. God forbid.

DEUTER. Is your wife in?

THEOBALD. She's at church.

DEUTER. Herr Scarron is out?

THEOBALD. A flowered dress you happened to wear last night seemed to him an admirable subject for conversation. He even thought of a word for you.

DEUTER. Which was?

THEOBALD. *Popote.*

DEUTER. What does it mean?

THEOBALD. I don't know the definition, but the word *has* something. What's that you're holding so tight?

DEUTER. Nothing for you. I find Herr Scarron's description of me absurd. I see nothing nice about it.

THEOBALD. I like it. I think it fits.

DEUTER. As you don't even know what it means . . .

She sits down on the couch.

THEOBALD. It's the sound of the word . . .

DEUTER. The sound?!

THEOBALD. The images it conjures up. Makes you think of little round arms—oh, all sorts of things.

DEUTER. Quite absurd. You call a lady either plain or pretty.

THEOBALD. Let's say: either spindly or *popote.*

DEUTER. Spindly! Oh dear, an old maid like me.

THEOBALD, *who has taken her package and opened it.* Underpants! And what underpants! Pink silk ribbons, material like a spider's web. The woman who wears these and talks of old maids is fishing for a compliment!

DEUTER. You think so?

THEOBALD. Why would a battered old ship sport silken sails?

DEUTER. So as not to seem battered and old.

THEOBALD. In fairy tales only. In real life, they save themselves useless expenditure.

He holds the pants up, spreads them out.

They have zing. And when they fit their owner as if she'd been poured into them, they will give rise to some very pretty notions.

DEUTER. Herr Maske! I don't know this side of you.

THEOBALD. You don't know any side of me. One might even say you and I didn't see eye to eye before today. And it didn't really bother me. But then yesterday you came with that devil of a dress—and today you come in these tricky underpants . . .

DEUTER. *Carrying* them chastely on my arm to show to your wife.

THEOBALD. If all is to be as it should be, they need complementing by white stockings.

DEUTER. The things you think of!

THEOBALD. My good girl, how do you know I haven't been thinking of you—before today? I'm like that. Now you've got me discussing such delicate topics, you'll find I am by no means as indifferent to your many qualities—qualities which, by Heaven, a man can't help noticing—as thus far it may have seemed.

DEUTER. If your wife knew this!

THEOBALD. She knows nothing. I wouldn't permit myself to tell her—it would only trouble her. I do such things very much in secret. And not often, though with great pleasure.

DEUTER. Human beings are only human beings after all.

THEOBALD. Not after all. I began at the age of fourteen.

DEUTER. I'm thirty-two. A girl doesn't have it so easy.

THEOBALD. But almost.

DEUTER. My parents were more strict than I can say. Father beat me for being a minute late, and didn't die till I was twenty-nine.

THEOBALD. That's tough.

DEUTER. Then I came here. But under the eyes of all these old women . . .

THEOBALD. Did you leave your apartment unlocked?

DEUTER. I locked up when I came here. This house is all spies.

THEOBALD. Twenty past ten . . . I have it: one evening I

found myself looking down at you from our windows while
you——

DEUTER. I must go. Your wife will be back.

THEOBALD. Not for another hour.

He stands in the open door of the bedroom.

Do you notice how clearly one can see your room from near
my bed?

DEUTER, *going toward him.* Really?

The door closes behind them. SCARRON *enters by the hall
door after a moment and looks enquiringly about. A knock
at the hall door.* SCARRON *opens it.*

THE STRANGER. They tell me downstairs there's a room for rent
here.

SCARRON. The tenant isn't in. Maybe you should come back
later. But there are no rooms free so far as *I* know.

THE STRANGER. The janitor's wife says the opposite.

SCARRON. Of course I can't tell you for sure.

THE STRANGER. Are there many children in the house? Is there
a piano? Can you tell me these things?

SCARRON. No.

THE STRANGER. Thank you very much. When will the tenant
be back?

SCARRON. I'm afraid I can't say.

THE STRANGER. Good-by.

Exit THE STRANGER. SCARRON *goes into his room.*

THEOBALD, *peeping out of the bedroom.* Who was that?

Goes to SCARRON's *door, listens, and runs to the bedroom.*
Come on. Scarron is back.

DEUTER, *coming.* Do you love me? When shall I see you again?
Today? Early tomorrow morning before you leave?

THEOBALD. Now don't let's overdo it. I'll be thinking over how
things should be arranged. Perhaps, after all, we should fix
on a certain day of the week. I'll make all the arrangements.

DEUTER. Am I to see you only once in seven days? What shall

I do with the others, now that each minute without you seems an eternity?

THEOBALD. Pull yourself together, your impatience may spell disaster. If you can only be content with a few times, the pleasure of each particular time will be the greater.

DEUTER. But . . .

THEOBALD. Not another word. And I'll send my wife down-stairs if you want to talk with her.

DEUTER. Actually, I've nothing to say to her now.

THEOBALD. So much the better. And remember: no scowling at her! No snide remarks for her to overhear!

SCARRON, *entering*. Good morning all! There was an elderly man here with a full beard. He wanted to rent a room.

THEOBALD. Ah! This business has possibilities. We are making headway!

DEUTER. I'll be going.

THEOBALD. Maybe I should have let Mandelstam go.

DEUTER. Where did I leave my parcel?

SCARRON *hands her the underpants wrapped in paper.*

Voilà! Thank you so much, Herr Scarron. Good morning.

Exit DEUTER.

THEOBALD. Are you better?

SCARRON. You left me for dead in my doorway—you have the right to ask. But what happened will very much surprise you. The need to elude the grasp of a senseless theory became more imperative than the demands of my prostrate body. And so—as you staggered off home . . .

THEOBALD. Don't worry about me. Just a little bellyache.

SCARRON. The clarity of your view of things had struck me most forcibly and, exhausted as I was, brought into doubt the accumulated conclusions of many years.

THEOBALD. The view of a petty official, Herr Scarron.

SCARRON. A view that, for me at least, was an event—an event that required me to re-establish the truth of my own gospel without a moment's delay.

THEOBALD. In the middle of the night?

SCARRON. God was merciful. As I ran up and down the river-bank—my brain confused and affrighted—all of a sudden I saw a shadow following me.

THEOBALD. Oh!

SCARRON. When I came to a standstill, there before me towered—a woman.

THEOBALD. Towered?

SCARRON. Don't interrupt. She stared at me out of vacant eyes.

THEOBALD. I'll be damned.

SCARRON. The quest for bread and God in human form! Those first minutes! That exquisite eloquence of the eyes! She administered more than a sacrament: she poured herself into me, body and soul, she let me into the secret of her thousand shames. Understand this, my dear fellow: it was a miracle. Never was chastity so fervently close to me—running around with children, kneeling before the madonna—as with this whore. I soon reached a conclusion: your view that values are immutable—for that, surely, is your view of life in a nutshell . . .

THEOBALD. It is?

SCARRON. Yes, it is. And it was proved forever invalid by this woman. Year after year I had maintained, nay, strengthened my faith in humanity's power to develop. Year after year I had endeavored to educate and improve my own powers of understanding. Now I knew: it was not in vain.

THEOBALD. You knew?

SCARRON. I followed her to her miserable dwelling, and there in the light of a quavering lamp I drew from her locked and bolted breast such a confession of high, new, undreamt-of Greatness that I fell on my knees beside her straw mattress . . .

THEOBALD. She was already on the straw?

SCARRON. And uttered prayers full of a fearful strength and humility. I wouldn't have lifted my head even if she'd trodden on it with her thorn-torn feet.

THEOBALD. Which happens sometimes.

SCARRON. How far from appreciating such a feeling you are,

all of you! Every hour she sacrificed her body to the base-ness of men, and every day she raised herself, by her sorrow, nearer to the Omniscient One.

THEOBALD. These girls are very goodhearted.

SCARRON. When the morning sun surprised us, she found me unworthy of her.

THEOBALD. But you did pay?

SCARRON. I shall not take offense at your question: we are oceans apart. How you'd laugh if I told you I wouldn't have *dared* ask her to marry me!

THEOBALD, *worried.* You still haven't slept? You seem in a bad way.

SCARRON. There will be no sleep for me till I see this woman's soul so clearly that I can re-create it for all mankind. Would you believe that, yesterday, I was intending to make you, Herr Maske, the hero of a work of art? Today I feel with greater conviction than ever before: the artistic viability of any object depends solely upon that object's psychological volume.

THEOBALD. Viability? Psychological volume?

SCARRON, *smiling.* Poor fellow! I forgot. You must have diffi-culty following me?

THEOBALD. I got some of it. You were with a woman last night.

SCARRON. An angel.

THEOBALD. A fallen angel.

SCARRON. You are a philistine.

THEOBALD. You're not going to tell me about psychological volume?

SCARRON. Nothing is immutable. Not even good and evil—thank God.

THEOBALD. Man alive, that sounds dangerous!

SCARRON. It is. Thus have I lived, and thus will I die. . . . And there's something I hope you won't take amiss: I shall have to leave you.

THEOBALD. But you signed a lease for a year.

SCARRON. I'll honor it. I'll pay you twelve times twelve thaler in advance—a hundred and fifty

Which he pays.

—and I've no objection in the world if you wish to rent the friendly little place all over again. Your personality—however auspicious in your own sphere of life—might affect my next project unfavorably. You understand?

THEOBALD. This is six thaler too much.

SCARRON. Think nothing of it.

THEOBALD. You're an unusual character.

SCARRON. A man of action, that is all: I can leave nothing unfinished. That is why I am drawn to this woman—irresistibly. I must be the intimate witness of her life and her milieu. It is my God-given duty to plumb human relations to the depths. Accustomed as I am to the heights, I must consent to descend into the abyss. Who knows what unheard-of joys await me?

THEOBALD. You're a bit of a rascal.

SCARRON, *severely.* Unheard-of joys—and unlimited torments!

THEOBALD. *I* see! One should take care not to fall too low too soon. A certain regularity is required.

SCARRON. A certain *ir*regularity is required. Or I'd hang myself.

THEOBALD. One can be irregular—with a certain regularity.

SCARRON. In a short time I hope to send you a book that will make you sit up.

THEOBALD. And if you have a well-to-do friend who needs a room, send him to us. What you need first, though, is a couple of hours' sleep.

SCARRON. Herr Maske!

THEOBALD. You do.

SCARRON. Well, Heaven knows, it may be sound advice. I begin to feel a little fatigue. Good luck go with you!

THEOBALD. You'll be with us again sometime.

SCARRON. Where can I find a cab in this neighborhood? That damned winding staircase.

THEOBALD, *laughing.* Your poor old legs! But you'll sleep it off.

SCARRON, *encountering* THE STRANGER *in the doorway.* Here's the gentleman who wanted the room.

Exit SCARRON.

THE STRANGER. The janitor's wife told me you were bound to be home. You have a room free now, I hear?

THEOBALD. As chance will have it, yes. Twelve thaler, breakfast included.

THE STRANGER. Expensive.

THEOBALD. A large room. See for yourself.

THE STRANGER. Any pianos in the vicinity? Little children? A sewing machine? Canaries?

THEOBALD. Nothing in that line at all.

THE STRANGER. You keep cats or dogs?

THEOBALD. No.

THE STRANGER. You have marriageable daughters?

THEOBALD. No.

THE STRANGER. You're a married man: is your wife young?

THEOBALD. Yes.

THE STRANGER. Flirtatious?

THEOBALD. There'd be hell to pay.

THE STRANGER. So you're constantly on the watch?

THEOBALD. Absolutely . . . The conveniences are halfway up the stairs.

THE STRANGER. I reduce personal contacts to the minimum. The maid will knock three times before entering. Instead of coffee, I shall take tea, which I supply myself. I suffer from constipation, but that is my affair.

THEOBALD. Your affair entirely.

THE STRANGER. Under these conditions, I'll come here for a trial period of one month. I can give notice as late as the fifteenth. My name is Stengelhöh, my field is science.

THEOBALD. Agreed.

THE STRANGER. When the maid comes in, her clothes must be proper: nothing torn, nothing transparent. My things will be here in one hour. Good morning.

THEOBALD. Good morning, Herr Stengelhöh.

Exit THE STRANGER.

I'll take out "Joseph Before Potiphar" and hang instead "Boa
Constrictor in Combat with Lion."

*He gets a picture from his bedroom and carries it over to
what had been* SCARRON'S *room. Enter* LUISE.

Did you see Herr Stengelhöh on the stairs? A man with a
full beard?

LUISE. I believe so.

THEOBALD. He's our new lodger. The business is making headway. Nothing can stop it. He takes tea, which he'll supply,
and his field is science.

LUISE. Scarron?

THEOBALD. Ah yes, Scarron. I saw through him. He is tired of
us. He's vanished, never to return, after paying one year's
rent in advance. He expressed a wish to be cordially remembered to you. I could tell you other things about him, but
Heaven preserve one's wife from such ridiculous fanfaron-
ades. He was a clown and a poltroon, he stank of violets.
Mandelstam, on the other hand, is staying for a year, and
I'll fix it so he'll barber me for nothing. Did it do you good,
going to church?

LUISE. The dear old Holy Catholic Church, Theobald.

THEOBALD. No empty dream, you're right.

LUISE. We've been married just one year today.

THEOBALD. How time flies!

LUISE. What shall I cook for you?

THEOBALD. I know very well you have a tasty pork roast tucked
away somewhere.

LUISE. I'll serve it with sauerkraut.

THEOBALD. You might risk adding an onion. And now I'm going to come right out with my big secret: those two men
that stumbled on this apartment, so to speak, have put us
in a position finally to—to what, Luise?

LUISE. I don't know.

THEOBALD. You don't even guess.

Gently.

I can manage it now: I can give you a child. What do you say?

LUISE *starts cooking in silence.*

Handle him with kid gloves. He's peculiar, Stengelhöh. He wishes to have no personal relationships here. Asked if you were flirtatious. Suffers from constipation.

He runs around the room.

The clock isn't wound up—as usual—for all my appeals. The flowers need water.

He pours some on them.

Fräulein Deuter was here an hour ago. Wanted to show you some underpants she's made herself. They're using snap buttons now instead of ribbons. Look into it. With these snaps, the confounded incident that gave us so much trouble need never have happened. With you so lascivious, it's good we can avoid big trouble at so little expense.

He sits at the window and takes a newspaper.

Behind the wallpaper of life, so to speak, strange things happen. I still have that bellyache. Mustn't go on the spree in future . . . Snaps . . . The human race invents something good and sensible once in a while. I believe I read you this before: They say the sea serpent has turned up again in Indian waters.

LUISE, *mechanically.* Good Lord! And what does such a creature live off?

THEOBALD. The experts disagree. And anyway I find reports of weird things like that repulsive. Repulsive.

NOTES

LEONCE AND LENA

Georg Büchner submitted a draft of LEONCE AND LENA in a publisher's play contest in 1836 but continued to work on the play almost until his death (in the following year). There were, finally, two MS. versions, neither of which has survived. Scholars have made different dispositions of the available materials. The present translator, claiming no right to an opinion in this field, has simply followed one of the most authoritative editions, that published by Inselverlag: Georg Büchner's *Werke und Briefe* (Leipzig, 1949). A. H. J. Knight's *Georg Büchner* (Blackwell, England, 1951) contains an admirable 20-page section on the play. A previous English translation appeared in Geoffrey Dunlop's *The Plays of Georg Büchner* (1928, reprinted 1952). One of the plays Büchner has drawn on in this work that has often been considered chiefly a plagiarism is Musset's *Fantasio*, which appears in *From the Modern Repertoire*, Series One. Another is Clemens Brentano's *Ponce de Leon*. While Léonce is an accepted French form of the name Leo (Leon, Leontius, etc.), it has been suggested that Büchner arrived at it by putting Ponce and Leon together; at any rate, a joking literary allusion to Brentano may lurk in the name. *Leonce and Lena* was first performed in 1911 at the Residenzbühne in Vienna. Karl Walser's design for a later performance at the Lessing Theatre in Berlin is reproduced as Color Plate 3 in Oskar Fischel's *Das moderne Bühnenbild*. Peter Larkin's drawings were commissioned expressly for the anthology *From the Modern Repertoire III*, now out of print.

SPRING'S AWAKENING

In 1911, Frank Wedekind wrote down some notes on his various plays under the title *Was Ich Mir Dabei Dachte* (What I Thought about It). His comments on *Spring's Awakening* follow:

"I began writing without any plan, intending to write what gave me pleasure. The plan came into being after the third scene and consisted of my own experiences or those of my school fellows. Almost every scene corresponds to an actual incident. Even the words 'The boy is no son of mine,' which brought down upon me the charge of gross exaggeration, were really spoken.

"During my work on the play I rather prided myself on never dispensing with humor in any scene, even the most serious. Until it was staged by Reinhardt the play passed for pure pornography. It has now been decided that it is the dryest exercise in pedagogics. Everyone still refuses to see humor in it.

"It went against the grain with me to conclude the play among school children without supplying any image of the life of grown-ups. I therefore introduced a Man in a Mask in the last scene. As model for Moritz Stiefel, the incarnation of death, who has risen from his grave, I chose the philosophy of Nietzsche. . . .

"Did the critics of twenty years ago know what *Spring's Awakening* was? On the contrary: even today they haven't an inkling of the nonpartisan humor to which I gave expression in all scenes of the play except one. I wouldn't like to judge these gentlemen's lack of understanding too harshly. A scoundrel does his best—or even more! What can they do about the frightful lack of humor which is the legacy of our foolish tribe of naturalists? In my theatre, so a famous Berlin theatre magnate told me, the audience may laugh only when laughter on stage gives them the cue to do so. And the humor in which I soaked *Spring's Awakening* has up to now been just as little appreciated by the audience as by the critics. For ten years —1891 till about 1901—the play was generally regarded as unheard-of filth. The exceptional people who set a value on it were few. Since about 1901, above all since Max Reinhardt put it on the stage, it has been regarded as an angry, deadly earnest tragedy, as a thesis play, as a polemic in the service of sexual enlightenment—or whatever the current slogans of the fussy, pedantic lower middle class may be. It makes me wonder if I shall live to see the book taken for what, twenty years ago, I wrote it as—a sunny image of life in every scene of which I tried to exploit an unburdened humor for all it was worth. Only as the peripety of the drama did I insert, for the sake of contrast, a scene that was stripped of all humor: Mr.

and Mrs. Gabor quarreling over the fate of their child. By this time, surely, the joke had gone far enough. The Dismal Day scene in *Faust*, Part One, had served me as prototype."

LA RONDE

LA RONDE (1896–97) first appeared in America as *Hands Around* (New York, 1920); the translation is unsigned, the introduction is initialled by "F.L.G." and "L.D.E.," and the copyright is in the name of A. Koren. This edition was privately printed. The second American appearance of *Reigen* came in 1929 with the printing of a version by Keene Wallis. A little later an anonymous version was included in a Schnitzler volume in the Modern Library (1933). The Keene Wallis version was reprinted with a few editorial changes in *From the Modern Repertoire*, Series One, edited by Eric Bentley (Denver, 1949). The first British edition appeared in 1953 as *Merry Go Round* (translators: Frank and Jacqueline Marcus). The Bentley version was first published in The Modern Theatre II, 1955, now out of print.

THE UNDERPANTS

"Full to bursting with the impressions of thirty-one years of conscious living I sat down at my desk on the 7th of July 1909 and by the 18th of July 1910 had completed my first 'middle-class comedy,' THE UNDERPANTS in Four Acts": thus Carl Sternheim in his autobiography, *Vorkriegseuropa im Gleichnis meines Lebens* (1936). When Reinhardt produced the play in 1911, Carl Sternheim became a national figure. The process of becoming an *inter*national figure was slower and is still far from finished. The attempts to render Sternheim in English were few. Alfred Knopf published his novelette *Fairfax* in 1923. Ashley Dukes translated his *Die Marquise von Arcis* (*The Mask of Virtue*) for a London production in 1935: Vivien Leigh played the lead. In the twenties Eugene Jolas brought out his own version of *The Underpants* in his magazine *transition* (nos. 6-7-8-9). The play is the first part of a trilogy. The second part—*The Snob*—was translated by Winifred Katzin and Barrett H. Clark and included in the anthology *Eight European Plays* (1927). Another version was made by Eric Bentley and included in his anthology *From the Modern Repertoire* I (1949).

A word on the title of the play. The German word *Hose* refers to either the overgarment or the undergarment on either the male or the female body. An English translation has perforce to limit itself to one garment on one sex. But fashions, even in undergarments, change, and words to describe these garments proliferate. Sternheim was born in an age when they were quite often referred to in English as "unmentionables." *Hose* is, by contrast, a four-letter word: hence its shock value in 1909. In 1959 all words have lost their shock value, and Sternheim can no more get his original effect with the word *Hose* than Bernard Shaw can get his with *bloody*. One foregoes fireworks and settles for mere plainness. *A Pair of Drawers* was Mr. Jolas' title in the twenties. But today it is hard to make of *drawers* anything but part of a *chest*. *The Underpants* was chosen as the most straightforward solution. But it would not work in Britain where a *Hose* for ladies is called a pair of knickers. *The Knickers* would be the British title. . . .

Truly, an inexhaustible subject!

At points where the Aufbau Verlag edition of 1947 differs from the Insel Verlag edition of 1919, the present translator of *The Underpants* has generally followed the Aufbau edition.

TWO STATEMENTS BY CARL STERNHEIM

1.

Preface to *The Underpants* (1919 edition)

When, in 1908, I brought out a comedy of middle-class life, the German theatre had finished with Gerhart Hauptmann's naturalism and now knew nothing but the old fairy-tale king, the young queen, and the page,[1] who in various guises repre-

---

[1] Sternheim calls the page "famos," a word which implies both excellence and notoriety. King, queen, and page are all found in Heine's poem *"Es war ein alter König."* E.B.

sented neo-romanticism. Richly clad, they talked (unreal) magnificence and enacted sublimity. In my play a woman of the middle strata lost her underpants, and on the stage the talk—in naked German—was of nothing but this trivial subject. The world gave its verdict on such simple-mindedness. How could it be literature? Middle-class underpants and five Philistines arguing about it? Where was the accustomed (fake) magnificence? What had happened to the (pseudo) naturalism? The characters, moreover, spoke of this nonsense in language never seen in book or newspaper, never spoken by any well-bred acquaintance.

His intentions being obvious, the author followed up this comedy with several others which added nothing essentially new to the first. There was more talk of banal matters, and insignificant things were discussed with such emphasis and eagerness as never before had been attached to the middle-class world.

This world, however, not wishing to play any part in public life, but leaving the honor and the burden of responsibility to others, grew flustered as it felt upon it the spotlight of an inquisitive eye—caught offguard, as it were, in that bright beam. They accordingly shrieked their denunciations at the disturber of the peace. The press dutifully prepared to attack.

Around the year 1910 one could read all the reviewers saying with one voice: We won't stand for such heartlessness! To present backward nobility and modern proletarians was permissible—they are not of this world. The solid, middle-class citizen, however, brings us face to face with the risky reality of business drafts and certified checks, concealed as they may be behind a rampart of agreed ideologies, clouds of gassy apotheoses, and trenches of metaphors.

Between 1908 and 1913, I wrote seven comedies. The last, which bears the name of the year before war broke out, shows, where possible in all naïveté, what effect the solid citizen's business transactions had led to. Reality spoke for itself; there was nothing for the dramatic poet to add.

Despite the many public performances, despite the circulation of my works in print, no one noticed in these works the direction of the author's will. Periodically, it is true, Franz Blei failed to contain his delight and thereby threatened to call a more general attention to me, before in sheer reality the age

would exact from the solid citizenry precisely such actions as
I had shown their representatives performing upon the stage.
In all my comedies of "middle-class heroism," as well as in all
the stories that followed and that will soon appear as a *Chroni-
cle of the Onset of the 20th Century*, the whole middle class,
its hero included, gets out of step, so to speak, with its own
ideology. But the main character in each work, in conflict with
society, and seen against the background of the All Too Many,
is a man of passionate, heroic will, rooted in himself, in the
primitive sources of his being.

He is not overendowed, it is true, with such hackneyed,
picture-book virtues as the poets have sung and continue to
sing. Instead of the habitat of middle-class decadence painted
in pastel colors, he brings us his fanaticism; he is possessed;
his point of departure and his goals are alike his own. Schip-
pel and Maske, making a triple appearance, and also Meta and
Busekow—these are not the illusion-ridden Germans of former
days. They have been awakened to actuality. It did not take
long for their peculiar way of taking the world in hand to
arouse general astonishment.

Hence, despite the newspapermen and the mob that par-
rots them, my writings are not to be regarded as irony and
satire: they teach a lesson which the public has yet to learn.
To preserve his strength, man must not listen to outdated
clichés but to his own fresh, individual voice. And if this voice
at times has brutal things to say or to imply he must not
trouble himself about the public response.

My advice to all who live was to do so according to their
distinct and unique nature so that the word "community" may
not signify mere numbers but rather the determination of in-
dividuals to live their own lives. Only thus can a nation—or
humanity—reach a goal. Public announcement of this, my sole
intention soon gave me a certain influence. To that influence,
resistance was then organized. It is not astonishing that my
opponents belong chiefly to the youngest generation of writers,
for our youth sees its future less in spiritual allegiances than in
incisiveness of attack.

And now, in 1918, a flood of writing in books and periodi-
cals bears witness to an irresistible demand for human feeling,
to the existence in every human breast of a daimon that sends

us out to see our neighbors. The point is that the whole world is pregnant with some great manifestation of love.

The success of this young generation and the trust that the educated class puts in it will need strengthening by the peace which surely, some day, must come.[2]

(Translated by Eric Bentley)

2.

What all my plays are about

A Word in Advance prefaced to *Carl Sternheim und seine besten Bühnenwerke, eine Einführung,* von Dr. Manfred Georg. Berlin, 1923.

In order to be happy, the human being must not trot on a leash or believe absolutely that 2×2 is four.

That is to say, if one behaves outwardly and adequately in the conventional manner of the good citizen, one can resolutely be oneself, a fellow with the self-will of a Cyclops, and eat the pastures of life completely bare for one's own pleasure and profit.

It was in 1908 that for the first time in my comedy *The Underpants* I kicked open this door into freedom for the timid plebeian of our day. Whereas up to that time the play-hero whom the dramatist had made responsible paid the penalty for his struggle between the duty to others and his liking for himself by infallibly dying in the last act, at the end of every play of mine the swollen-chested actors took the final step that brought them abreast of themselves.

In a dozen comedies from 1908 to 1920 I established the "heroic life of the middle-class citizen," the avowal of his unique individuality. He *was* a hero, because he played his way out of social and casual compulsions, in the face of opposition, more and more into the personal freedom of his character, into his own incomparable "way of being." So for example, as far back as *Perleberg,* when the hash-slinger Friesecke has his attention called to the unsociable atrociousness which annoys people to death, he announces in victorious

[2] Written early in 1918.

accents, "That's the way I am!" Or finally there is Ständer in
Tabula Rasa, who closes the play with the words, "All I want
now is to explore my own breast without dependence on community ideals, and to seek the teachers whom my nature demands, even if I have to find them in China or the South Seas."

Unfortunately the critics, unmanned and maddened by the
red rag of freedom, succeeded in gumming up for the public
my clear intention with the sweet syrup of their phrases, especially when they could praise my skillful imitators, who
copped onto and copied everything except that revolutionary
rush toward freedom. Now however the time seems to be no
longer distant when the German, whom it takes a long time
to talk into anything intellectually out of the ordinary, will
take with hook and sinker the food of freedom which I have
predigested for him in about twenty books of plays and prose,
and will gobble it down and like it.

                        (Translated by Bayard Quincy Morgan)

                              ****

    The above Note on *Leonce and Lena* is reproduced from
From the Modern Repertoire, Series Three, Indiana University
Press, 1956; the Note on *La Ronde,* from *The Modern Theatre,*
Volume 2, Doubleday, 1955; the Notes on *Spring's Awakening*
and *The Underpants,* from *The Modern Theatre,* Volume 6, Dou-
bleday, 1960. The following Notes were added for the
Applause presentation in 1985.
    The attention of Büchnerians, now numerous in America,
is drawn to the following items, listed in chronological order:
    1963: *Georg Büchner, Complete Plays and Prose,* translated and
        with an Introduction by Carl Richard Mueller
    1964: *Georg Büchner* by Herbert Lindenberger
    1967: *Georg Büchner: Sämtliche Werke und Briefe,* Vol. I (a new
        edition in German edited by Werner Lehmann)
    1977: *Georg Büchner: The Complete Collected Works,* translated by
        Henry Schmidt.
    Even in 1985 Wedekind is known to the broader public in
America indirectly — through Alban Berg's opera *Lulu.*

But note should be taken here of:

Frank Wedekind, The Lulu Plays, newly translated and with an introduction by Carl Richard Mueller, 1967

Spring Awakening, translated by Edward Bond, 1979

As for Arthur Schnitzler, theatrical producers realized that, as of 1981, they could produce his plays without payment of royalties to the Schnitzler Estate. This fact created a Schnitzler revival. The Bentley version of *La Ronde* came back into print as part of *Arthur Schnitzler: Plays and Stories* (Continuum, 1982), otherwise there had for years been only a Samuel French acting edition of this item.

Five plays of Carl Sternheim were included in one volume by Calder and Boyars of London in 1970. Eric Bentley's translation of *1913* was published in the magazine *Canto*, Spring 1977.